# THE NAM WITHIN

by

## Leonard D. Reese III

*To Burt & Charlotte*
*My very best of friends.*
*I hope that my words have*
*some meaning to you.*

*Leonard Reese*

Cover Design by Leonard Reese IV
Formatted by Enterprise Book Services, LLC

# Chapter One

## DATE: The Present

I did the best that I could to tell my story with all of the truth that I have within me. Almost fifty years have passed since my thirteen-month tour of duty in Vietnam from 1969–1970. I still see some of those images as clearly as if they were happenings within a blink-of-an-eye past. While others, partially confused and shaking like a pile of pick-up-sticks awaiting the next attempt at success or tragedy, arrive within the shadows of the night, blurred and weighted by the evening's dew.

Incorrect names and misplaced trails, rice paddies, and small areas of high ground dot these pages as if they were paint sprayed across canvas. Yet, in my mind's eye they are accurate and certain in their descriptions, and even more clearly, in their grip upon my scared soul. Please know that these lines are much less about the fight than they are about the emotions of the men who did the fighting. We were more than just sand-box warriors moving from one pile of windblown up-turned-bucket encampments to the next moment's instant rebirth, within a new pack of forest green plastic men preparing for counter attack or ambush.

It is the feel for the war as it happened, and continues to happen, to this one man trapped within his memories, and that, I pray, might open at least one lone person's eyes, or increase a loved one's ability to understand his self-imposed blindness. I want you to experience the loss of self that many like myself went through so that you might

1

more accurately understand the ghosts that continue to walk a kill-radius behind, or to our front.

# Chapter Two

## The Walk

**DATE: 1969, Vietnam**

A rocket-propelled grenade races over our position and explodes with a deafening roar to our rear. Shrapnel slices through the elephant grass on all sides of us. The "crack, crack, crack" of AK-47s comes from the rice paddy dike to our left. Out of the corner of my eye I see Fontana squeeze the trigger-key in his hand and watch the back-blast of the Claymore mine to the front of our position, exploding in a cloud of dirt and dust and gravel into the air above our heads. Chemicals from mosquito repellant and camouflage paint mix with the sweat from my forehead; my eyes sting in rebellion as I turn to my side and change a spent magazine to a full one.

I jam the magazine into my M-16, pull back the lever to chamber a fresh round, and slip the selector with my thumb a quarter turn from off to semi-automatic. I pull my rifle to my shoulder and raise my head. Through a cloud of gunpowder and smoke, a silhouette rises from behind the cover of a lifeless body that lies, face down, on the trail. Another pair of eyes turn from the left and look directly at me. I see the same fear in their glassy stare that they must see in mine. A rifle's aim begins to turn toward me. My breath stills, and my heart races.

I fire first.

*********

I open my eyes, lost and confused by a deafening silence. Reflexively, I reach for my rifle but find my shaking hands empty. Instead, I sense a body beside mine and jerk away. The sudden movement parts the fog and I begin to feel a slow warmth and comfort as another's hand reaches through the darkness to take mine. I recognize the touch as that of my wife, and I am home again.

My breathing calms and I lay back to wait for the late autumn dawn. The gentle, rhythmic sound of her breathing at my side reassures me. My mind begins to drift, and I find another time warp that carries me to a different, kinder day. A smile crosses my face as warm images fly me once again to the first time she took my hand in hers.

**\*\*\*\*\*\*\*\*\*\***

## DATE: March 1974

It is the spring of 1974. I attend Stephen F. Austin State University on funds from the GI Bill. Devoting all my time to studies, I eke by living in one of the oldest, least expensive dorms on campus and limiting myself to one meal a day. A young lady in my Latin American History class possesses a soft beauty that steals my attention each session. One morning I wait to turn in my test papers until after she rises to set hers on a desk by the door. In a quick glimpse, I read her name incorrectly, and now, when I look into the garden of her eyes, she struggles to suppress a laugh when I say, "Hi, Cathy."

"My name is Cindy," she smiles and corrects me.

I think: If only she had better handwriting, or I better eyesight, I would have missed the blunder that finds me standing in the shadow of this smile.

Later, as we walk through the serving line of the Vista Inn Café on campus where she works as a cashier, I can almost taste the smell of hot grease from the griddle as it sizzles in the small cooking area behind a Formica countertop. I order a cheeseburger with fries, then hesitate while those in line behind me wait. "If you have a break soon, would you like to sit with me and talk for a few minutes?" I ask.

She reaches across the counter and takes my hand with a gentle touch. "I'd like that, too," Cindy responds with a smile that carries a small trace of red blush as it dances along the curve of her cheek.

Her break arrives, and we talk about anything and everything. I know I don't want these moments together to end. "When you get off work, if you have the time, would you like to take a walk? It's a beautiful day and the azaleas are blooming on Raguet Street."

"I'd like that, too."

As we move along the sidewalk, the colors of spring rest their hands on our touched shoulders. The miracle of the blooming brilliance sets our private world aglow. Purple and pink blossoms melt with an impressionist's paintbrush of redbud and dogwood. The vacuum of her delicate steps steals my breath, and I feel only her presence at my side.

We stop to rest and sit on the woven, manicured comfort of a Saint Augustine grass blanket beneath towering East Texas pines. We are at peace with the familiar assurance only silence can add to a moment when words are shamed by their inadequacy. We drink in the nature that holds us in a warm embrace of new life and bathes us in the fresh smell of fertile soil with the promise of renewed growth.

After a brief eternity, I stand to return to campus to make my afternoon class. I take her hand and help her to her feet. "That was nice," she says and keeps her grip in mine. I know I will always remember the sound of her laughter and the warmth of her touch as we walk hand-in-hand through this beautiful spring's symphony.

**********

Her love and comfort still accompany me. The mistress of Vietnam continues to ambush my nights and mock my dreams, violating my soul. But now, at the touch of my wife's hand, my enemy retreats into the underbrush of a jungle trail to regroup until its next assault.

My eyes water as light enters our bedroom and shakes her awake with a sunbeam's soft touch. She turns her face toward mine and sings the same smile, my sanctuary since that first day. "What would you like to do today?" She yawns.

I pause for a moment. "Would you like to take a walk?"

5

She gives me a playful wink, pulls my hand to her lips, and gives the back of my fingers a soft kiss. I pull her close. She rests her head on my shoulder and whispers, "I'd like that, too."

# Chapter Three

## The Day Before Yesterday

**DATE: June 2008**

It is the day before yesterday. One of my best friends, John "JJ" Jerabeck, contacts me and asks a favor. His request causes me to spend a few hours with an assemblage of men and women on a mission of honor and remembrance. The "Run for the Wall" motorcycle riders begin their journey on the West Coast and end their ride in Washington, D.C. on Memorial Day. Their noble mission brings attention to the thousands of men and women still unaccounted for from all our wars. It also serves as a welcome home healing process for veterans.

Although the motorcycle riders who stop to break bread with local supporters represent men and women young and old alike, I relate best to a subgroup of combat vets from Vietnam. We are now overweight old men: mustached to divert attention from hairlines like low tides, withdrawn far beyond receding.

The Run for the Wall participants wheel in on weighted-down motorcycles like veldt-roaring beasts of prey. Volunteers direct them to park in assigned spaces on the heat-rippled, oil-topped lot surrounding the Veterans of Foreign Wars meeting hall. The local post is hosting an afternoon meal and temporary respite from the Texas summer heat. In refrigerated-air comfort, warriors rest and visit with friends and well-wishers.

Bearing the load of changes of clothes and changes of life, the men also carry the added baggage of memories far beyond any that might fit within their polished-leather saddle packs. Baby-fine, thin, gray hair spills out from beneath their sweat-stained caps. They remove Willie Nelson-esque bandanas as they park, cut engines, and dismount on unsteady, childlike, first steps. The tired travelers then stretch and twist their time-stiffened shoulders and age-compressed backs.

The mission begins with a call from JJ requesting that I run one last patrol for him. "There's this guy was with me in the Nam," he explains. "I wanna help him. You gotta make it happen. He still struggles with demons like you 'n me. He's just as Nam crazy as us." JJ drops the phone and the sound causes me to wince and pull away. In a moment I hear, "Red, ya still there?"

"What the hell was that? You're messing with my nerves, JJ."

"I'm sorry, man, I was opening a beer and the damn thing jumped out of my hands. Okay, where was I? Oh, yeah. We call him Fish. Anyway, Fish is riding all the way to 'The Wall' in Washington this year for the Memorial Day ceremony. I told him I would meet him in Longview to bike along for several days. I haven't seen him since they sent me home."

"God, it's hard to believe that was forty years ago, JJ." I walk around the house with the wireless phone. I pick up a tennis ball in my son, Downs', room, throw it in the air, and catch it. "Okay, JJ, what can I do?"

"I've been helping him with his veteran's claims. Agent Orange, PTSD—all that sort of shit." The sound of another beer tab popping and fizzing lets me know that JJ is on a roll. "He asked me to meet him. I told him I'd be there, but now I can't make it. You're the only one I can turn to."

"It's done, brother," I interrupt. "No problem."

"I'll e-mail you his picture. That'll give ya something to go on. Won't be easy. There'll be between five to six hundred bikers by this stage in their ride from LA to DC." He laughs from his side of the phone. "If it is to be done, then 'you be de one,' Red Man, 'you be de one.'"

"It's already taken care of, JJ. It'll be good to saddle up once again for this one."

8

I think back. What smartass little turds JJ and I were, growing up together in Houston. We embarrassed ourselves with more young girls than I care to count. Shit-faced drunk, we rolled backward, trousers down, and lit blue-flame farts together in the campfire's glow of Galveston's darkened West Beach sand. We laughed till we ached, at nothing at all, then threw up on each other and laughed even louder. We fought for the same girls—who ignored us—and dropped the ones who paid us any mind. We gave the same book reports two years in a row at Spring Branch Jr. High and four years running at Memorial High. A humiliating final semester found us in freshman physical science as seniors needing a last credit to graduate. Oh, we were sweethearts indeed!

I visited JJ in the hospital following his numerous car wrecks and snuck in beer and girlie magazines with each of his challenges to bulletproof adolescent invincibility. He was one of only a few of my eighth-grade friends to attend my father's funeral, an act that bonded him to me for the duration of whatever endures in the deep recesses of our remembered teenaged years.

We both went to Nam in 1969. I joined the Marine Corps in a skewed response to TV coverage of the Tet Offensive of 1968 and daily footage of the siege at Khe Sanh, and JJ volunteered for the Army soon after. From the wealthy Memorial section of Houston, I believe there were only three of us out of the class of 1966 who went to Nam: JJ, myself, and a fine boy man named Lee Wolf.

JJ and I lived on beyond Nam, yet remained to fight the war with each night's tortured sleep. Wolf threw snake eyes fighting his final battles after we'd returned home.

I wait in front of the VFW in Longview, Texas. A poster emblazoned with "Fish—John Jerabeck" sways above my head as I move it back and forth. I stand in a spot where the bikers will pass by. Beside the road in front of the post, a troop of Boy Scouts wave American flags. These are good boys, certain and proud of their merit-badge-decorated uniforms. Red-white-and-blue ribbons and religious sayings cover a small van across the street. Patriotic music plays from a loud speaker on its hood.

The iPod I borrowed from my son provides accompaniment to this afternoon's parade as it plays for my ears only. I mouth David Bowie's line from *Under Pressure*: "Watching some good friends scream, 'Let me out.'" I sway to the Guns N' Roses cover of *Knockin' on Heaven's Door*, using Dylan's words to plead, "Momma, put my guns in the ground; I can't shoot them anymore." I sing along, loud enough for the Scouts to turn and stare at the screwy old man in the clown's face, with Bob Seger's *Against the Wind*, reminding me that, "I wish I didn't know now, what I didn't know then."

As more and more riders assemble amid long-overdue cheers, waving flags, and thumbs-up gestures of approval, I hold my sign higher with the passing of each motorcycle. The leader of the bikers 6th platoon rides through the entrance, and I receive a shouted response of, "He's with us." He points at my sign and gives a wave of recognition. Then five or six riders later, I breathe a sigh of relief at the smile of recognition that arises from a proud, tired rider. He yells back over his shoulder, "I'm Fish. I'll wait by my bike."

I leave my spot between the Scouts and the van and follow the Harleys and Hondas behind the building. They glide past the oil-drum smoker and the day-rental portable potties while I trot behind hoping not to get run over. Finally, I turn the corner and catch the stranger of my mission. He is the friend of my friend—the brother of my brother.

"I don't know you, do I?" he asks.

"And I don't know you." I stare at him. "But my friend, John Jerabeck, asked me to find you." Rolling the poster into a tube, I begin to tap it against my leg. "He told me you fought together. He said you were brothers."

"JJ's name is all I need to know." He sees the 1st Marine Division, Vietnam patch I wear on my cover and adds, "Welcome back to you, my brother."

I respond with outstretched arms and say into his ear as we embrace, with a redundant necessity, "And welcome home to you, once again, my brother." We hold on a little longer.

He pushes me back to arm's length. "Are you okay?" he asks.

"Better by the minute, better and better, and better by the minute," I answer. My lips curl into a smile. "Yes, I'm fine. JJ requested that I give you his contact information." I reach into my pockets and search for a piece of paper. "He wants you to know that he'll meet anywhere you want on your way back home." I finally find the paper in my wallet. It contains JJ's phone number and e-mail address. "Here ya go." I hand it to him along with a picture of John's daughter.

He checks his watch and excuses himself to go inside and eat. We say goodbye and I step away. About thirty minutes later the group of riders prepare to depart. The roar of their engines causes me to back even farther away. Time plays another game with the pictures in my head. Images from now merge with those of then. I look backward, clock-locked, through the squinted eyes of a confident nineteen year old in the full prime of promise. I see a time in which all things are possible. There, in the face of my new brother, I see a young man's innocence, and I smile. I look about me at what, a moment before, were the misshapen memories of past triumphs and tragedies. Now I see, within this wrinkle of time, young men all.

I feel myself standing a bit straighter, time decompressed an inch taller, muscle-flexed many years tighter with the catch in my get-along flown on the surf of this May afternoon's southern breeze. We, each of my brothers and I, stand once again erect, brave young men all. Mustaches curl in thickened waves and gray turns to darkened shades of black and brown and surf-bleached blond. Slumped, stiffened steps turn to patrols with fifty-pound packs in the humid, drench of sweat within the bitch—the nasty-assed bitch of the Nam.

And we are all here together again, joined in the knowledge that we walked through Tennyson's "jaws of death," we came back from combat's "mouth of hell," and we are all, once again, a part of another day's patrol backward to that moment in time before our brothers: brave, unscarred, young men all.

It is the day before yesterday: Before Big Al from Nebraska, Midwestern and lanky, walks past the grass-mound bunker and falls face forward into the mud—into the stink, leech mire, never knowing the origin of the round that tears his future, his dreams, and his children's dreams to come, through his chest.

It is the day before yesterday: Before rocket-propelled grenades shatter the night and Duvol swagger-sways on both his legs while Frank still writes letters home to the beautiful, Kodachrome image of the sweet Jeanette. It is the day before yesterday: A time before we ambush an enemy patrol, including two female nurses, and a day before we...the day before we...

It is the day before yesterday: The day before instinctive diving toward the ground with each loud noise of a normal man's afternoon walk in a park steals our own stroll of peaceful solitude. It is the day

before yesterday. Or maybe not. Perhaps it is the day before that—
I'm not so certain any more.

# Chapter Four

## Waltzing Matilda

**DATE: November 1969**

As I go back to the bush after a stay in the hospital at First Med in Da Nang, I never imagine it's possible that I will ever live to take breath in the real world again. I figure I am a dead man walkin' and my time is slippin' through my hands. At this point, I have six more months left in my tour before my rotation date comes around. Now, I don't know if this makes any sense to anyone else, but I feel that there is this big semi-truck heading straight for me and I am stuck in the mud up to my neck, like the painted Indians used to bury the cowboys in the Saturday afternoon Westerns of my youth.

It seems that I am just waiting around to see what it's like to experience the "whomp" of the big rig's impact, and to know what it feels like to be within that death sequence when it comes to pass. I'm not even that scared. I just want to know what it will be like to die, to just depart and fade away. No shit, I know this sounds strange, but I just want to know. I need to understand what that last round or stray piece of shrapnel feels like. I want to sense what the concussion whiplash after the tickle of a tripwire brings. I swear to God I have lost my fear, and I just have this strange longing to know what the moment of the long goodbye is going to be like.

I spend the night at an in-transit hooch at 11th Motors so I can catch a chopper or hop on a convoy truck out to our firebase at An Hoa tomorrow morning. I get lucky and they have a USO show on

13

the small stage they built there for their enlisted men's club. It is an Australian group that has a pretty good band, and three go-go girls are the main attraction. God, the guys go ape-shit over these dancers.

During an intermission, while the band rests and the girls change outfits, they have this old woman come out and talk to us. She sings solo, with only a guitar player as accompaniment. I guess she is some sort of famous Australian singing star or something like that. She is at least in her sixties and seems even more out of place than the go-go girls on the wooden stage that is reinforced and protected by weighted barrels and sandbags.

She is a big woman, and her long dress is brown with a yellow-and-red flower pattern. Her hair is gray with curls and her face is plain. She doesn't wear much makeup. The few jokes she tells are worn and outdated for our age group. Most of the guys have never heard the songs she sings from a time before we were born. Everybody is nice and claps for her, but the truth is that we all just want to look at the go-go girls again.

She says some nice stuff about how much she appreciates what we are doing and what we are fighting for. Then something special comes out of nowhere. Taking the mike from its stand, she walks to the front of the stage. She sings this song called *Waltzing Matilda* I once heard in an old, World War II movie when I was a kid. I know this sounds stupid and weird and all, but I gotta tell you, it is one of the most beautiful things I've ever heard in my life.

I mean, her voice isn't what it must have been like when she was younger, but it is real nice and sounds trained. It isn't so much how it sounds, you see, as much as it is all about how I can tell she feels all sincere and deep-down honest about it. I can't help but get caught up in the truth of her emotions. The other band members come out and start to sing along with her, and the dancers come out and sing along too. The girls aren't acting sexy anymore. They are just a part of some old song that is bigger than each of us individually and much larger than all of us collectively.

And hell, after a while I stand up with everybody else and sing along. I feel these damn tears well up in my eyes, and it's okay and I'm not ashamed a bit. It is all right. It's as if, for at least a brief melody in the warm night's breeze, I feel that somebody actually gives a shit about us, and I am proud about heading back to the bush in the morning to join my squad and be in the real fight and all.

I've always been proud to be a Marine, but I think I've never been more so than during this isolated slice of an old woman's memory, caught in a time warp and singing along with her wounded soul that is still trapped in the war of our fathers. I find myself thinking about my platoon and the bond we share in the here-and-now, and I miss each one of them and feel a loneliness cover me like wet paint.

I really like this old lady and I'm certain I never will forget her. Isn't that funny? I doubt I'll remember much about the go-go girls and their teasing miniskirts, but I expect to close my old man's eyes some day, if I ever get out of this damn place, and still see this grey-headed, feisty old lady singing this song: "You'll come a-waltzing Matilda with me." Hell, these are all the words I really know.

She stops in the middle and the whole damn crowd listens, back-row-Baptist still, while she explains what the song is all about and how Matilda is some sort of a fighting man's backpack. She tells how her old man fought in World War II, and how he is now long gone from too many unfiltered cigarettes and his unforgiving war wounds. She pauses and cries a short while in the silence.

She pulls a handkerchief from her pocket and asks us to forgive her. She explains how much it means to her to sing to us this night. She tells us how it makes her feel close to her old man and how it makes her feel important and meaningful and even a little bit young again. Then she thanks us, and you can tell she means it deep down inside. She's the one who thanks us—figure that one out.

Isn't it strange how your mind works? I shot and killed a man a week before and it doesn't seem to bother me much right now, but here I am sniffling about some Australian fighting song and some old woman and her long-gone old man. Figure that shit out, and let me know about it when you do. I can't quite seem to get a grip on any of it. It's like trying to pick up your grandmother's hot cookin' skillet by the bacon-grease-splattered handle and feeling its iron weight pulling it downward from your grasp and thinking as it falls: *Shiiiiiiiiiiiiiiiiitt!*

I know I'll get on the chopper and go back to the bush in the morning. I recognize what I'm stepping back into, but all I can feel is an incredible pull to be with my brothers of the 2nd Platoon again. I sense that these men need me more than anyone else ever has. My absence leaves their backs less covered and I feel important and significant stepping back in the fire with them.

# Chapter Five

## Problems

**DATE: August 1969**

Fontana shows up and, as usual, he's carrying bad news with him. "Hey, Plant," he shouts. "Sergeant Matt says it is 2$^{nd}$ squad's day for the Observation Posts. You guys be it, so don't even start bitchin' and just get your shit together."

Plant crawls his ass out from underneath the shade of two ponchos snapped together. We make these huts by hanging them over a bamboo pole with ends propped up by two smaller sticks. They look like a child's clothesline-and-blanket tent in a summer's yard back home. Plant is out and whining like a baby.

"I might, but I kinda fuckin' doubt it." He stands in defiance, his skinny chest out. "What about O'Bie's fire team? Why can't they take the damn OP. We were on the Listening Post last night. Oh, man, this is out-fuckin'-rageous." He paces back and forth like he's waiting for a new baby's arrival. "This ain't right, man." He jerks his helmet off, tosses it to the ground, gives it a hard kick and watches it fly into our fighting hole. "There is no way this is right."

Fontana sticks his hand out straight, stoppin' Plant and looking like Diana Ross in that song of hers with those Superettes or whatever the hell they call 'em. Goofy ol' Plant starts jumping up and down, hopping from side to side. His freckles blur in these jerky movements. They make his face take on an orange, kinda dried-up pumpkin look.

16

Fontana's loving this shit. He stands there rubbing his hands together, watching Plant go nuts. "O'Bie's team is already out at Observation Post 2, so quit your damn bitchin' and get on with it." He bends down and squats on his haunches. He draws circles and squares with his fingers through the dust, and smiles while Plant continues to holler shit at the clouds that must be laughing down at him too. "Plant, if you don't like it, then go tell Sergeant Matt. Hell, he'd love to sit down and discuss his plans with you." He reaches down and grabs a small dirt clod and tosses it at Plant's feet. "Yeah, you go on over and talk with Matt. That is just a super idea." He throws another clod that causes Plant to turn and dive for the cover of the hooch.

Fontana's voice grows louder in anger. "And Plant, you be sure to take your time, too. Oh yes, Sergeant Matt lives for your advice. Yeah, he abso-fuckin'-lutely loves sittin' 'round and waitin' to talk over the day's plans with your sorry ass." Fontana shakes his head as if he's trying to clear cobwebs from his attic. "Plant, I love ya man; even in this shit-hole of a place, you make me laugh. Man, you are something else."

Plant crawls back outta the hooch and pulls on his boots. One snaps as he tugs it on, so he ties the broken pieces together in an inept granny knot. "Shit, shit, and more shit, this is un-fuckin'-believable," he says. "All we get is crap and they won't send us any more of anything to fix the shit we got."

He points a finger in the direction of our firebase at An Hoa. "All those assholes back there in the rear keep the good shit and send us whatever the fuck's left over. Shit, those mothers don't do diddly-squat back there." He shakes his finger in accusation, aims it in a poking jab, and works it like a piston. "They just lie around all day, eat hot chow at the mess hall, and then take turns, half-assed, standing lines at night." He lowers his arm but continues to stare to the north. "Shit, I say, fuck 'em!"

"That's a lot of 'shits' for a skinny boy," Fontana says. "Damn you're a sweet-talkin' son of a bitch, Plant." He's proud of his humor and looks around at the rest of us for some approval. "And you're abso-fuckin'-lutely right: An Hoa is a damned paradise. That's right. It's a fuckin' Disneyland." He starts to laugh and the rest of us join in, agreeing with that assessment of the news. "Hey, Plant, what ya do last time you were in the rear?" He stares and waits. "No, don't

17

tell me, I know. You burned shitters, didn't you, Plant? Sure, you did. I can see it now, Plant in fantasyland pullin' those stinkin' barrels out from underneath the four-holers." Fontana gives a faraway look and shakes his head in slow confirmation that this image brings to life. He points to the distant clouds. "Oh yeah, there you are lightin' those damn barrels of kerosene and shit, usin' a stick and a string of toilet paper, lit and danglin'." He moves his arm and points across the horizon of his picture.

"I can see ya now, movin' closer to stir 'em round and round. Yep, there ya are, scoopin' with an old broom handle to make sure all the lumps reach the top to burn away." He looks down to face Plant. "No doubt about it, you were havin' a real, good ol' time playin' in that crap all afternoon."

Plant gets angry again and tries to explain it to the rest of us. "It's all 'cause the Gunny don't like me, that's why," he says. "Yeah, Gunny's just after my ass 'cause of that fuckin' bullshit with Dutch. It's all Dutch's fault. He didn't have to tell the Gunny that shit. Hell, Dutch kicked my ass sideways. But no, that wasn't enough for that sadistic son of a bitch."

"Ya want me to tell Dutch you been callin' him a son of a bitch when he gets back from patrol, Plant?" Fontana asks. He moves closer to Plant and gets into his face like he's trying to see how near he can get without touching it. "Huh, Plant?" Plant throws his hands up, then takes a step away for even more protection. Fontana cocks his head to the side and adds in a softer tone, "Is that what ya lookin' for, Plant? Huh, is that it? Ya want another run-in with Dutch?"

Davie walks over and pulls his flak jacket and helmet out of the makeshift hooch. "Yeah, Plant, let's tell Dutch you're tired of his bullshit," he says. "I get a real kick out of watchin' him slap your silly ass around. Yeah, in fact, I'll just tell him for ya, Plant, if ya really want me to." He turns to look over his shoulder toward the Command Post and jerks his head in that direction. "They ought to be gettin' back any minute now. I'll look him up for ya."

Plant starts to freak out and looks around from side to side. "Damn, Fontana, I was just shittin' with ya, man. You know that," he stammers. "We're going. We're going. Don't get your bowels in an uproar. Come on, Davie, let's get our shit and get ready to move out."

"Red, get your ass over here!" Davie hollers to me. "We gotta relieve OP-1 right away, man, double time. Come on, get ya ass over here and grab your stuff."

"See guys, I was just playin' around," Plant tries to explain. "I was just fuckin' with you guys, that's all, that's all." He paces around with no real direction in his movement. "Shit, can't you take a joke? I was just kiddin'. I was just screwin' around, that's all." He starts to breathe hard and his sunburned face turns even redder. "Shit, ya'll know me. Am I right, or am I right?"

He grabs Fontana's arm. "I'm a bullshitter. Fontana, ya'll know me." Fontana looks down at the hand on his arm, which causes Plant to pull it away. "I'm just a bullshitter. Just an old bullshitter, Plant. That's me." He jogs over to me and gives a light slap to my shoulder. "Red, you guys know that. Hell, everybody knows that." His voice cracks like a twelve-year-old boy's. He's scared and can't seem to quit going on and on.

"Don't tell Dutch. Come on, guys, just give me a break this time, okay?" He spins in a slow circle to make eye contact with each of us. "Dutch's crazy when it comes to me. Y'all know it's the truth. He won't understand that I was just bullshittin' around."

You see, Plant fucked up big time about two weeks before when Charlie 2 took up a perimeter for the night at Henderson Hill out near Phu Loc 6. He fell asleep on watch while Dutch was checking lines. Dutch caught him with his head drooped down and his chin sagged against his chest. Hell, he was even snoring.

Dutch knocked Plant's helmet off with the butt end of his rifle, then began to beat the living shit out of him with his bare hands. He went ballistic. He bitch-slapped Plant, slugged him with his fists, and kicked him in the ass more than once. And then, when Plant was lying on his side, Dutch just kept on batting him around some more. Plant balled up into a fetal position with his hands over his head. But Dutch kept it up till O'Bie grabbed his arms and pinned him back. It's one of those times that seemed to go on forever in slow motion, like you're caught in a nightmare with slip-sliding feet and you scream for help but the words won't come out.

But you really can't defend Plant. Dutch caught him guilty as Cain. His lack of discipline put all our lives in trouble that night. You can't crash on watch. You just cannot ever, ever, crash on watch. But Dutch, sadistic son of a bitch that he is, went overboard with his reaction. He beat Plant beyond what was necessary to make his point. Hell, Plant is a fuck-up. We all know that. But Dutch is getting to be a mean bastard and Plant is a far-too-easy target. To top it off, Plant is scared shitless of Dutch, who goes even more nuts when he smells fear. Fear to Dutch is like blood to a shark. It makes him more and more frantic with each sniff of the stuff. He gets off on it. I swear he does.

# Chapter Six

## Relief

**DATE: August 1969**

Davie, Plant, and I get our shit together. Fontana coughs to clear his throat. "You guys will be the last relief for the day," he says. "We'll call y'all back to the perimeter 'bout an hour or so 'fore dark." He coughs again and spits to the side. "Grab a box of C-Rations from the Command Post. Make damn sure ya got some water 'fore ya leave out. And lighten up a little bit, will ya?"

I think, *Fuck Fontana—I'm getting a little tired of his "take it easy" bullshit.*

We pick up our flak jackets and a couple of bandoleers of magazines. We decide to grab some extra frags (grenades) when we stop by the CP to get our C-Rations. I take point and start off down this corduroy-rutted dirt road toward Observation Post 1.

During the dry season, dirt gets a color like rusted dust and it seems to explode with each step I take. It's as if I'm a kid splashing through puddles by the side of the road. I'm walking point, Plant follows me, and Davie covers the rear. I feel better with Davie behind me. He's got his shit together. He's able to feel the pulse of the Nam inside him. Seems there's a spark in his body. It shows in the way he walks with a short-man chip on his shoulder. He rubs his thumb and forefinger together as he moves along.

There's this look about him, like he's a gunfighter at high noon. He looks like Paladin walking out of my Uncle Pat's old black-and-white TV set. He wears a know-it-all smile and glances around like a card shark playing big-time poker. You can tell he thinks he can do anything—and shit, I believe he can too!

We try to keep a twenty-yard kill-radius between us. It isn't too long before I see Gino's fire team sitting in the dirt just off a sharp curve in the road at Observation Post 1. Gino sees us and waves. I raise my M-16 over my head to let them know we see them. When we get there, we take awhile to look around. I can see down the road about a half mile southward and I get a clear view to the east toward the low paddies near the river. The muddy fields sweep back north for a good piece toward the company's perimeter.

The damn place earned the name "Alamo" a long time before we got here. They say it's because Marines always find themselves outnumbered and making last stands on its small area of high ground. This information just doesn't make a new boot like me feel all that great inside.

The day's so hot I taste chili peppers on the tip of my dry tongue and feel the dust crawling on my skin, mixing with my sweat. The gooey grime it creates covers every inch of my body. It's like I'm taking a bath in used motor oil. There's a stream of the nasty shit flowing from the back of my neck to the chafed crack in my ass.

"Shit, fuck, and damn it. Where the hell have y'all been?" Gino says. "They radioed we were going to be relieved an hour ago. There isn't any fucking shade from anything out here—nothing." It surprises me how mad he is, and my mouth hangs open. I just stare at him. "There isn't shit to break the heat, damn it. We've been frying here, man." Gino's cheeks are bright red from the relentless sun, his face on fire. He kicks the dirt at his feet and some of it flies up and hits my arm. He's really pissed so I don't say shit about it. "My granny used to say her mouth was so dry she could spit bricks," he continues. "Well then, it's a granny day out here for sure. It feels dry enough to spit a brick shit-house. This place sucks, man. It sucks big time."

Gino slams his helmet down like one of those TV wrestlers, and Plant jumps back to stay clear of the bounce. "Did I tell you that? Did I tell you how this fucking place sucks?" He looks around and sees the rest of us staring at him like he's nuts or something. "Would I shit you? Look it up in the dictionary under 'Marine Corps,' or

'Vietnam,' or 'green motherfucker.' I don't give a shit. It'll be there, trust me."

He looks from me to Davie and then back to Plant. "Shit, Plant, it's your fucking fault we've been out here so long, isn't it?" he adds. "I might a known you'd be a part of this cluster fuck. Hell, it takes your snail-ass so damn long to shake your dick dry after a piss. Probably because you have so much trouble finding the damn little thing." He holds up his right hand and shows an inch and a half between his thumb and forefinger. "You're such a jerk-off, Plant. It must have taken you half that time just to get your hand out of your pants. No shit, you really put me off. I'm not fucking with you, man. This shit really pisses me off!"

Gino works himself into one of his crazy fits. His hands and arms go all over the damn place like he's swatting at bees. Let me tell you, when Gino lets himself fly off the handle, he is, without a fuckin' doubt, nobody you want to screw with. We all know from experience that just letting him blow off steam however he wants is the best way to get through the Roman Legion crap where he thinks he's some sort of bad-assed "Caesar of the Nam." Poor Plant; just being his sorry-self places him in the eye of the storm every time.

Davie is one of the few guys who can calm Gino down when he gets this way. "Gino, lighten up and lay off Plant," Davie tells him. "It isn't his fault. Least ways this time, it ain't. They just told us about this damn relief thing a little while ago. We came right out. If you want to get in someone's shit, take it up with Sgt. Matt or whoever is on the radio back there. Don't drop all this cheap crap on Plant. Remember, this isn't our idea of a picnic, either, my brother, so you might think about cooling down and backing off."

Gino's still looking for somebody to blame. "It's probably that fucking Short Round. Yeah, that's who it is. He's been on the radio all day since 1st squad took a patrol out to the south this morning. He went and forgot all about how long we've been out here. I don't think they replaced OP-2, either." He kicks his feet again, and red clouds fly up all around us. We can see he's coming down from the worst part of his rant, like a party balloon losing helium. "It's okay men, no biggie," he explains. "No sweat, brothers, no sweat. I'm okay now."

Gino does a change in mid-thought and turns a complete circle with his arms sticking up like a saved sinner at a revival. When he stops, he's in a new type of day. "Hey, did the convoy from Da Nang drop off any mail when they went through?" Gino asks. "No shit, I'm going fucking funny-farm loony here. I need some tie with the world or I'm gonna lose it, man. Look into my eyes. Davie, Red Man, all you fuckers, look at my eyes. If they seem even half as bad from your side looking in as they do from my side looking out, I'm fucked. No shit, it's all fixing to slip away big time, right here, right now."

His eyes take on the damned thousand-mile stare, and he squats down and plays with the dust at his feet. "Red Man, it's sand through my fingers, brother. It's all just falling through the cracks in the floor." He lets us watch the dirt seep from his hands. "You know what I mean. I brush the broom over the slats and it all appears clean, but it's only falling through the gaps in the boards. It's all still there underneath, piling up. It never fucking goes away. It's always gonna be there."

Davie steps closer to Gino and squats down in front of him. "Yeah, they did drop off a mail bag," he says, then flops on his ass to sit cross-legged. "They must still be sorting it out, or maybe they are just waiting for the patrol to get back in. Who the fuck knows?" Davie plays in the dirt, too. He sweeps his hand to create a smooth surface and draws designs with a small stick. "They should be there by the time you guys get in. They'll pass it out then, Gino. It's gonna be okay; it's gonna be all right."

Davie picks up some dirt and lets it filter through his fingers, watching the sliding grains of time. "Gino, this isn't you, man," he says. "Look at me! Hey, my brother, it's me, Davie. What's troubling you, man? Are you expecting something special from home?"

"Nah," Gino starts and then takes a deep breath and corrects himself. "Well, shit-yeah. You're damn right I am." He puts his hand to his eyes and runs it across his face. "I've been thinking that my girl might send me something—you know, a letter, or maybe some of those crumbled-up chocolate chip cookies she used to send all the time." He looks from Davie to the rest of us. "Remember, they were so bad last time that I couldn't even give them away?" We laugh with him but get quiet when he stares at the dirt again like he's in some sort of trance. "Shit, Davie, I think it's all falling through. It's like there's a hole in my bucket, and I'm getting sucked down into it. The more I fight, the quicker the whirlpool pulls me under."

Davie reaches over and slaps Gino's knee. "Damn, Gino, there isn't shit you can do about it from here," he says. "You know that as well as I do. You have to let it slide. Be cool. Just, be cool, brother, and we'll get through this shit." Gino drops like a brick from his squatting position to the ground to sit cross-legged like Davie. "Shit, the fuckin' truth is—" he starts. "I think my girl has dumped my sorry ass for one of those junior college assholes from uptown. You know the ones—boys in their daddy's big cars—God's chosen wonder-kids." He looks at Davie, then back over his shoulder at me. In a softer voice, he continues, "Hell, I don't really blame her. I've been gone eight months."

He draws a new design in the dirt with a stick and doesn't speak for a minute. All of a sudden, he throws the twig at the ground and the damn thing sticks straight in, perfect, just like a pocketknife in a game of Mumbley-peg. "I don't think she was all that gung-ho about my ass in the first place. I mean, no shit, really. I think she thought it was cool to be at my side at first. There she was, dating a Marine in dress blues with shiny buckles and all that shit." He pauses again to stare at the twig sticking in the ground.

"When I was home on leave before shipping out to this fucking place," Gino explains, "there was a special 'newness' to it that she could touch and feel and taste. It was alive to her. It seemed to fire her up. No shit."

Plant walks away from us and starts to talk with Hank and the Mexican. Gino watches him leave without comment then continues, "It was good and all, don't get me wrong. But I felt like there were three of us in the backseat of my daddy's Ford Fairlane company car. It was like, there she was getting high with the scent of danger and musk. I almost felt like I was the one pushed to the armrest as the odd man out."

He gives one of those far-off looks toward the river that takes him a hell of a way further beyond the far bank. "In the fogged-up rear-view mirror I saw something more. It wasn't me she was giving herself to—it was the Nam. I ask you now, isn't that a trip? She was screwing the damned Nam." He laughs loud and stares back down at the ground. "And now here I am, and the fuckin' Nam is screwing me. Go figure that shit out for me, will ya?"

He shifts his feet in the dirt and I sit down beside Davie and him. "I left the world for this damned place, and she goes on and graduates from high school," he adds. "That's when she started classes at the junior college. And that's when the letters began to fall off."

"Hell, I think more than half those draft-dodging fuckers are just there for the student deferment."

Davie chimes in, "I bet they all just sit around and bad mouth the war. My brother wrote and told me that they call us a bunch of baby killers and shit like that. I bet it was them assholes who done it. They all wore her ass down with that kind of bullshit. You know, her having to explain how you was in the Nam, and all."

"I don't think she's ashamed of me, but she don't know anything to say to defend me, either," Gino says. "At least not with anything that wouldn't put her in the same boat with me—with us. Hell, I can't really tell it right myself, so how can I hold it against her?" His hands shake, and he puts them under his legs. "And you can be sure, brothers, there ain't anybody standin' up for our asses back in the world."

He gets quiet again, then he speaks like we aren't there and he's just talking to himself. "I think that shit just got too much for her to handle. I'm okay with her, no shit. It's just all those other fuckers beating us down." He looks at Davie and me for us to agree, and we nod our heads. "Here we are in the fucking armpit of the devil. And we can't do shit about any of it." He gets fired up again and talks louder. "Now, that's what burns my ass up. Know what I mean? It just lights my ass on fire, big time."

Gino's words tick Davie off, too. "Fuck 'em, fuck 'em all," he says. "I'd like for one of those little pricks to say that shit to me. I'd kick ass and take names, man—no shit. Asses and elbows. That's all you'd see, just asses and elbows sneaking away like chicken-shits into the bushes. This crap really sets me off, too. No shit, it burns my ass to no end."

Without looking, Davie throws a handful of dirt my way that I'm able to duck just in the nick of time. I say, "Whoa Davie, it isn't me. I'm on Gino's side, man."

"Fuck that bitch and the horse she rode in on," Davie goes on like he never even heard me. "You tell her I said that. You tell her that if we both make it back, I'll come see ya. We'll go out to that fucking pansy-ass, junior college together. Then we'll see if any one of those 'peace' assholes has got the balls to say shit to us." He laughs and spits to his side. "Peace, my ass! Those chicken-shits just want a P-I-E-C-E. They all just use this war as a quick trip into our girls' satin panties while we're gone. I mean, no shit. Assholes. Fuck those wimpy sons of bitches."

Plant wanders back and stands beside us again. "Junior college?" he asks. "What sort of big deal is that anyway?"

"It's like they wanna be in a real college but they're not tall enough," says Gino. "They're all whining because they can't get on the big-kid rides at Disneyland. Shit, the tops of their heads probably won't reach the height-line on the wall, or some shit like that."

"I agree—fuck them!" adds Plant.

"Plant, what the fuck do you know 'bout any of this shit?" says Davie. "Keep out of it if ya don't got nothin' worth shit to add." Plant steps away with his head down and goes back to bug the Mexican and Hank again.

Gino decides it's his turn to try and calm Davie down. "Hey Davie, man, cool off, brother—it's okay," he says. "Really, it's no big deal. I'm okay with it, no shit." He looks over to me. "We've all got to keep our heads on straight. Right here and right now, men. We'll never get back to the world in the first place if we don't. That's what we got to worry about, brothers. We take it one step at a time. Just, one step at a time." He looks back and forth between Davie and me. "We can't let this shit get to us. Hell, I'm the one getting it in the ass, man. It'd be nice to hear from her, but shit, what the fuck you going to do?"

I watch the Mexican and Hank put their gear on and make their way over to us. "Hey, you got to get a room and save dis bullchit for later," the Mexican cuts in. "Take it up with dat bitch, Dear Abby, or some chit like that. Come on, Gino, give 'em de fuckin' radio and lez get back to de lines."

Gino stands up, grabs the radio, and hands it to Davie. The Mexican looks up at the sky like he's praying. "I need to get out of dis sun and crash awhile, man. I'm a Mex'cun; I need siesta, *amigos*. Who de fuck knows what sort of chit dey got for us *este noche*? Come on, lez get de fuck out of here. I've got a *muy malo* feelin' 'bout dis place." He passes by me and slaps the hell out of my back. "Chit, I'm Mex'cun and dey put me in a place called 'de Alamo.' Don ja hear me, dere be *mucho* bad vibes here *compadres*."

"Yeah, me too. I'm a Tenn-a-fuckin'-see-an, guys," Hank says. "Don't forget, that Alamo was not a very good place for white boys from Nashville, either. Let's get out of this shit, now. Y'all can have it." Hank reaches out his hand, grabs me by the arm, and helps pull my ass off the ground. "The only thing we've been seeing is those gook kids. Look at 'em down there close to the river working that paddy back and forth."

He shakes his head. "Watch 'em. Shit, the little baby-san's been sprawled across that water buffalo's neck for the past two hours. He's been sound asleep the whole time." He points toward the rice paddy they work through. "That other kid's been leading it up and back, and up and back. Looks like he's fucking mowing the lawn or some shit like that. It's a fucking ping-pong match—back and forth, and back and forth. They keep wading through that mud and slop. I just don't see how they do that bullshit all day long."

We all stare down at the paddy and shake our heads to agree with Hank. "These people aren't real. No shit, they are like ghosts or some crap like that. That's who they are, ghost people. They've been doing this shit for-fuckin'-ever man. Not just for today and yesterday, but last year, and the year before that, and the year before that, and lifetimes before that. It's fucking not human, man. It freaks the shit out of me."

Gino breaks in, "You guys keep sharp. We've been hearing first squad's patrol call in radio-checks. They been seeing all sorts of signs of gooks. Said they came across some old momma-san in one of the Phu Loc villes toward the hills. Said she was acting all weird and scared as shit. Like somethin' is gonna happen and she's caught in the middle of it."

"Well, there's no doubt about that, this is a bad place, man," says Davie. "I don't like anything about it at all. This is where Delta Company got their fucking asses kicked last month. They lost a bunch of grunts, man. No, I don't like this place, neither."

"We'll see y'all later," says Gino. "We're gone." He motions for his men to move. "Hey, Mexican—you take off on point. I'll follow you, then Hank, bring it on up from the rear."

"Let's do it," says Hank. He doesn't play around much with words, but he's a hell of a badass in a firefight.

"No shit, don't fuck around, keep as low as you can out here." Gino looks back at us and says, "This is as fucked an open place as you can find. Stay cool."

"Yeah, 'cool.' Right, we'll 'stay cool,'" Davie says to me and Plant. He yells to their backs as they head away, "What the hell is that supposed to mean? 'Stay cool.' That's a good one, Gino. Fuck you, you Italian pasta-head." Gino flips his middle finger in the air and doesn't even look back toward us.

"Red, you figure that means he thinks I'm number one?" Davie asks me.

Davie takes the radio and calls back in to the Command Post to tell them that Gino's team is on their way in. He reminds them to be sure and pass the word so nobody will shoot their asses when they get near the lines. They slip outta our sight below the hill and we settle in at the post. After the rush of being on our own clears away, we calm down. Plant and Davie lie on their sides while I stand first watch and look down from the high ground toward the two kids in the paddy. Gino's right, they look like they've been out here for hundreds of years. No, more than that, it's gotta be thousands of years, because shit, they seem like they're just walking out of the ark with that damn water buffalo by their side.

After an hour, it's Davie's turn at watch. I sit down beside him and try to get some rest. Ready to say something to him, I look up at his face. A small droplet of sweat forms on the tip of his more-than-once broken nose. I watch the moisture build like water on the lip of a leaky faucet. When it gains enough weight to fall, the drop dives and explodes on one of Davie's scuffed boots while he pays it no mind. His gaze level, his mind focused on the task before him.

# Chapter Seven

## Lions

**DATE: August 1969**

We do a radio check and call in to find that 1ˢᵗ squad's patrol made it back to the perimeter. I silently pray, hoping that Gino got a letter from home. It's getting even hotter, so we take off our flak jackets and trade our helmets for soft jungle covers.

"Hey, Red Man, you and Plant come look at this shit," Davie says. A series of small craters bore into the dry red dirt at his feet. Six or seven indentations lie three-to-four inches apart. They range from one-to-two inches in diameter and look like children's snow cone cups discarded on a carnival midway.

"What the fuck are they, Davie?" Plant asks.

"Just watch," Davie says and raises his hand in a stop motion.

We stand in the cruel joke of pounding heat from a laughing sun and stare at the motionless pits for several minutes. Like three-card Monte suckers searching for the card with a bent corner, we wait for the flip in Davie's game, but nothing happens.

Plant shifts his weight from foot to foot. "What the fuck is it? I don't see shit," he says. "Davie, am I gonna see somethin' here or what?" His excitement builds, and he rises up on his toes and bounces in the dust. "You're just screwin' 'round with me again, ain't ya, Davie? Shit, why does everybody think that every day's 'fuck with Plant day' over here?" He twitches his head in a circular motion on his neck. "It's the same shit every fuckin' day."

"Listen up, Plant," I say. "You are not the Lone Ranger; I don't see shit, either. Davie, what the fuck is going on, man? What kinda magic ya workin' on now?"

"Give it time. Patience, brothers, patience," Davie says. "Shit, that's what's wrong with city-boys. Y'all 'spect everything to jump when you say 'froggie.' The real world doesn't revolve around Disneyland wristwatches." He holds his arms out to a ten and four o' clock position. "It's not all 'bout Mickey's left hand and Mickey's right hand pointin' out the time. Leave it alone. It'll happen when it happens."

Davie steps back from the small holes in the ground and motions for us to do the same thing. "Pull away and give it time, city boys, give it time! Ain't no wonder townie girls love country boys. We know how to go sloooooooow." Plant looks at Davie like he's a preacher givin' him a sermon. Davie looks into Plant's eyes and goes on, "Like Tina Turner sings it, Plant boy: 'Nice and easy.'" He begins to talk in a soft voice. "Then, if they ask us, real pretty-like, we'll let them have a little 'nice and rough' for the road." He gives a wink to Plant, and Plant winks back, his eyes wide—the size of silver dollars.

After five more minutes caught in Davie's time trap, Plant's attention starts to lose its grip. "Oh man, this is some borin' shit, that's for sure," he says. "Come on, Davie, quit fuckin' with us. Make something happen, man." Davie gets a little bit pissed at him for saying this. "Fuck you, Plant. Like, where you gotta be, anyways? You got a hot date or some shit like that? Your Momma got dinner on the table? Huh, Plant?" Davie pushes Plant away from his place beside him. Plant stumbles and I catch him before he falls.

"Shit, there ain't a one of us got any-fuckin'-place to be in this whole silly, fuckin' world but right here and right now," Davie continues. "Mickey has got one of his three fuckin' fingers up your ass right now, Plant. There ain't no time tickin'. It's all stopped." I help Plant stand back up straight. Plant backs away until he runs into me. "It's all just standin' still," Davie adds. "This is all there is, Plant. This is the ballgame. It's all right here and right now. There ain't no spinnin' Earth, Plant. You better hold on tight to your nuts." He reaches his arm above his head and draws a circle in the air with his hand. "If you don't, they gonna drift on out into space like some kind of Buck Rogers bullshit. It's just the Red Man, me, and you, Plant Boy. Just us and these damn holes in the ground."

31

We bend over and stare at the holes, and we stare—and we stare. Not a damn thing happens—not shit. I'm even beginning to doubt Davie's country-boy wisdom. God forgive me, but I'm starting to believe that Plant might even be right for once. Then I think, nah, and keep on staring at the pits in the dust. Finally, from the left side of the area, we watch, we notice a lone ant. A little, red, non-descript, time-traveling ant is zigzagging its way nearer to the craters.

"Okay now, watch this shit," Davie whispers. "Keep quiet and don't move. Just keep eyes on the ant. Watch 'im scurry. Be a part of his life. Watch his fate."

The ant works his way between the first two craters, then stops dead still. He seems to be planning some sort of strategy, the way a rock climber might wait beneath a cliff and chart out a face-climb in his mind. The ant rotates his head from side to side. He seems to be envisioning his moves before choosing the steps he'll make. In a little bit, he moves again. He crosses with calculated steps between several craters without a problem. Then, at the edge of the third pit, his ass-end slips off an edge and he struggles against the gravity that's pulling him toward the center of the pit. As he struggles, the grains of sand give way and fall down the sides of the slope beneath him.

As a spark inspires a flame, from the crater's depths a geyser of small grains of sand shoots up out of the center of the hole. Plant and I jump back, and Davie laughs from deep within at our startled response.

"What the fuck?" Plant and I shout in unison.

"Wait, wait, it ain't over, it's just beginnin'," Davie says. "Just watch. Keep your eyes on the ant. Get in his head and try to feel his struggle." Davie stands up straight and towers over the drama at our feet. "Shit, can't ya see it? He's a fuckin' grunt just like us. He's exactly like us." He looks back and forth between our faces. "Can't ya see it? He's one of us, man. He's trapped in the middle of this silly shit, just like we are." He looks to us again for understanding. "It's just all lightning-strike bullshit. Anybody can get it, anywhere, anytime—for no reason at all."

Davie is a tent revival preacher. "Don't you see?" he says. "It don't matter if he got his act together or not. He can be king of the fuckin' ants for all the good it will do them." He shakes his head and continues. "If it's his time to go, don't matter if he jukes left or right. If he zigs when he shoulda zagged, it don't make no never mind. He's

just another dead grunt." Davie turns and takes a step away, then he
turns back around and opens his arms to the scene. "He's walking
through booby traps just like us, my brothers. He's just rollin' the
fuckin' dice with each step he takes. He's a damned grunt, I tell ya!"

The ant continues to wiggle and squirm in its futile attempt to
escape its destiny. But every effort he makes causes him to slide
farther down into the hungry mouth of the crater. My hands tingle.
It's like I can feel his terror in my fingertips. I begin to sense that his
spindly little legs are my own nails clawing at the side of the pit. It's
like it's me. I'm the buried man in a closed casket. It's cold and dark
and I feel like I'm the one with scraped and bleeding fingers. The
more the grains of sand slide to the pit's center, the more frequent
the eruption from the hole spits them back out, higher and higher
above the crater's brim.

I feel the ant's frantic struggle for just one more moment of
sunlight—one second longer of whatever the hell ant dreams might
hold. I know his certainty that it is a lost cause, but I also feel his
primeval call to the heavens: "Fuck this shit. If you want my ass, you
are gonna have to battle me for it. I won't ever just lie down and quit
the fight. Come and get me, asshole. Let me see your face. I'll spit in
your eye with my last ounce of strength."

Finally, the ant's struggles work him down toward the final brink
of the center of the hole. "Watch now, it won't be long," Davie
cautions. "Don't blink or you'll miss it. You boys ain't gonna believe
this shit." In a bit less than a flick, this ancient monster with hyena
jaws and a head half the size of his body slips up out of the hole and
grabs the ant in a vice grip. Then, just as fast as it appeared, it
vanishes into the depth of the abyss, pulling its prey along with it.

Plant turns a circle in the sand. "Whoa, that was cooler than shit,"
he says, jumpin' up and down. "That was bad. That was defi-fuckin'-
nitely bad." He looks over to see Davie's broad grin beaming back at
him. "What in the hell was that, Davie?" Plant is going nuts and he
can't sit still. He paces back and forth and throws his hands in the air.
"How did you get him to do that, Davie? How did you get him to
fuckin' do that shit?" Plant stops jumping and places his hands on his
knees to catch his breath. "That is the most un-fuckin'-believable
thing I ever seen! Wow, man, that was cool. That was very, very, bad-
assed cool! No shit!"

"That, city boys, is an ant-lion," explains Davie. "It's half-lion and half-ant. No shit! Look it up!"

"Now, Davie, where in the fuck am I going to look it up?" I say. "Like I'm gonna check the *World Book* out when I get back to the perimeter and see what I can find under 'A.'"

Davie laughs some more at us. "No shit, Red Man," he adds. "That's what they call 'em. Least that's what my Grandpa Martin tells me back home. He says the Cajuns in south Louisiana tell that the monsters have the head and aggression of a lion. And they got the worker's back and body of an ant. Says it has somethin' to do with voodoo or hoojoo, or some shit like that. Grandpa Martin never, ever lies to me. I mean, never." Artillery fire from An Hoa sounds in the distance, causing us all to look to our north. "Why would I pick this time, in this fuckin' hell hole, to lie to you, my brothers?"

I'm a believer. I know, without doubt of Sunday mornin' forgiveness for Saturday night's sins, that Davie believes it himself— one hundred percent. I can tell by the glint of truth in his eyes. Takin' my rifle strap off my shoulder, I hold my M-16 in my hand and step away from them to get a better view toward the paddies by the river.

"Oh, hell, man, this is some scary, bad-assed shit," Plant says. "Are they gonna fuck with us, Davie? I mean, do they, like, get any bigger in Nam? Is this some sort of fuckin' set-up like you guys are always playing on me or what?"

Davie understands the truth of his fear. "No, Plant, calm down, they just fuck with ants and little shit bugs that fall into their traps," he says. "But, you do need to remember that, long, long ago they did mess with people in the night. They'd sneak into in the dark places of their souls. There's this fire dance, or some weird shit they would do." Davie shrugs his shoulders like he's not sure what to say here. "But Grandpa Martin says that is only Louisiana Cajun truth. He says that anywhere else it has lost its hoojoo power, as far as he knows.

"Now that I think of it, to tell you the truth, Plant," Davie continues, "Grandpa Martin never knew much about the side of the world we're at now. Who knows, Plant, who knows?" The guns from An Hoa begin their roar again. Davie hunkers down and moves off to the side. "Maybe on this backside of the map there's a place. Somewhere you sail beyond the edge and fall off." He stops talking and slides on his flak jacket, then checks his pockets to count his frags. "Maybe the ant-lions will one day rule. Maybe one night they are gonna rise up out of the rice paddies. Then they'll pull every last one of us down under with 'em."

Davie begins to step closer and closer to Plant until he is up in his face. "Fuck all our gunships and napalm and B-52 bombin' runs. Fuck every last bitta fire superiority we throw at 'em. And fuck the gooks and all their spider holes and booby trap bullshit." He turns his back on Plant and faces down the road. Plant steps up to stand beside Davie so he can hear him as he continues. "One night the ant-lions are gonna reach up and drag us all under with 'em." In a whisper, so soft it causes Plant to lean in so near to Davie that he is touching his sleeve, Davie adds, "You better breathe deep while you still can, brother. That's all I've got to say."

Davie isn't just messin' with Plant, either. Davie believes this shit. You can see it in his eyes. "Now, watch this," he says. He reaches down, picks a piece of dried grass, and turns back toward the small area of ant-lion pits. He leans over and gives a light touch to the side of one of the reverse cones. The movement causes a few grains to fall downward into the center of the pit. The touch works just like an ant entering the trap. The disturbance meets the same spitting eruption we witnessed earlier in response to the death-sliding struggles of the ant. It's the slow, useless, eternal battle all over again, but this time, it is an invisible grunt walking point and the ant-lion loses. I'm sure it pisses him off. But fuck his sorry ass.

Davie and I take turns on watch for the rest of the afternoon while Plant continues to be fascinated by the ant-lion pits. He scrambles around on his hands and knees, catching random ants to drop into the craters. He watches in rapt fascination as they struggle against their predetermined fate. With each little giggle of glee from Plant, I think I can also sense the ant's final gasp of hope. I know the darting, lunging thrust of the ant-lion as it rises from the bowels of the earth and lays claim to another ambushed victim of random circumstance.

Finally, the call comes in from the CP informing us it is time to end the OP for the day. We saddle up and make our way back to the perimeter. After we enter the lines, we go straight to our fighting hole and to our poncho-sagging shelter for some brief moments of rest.

O'Bie brings the mail to us. Davie gets a note from his dad. I receive a letter from my sister that includes a scribbled little piece of paper with a greeting from my three-year-old nephew. Plant doesn't get shit. He hangs his head for a moment. Then he jumps up as if it is the dawn of a new day. "I'll be back in a little while," he announces. "I want to tell the guys in Gino's fire team about the ant-lions of OP-1."

After Plant leaves, Davie comes over and sits beside me on the edge of our fighting hole. "Red Man, you know, I feel sorry as hell for that silly shit, Plant. He is, no doubt, a fuck-up. Oh, I know he brings it on himself, but still, he's too easy a mark for some of the bullies we've got."

I watch the early evening shadows play with the distant tree line. Plant is like those damn, doomed ants. He's just zigzagging around in life without a clue. Hell, he can't take care of himself. It's like fate is holding him from above. He's trapped here, dangling by puppet strings that manipulate him back and forth. There must be some sort of twisted fate that keeps him from slipping into one of those pits. Hell, so many squared-away grunts get capped out of nowhere. Some snap unseen tripwires and get carried home by the fuckin' Man from Glad. But Plant? Silly, dip-shit, fuckin' Plant just keeps dancin' his Wonderland two-step. Like a blind bat in the dark of night, he maneuvers his way around the killing craters. He's able to sidestep that damn avalanche of the world caving in beneath his feet just waiting to carry him under. And then he smiles and wanders on without a clue. Hell, the joke's not on Plant; the laughing I hear is at me.

Davie shakes his head, stares down at his feet, and remains tree-trunk still for a few moments. "Fuckin' ant-lions, anyway. Fuck 'em," he says, lookin' back up into my eyes. "You know what I mean, Red Man? Fuck 'em. And fuck the horse they rode in on."

"I know what you mean, my brother," I say. "I know just what you mean, and it is all cool with me. Davie, it is all gonna be all right. Trust me on this one." We look at each other and break out laughing into one of those laughs that swells and becomes more than itself. "Davie, would I lie to you?"

# Chapter Eight

## Lessons

**DATE: August 1969**

On a daytime, squad-sized patrol near the small hamlet of Phu Loc 4, some Viet Cong surprise us. It isn't any sort of an ambush, we just happen to come upon them as we emerge from a tree line. As we move over a small rise of high ground, they fire on us first. They're not more than 500 meters away from us and, after their initial fire, they make a run toward the far tree line. In the excitement of the moment I lose track of where we are. With one of our fire teams ahead and to the left of us, I pull my M-16 to a firing position and pop off a couple of rounds. Davie reaches over and pushes the barrel of my rifle downward. Although our men are free from my direct line of fire, only a few meters of safe space separate us.

Instead of hollering, Davie pulls me to kneel down beside him. In a cool voice he explains where I went wrong. Even while the enemy's fire continues to fly around us, he takes the time to set me straight. The boot's mistake I made can cause men to die. There is no doubt about it.

When we get back to the perimeter after the patrol ends, Gino comes to our position on the lines. He is ready to jump all over me. "Back off, Gino, he's my man," Davie says. "His mistakes are my mistakes. This is my own damn problem and I'll take care of it." Davie walks up to Gino and stands toe-to-toe with him. "You mind your own team and I'll keep my house in order. That's all ya need to know about it."

Gino begins to say something more, but the look in Davie's eyes causes him to shake his head. They silently face each other for a few more moments, then Gino turns and walks away. Ashamed of myself, I feel the redness flush over my face as if I'd been caught smoking behind the schoolhouse. Davie turns to look at me. "Do we need to talk more about this, Red Man? Have ya got it straight? This is no fuckin' game." I nod my head and he continues. "We ain't shooting blanks out here, brother. These gooks are not the pretend enemy from Camp Pendleton training. This is the real shit, brother. I need to know that I can trust your ass with my life."

He motions for me to follow him. We sit down by each other at the edge of our fighting hole. "This is the Nam. When you fuck up, men die. Do you hear me? They fuckin' die, Red." He looks out across the rice paddies to our front. Reaching to his side, he picks up a dirt clod and hurls it far out into the field. Its contact with the muddy water causes ripples that soon disappear into the young rice plants. "The kind of dumb-assed shit you did today is over with. You got that? From this moment on, you don't do a damn thing before you think 'what would Davie do' first. Instinct comes with experience and what ya do just happens." He slugs me in the arm to get me to look over at him. "Do not fuck up again!"

I shrug my shoulders and stare straight into his eyes. "I won't, Davie. I give you my word."

"That's all I need to know, and you remember to take everything I tell you as the gospel according to Davie 'cause it's the book that keeps your ass alive."

"Thanks, Davie," I say. My arm hurts where he hit me, and I begin to rub it.

He gets silent for a few moments, then spits out words like they're a wad of my Uncle Angus's chewing tobacco. "Don't you ever thank my ass for this kind of shit again. What I tell ya is meant to keep my ass alive just as much as it's meant to keep you upright, too. You can bet ya momma's life on this fact. I'll whip your ass like a fuckin' stepchild if you ever again put me in the kind of spot you did today." He reaches over and uses my shoulder as a brace to help push himself up. "My life, and the life of these other men, comes before any loyalty to the friendship we've got. Don't you ever, ever, ever fucking forget that." He slaps the back of my head. "Have I made myself clear, Red? Do you understand what I'm saying?"

I only nod my head. It feels like Davie's my third-grade teacher, Miss Villarreal, sending me to the corner for chewing gum in class. Hell, there's nothin' left to say.

"Then that's the end of it, and don't you say shit to anyone else," Davie adds. "It's none of their fuckin' business. You remember, while you are in my fire team, if anybody is gonna fuck with ya, it's gonna be me. Got it?"

"Yeah, I do," I respond. "I know where I stand."

"Red Man, one last thing, brother," Davie adds. "Don't you ever fuck with me. I may be a poor boy from Mississippi. I might even be a little short for the size of the balls I carry 'round. But you need to always know that I am the one not to be messin' with." He picks up his rifle and flak jacket. As he starts to walk away, he turns around and adds, "You listen to me and I'll keep your ass alive. You fuck with me, and you will wish your momma never had ya." He laughs and slaps me on the back just as if he was joking with that last line.

I smile in return, but I have no doubt in this world that there is no joke or game about this conversation. I love this young man as a brother, but I am now, without a shadow of a doubt, a hell of a lot more scared of Davie than I am of any enemy in the bushes.

# Chapter Nine

## In the Bushes

**DATE: August 1969**

Plant, Brice, and I take out a Listening Post after first darkness. Like nesting hens, we settle into a thick clump of elephant grass and banana trees overgrown in an old bomb crater. The spot is to the side of a worn trail that crosses a section of high ground. The CP assigns us a general area where the vegetation is dense; we pick our exact spot when we get there. We'll hide and listen for enemy movement, then radio an early warning to the perimeter if any occurs.

Plant takes first watch while Brice and I lay back and try to get some rest. Brice pulls second watch, leaving me last man up. At one-hour intervals we will switch and hand over the radio to the next man in the sequence.

As a Listening Post, we are instructed to avoid contact with the enemy. Standing watch in our hiding place consists of staring out into the blanket of brush that wraps around and through us. We stretch the limits of our senses to see with our ears or to taste a misplaced breath on a breeze through the black depth that engulfs us. The close cover swallows us. Alone on watch, we filter out the every-night sounds of the bush and strain to pick up any miscue within the movements of the night.

Sleep overtakes me sometime near the end of Plant's watch. It feels as if I just dozed off when Brice nudges my side and hands over the wristwatch and radio for my time on guard. Before rolling over onto his side, Brice gives one last, deep look into my eyes to make sure I am awake and ready to go. The watch's illuminated numbers wink nine-o'clock through the scratches on its weather-beaten face. I pull my frayed, green towel over my head to fight the onslaught of determined mosquitoes. I leave an opening for my nose, ears, and useless eyes and wait to respond to the next radio check from the perimeter. When the call slips through the air it carries the voice of Sergeant Matt. "If there are gooks in the bushes give me two pushes, if there are none give me one." I respond with one squeeze on the key of the handset. Sergeant Matt replies to the broken static sound with a soft whisper, "Roger that."

I return my attention to the spider web that surrounds us. It plays in the wind over our heads like the thin weave of midway cotton candy, in the magic of spinning sugar. Creatures of darkness sing their timeless tunes of the bush in perfect harmony. Tonight, there are the additional sounds of muted gunfire from distant firefights. Rounds of illumination light the sky like shutter flashes of far-off August wildfires.

The three of us are cramped into the womb of this angry monster of circumstance. Brice sleeps with his head on my leg. Every now and then I give him a quick shake to still the first snorts of a larger snore: sounds I know will grow from his hand rubbing across his nose. Plant props his legs at an awkward angle on my shoulder. Trying to find some sort of comfort, I lay further back into the bed of broken leaves and bent grasses. My thigh cramps, but I fight the urge to snap it out straight. I refuse to interrupt my brothers' short time at rest. Both Brice and Plant are sound asleep, held in dreams from a world away. I pray they escape in images that carry them away to prom queens, back car seats with fogged windows, and pasture keg parties. With time, the pain in my leg dulls. I lie awake, alone in our small nest of bugs, brush, and the prying eyes of night.

I maintain the fragile protection of our camouflaged sanctuary. My sweat-stained utility jacket is buttoned up to the curve of my neck, its sleeves cuffed down and fastened at my wrists. The heat and mosquitoes threaten my strained ability to remain motionless. I taste the 'bug juice' repellent in the moisture that stings my eyes and burns my lips, and I repress the noise of a retch.

The incessant, monotonous buzzing of mosquitoes assaults my ears. Like a stubborn soldier, one might fall to a swat of death, but the rest keep charging onward. They play every obnoxious can't-get-it-out-of-my-head song ever sung as an off-tune hum in my ears. They goose-step in formation on my wet forehead and dance across my unshaven chin. Davie promises me he once saw a Nam mosquito bonkin' a water buffalo. He argues that, while the cow kept bellowin', the skeeter kept hollerin', "suffer, baby, suffer!" I believe the story.

I take the towel from my head and shift positions without waking Plant or Brice. The change only makes things worse. The bloodsuckers from hell continue their relentless call of chainsaws and jackhammers in my ears. I'm not sure how long I'm on watch when I hear a rustling to our west. It becomes a certain movement on the trail just above the thicket where we lay. The breeze twists directions. The distinct scent of hot spices within alien sweat catches on the tip of my nose. My enemy is passing by.

I hear murmurings that must be conversation in groups of twos and threes. The sound of whispers, like stolen notes in the rear of a classroom, reaches my ears. These fighters have likely paused at this point on the trail many times before, and tonight's dance with luck once again pushes the odds on their home ground. I know the fear they feel while waiting for the courage to cross the open road a bit further on down the trail. I share the dryness in their mouths and the catch that comes with difficult swallows. I know their fear seeks to touch good-luck tokens and letters from home. It reaches for reminders, like words of love from mommas and sisters and brothers. I understand their need for a tie to last promises of "forever love" from first-kissed sweethearts. They are taking a break from the dagger of danger that stalks them just as it does us. Several of them congregate a short distance above the indentation of thick undergrowth at our heads. Shadows hold us from their direct view.

I can hear the redundant words from Babel uttered in hushed tones. I know they move and speak as eternal fighters in the night, as if they were one of our own frightened patrols laboring in the false safety of a cloud-shrouded moon. I can feel their bitching and moaning within the few, universal laughs they mute with covered hands. Their grunts I distinguish as the syllables of fighting men everywhere.

I sense the bravado in their nervous voices. I understand the forced laughter that serves to cover internal fears with the false confidence of men trapped beneath the shadow of death. Their sense of smell seeks out our foreign taste of bug juice and beanie weenies as it seeps through the pores of our wet skin. I am aware that their eyes cloud in the frightened stare of "when will it happen?" as they scan the leaves over our heads for any trace of movement.

I know that I can't shift my legs or shoulders for fear of waking Plant and Brice. I flick the selector switch of my M-16 with my right thumb from safety to semi-automatic. Hour-hand-slow, I reach with my left hand and feel detached as I watch it crawl, like a chicken-coop snake through thin, octagonal wire. It works its way from the ground to my thigh, up toward my stomach and onto my chest. It moves as if it were a separated part of me in the sneak of a shaking, third-date hand up the back of a sheer, summer blouse. It crawls with inexperienced fingers in search of the unexplained hooks of a thin bra strap.

Time changes and moves faster. My disassociated hand races to unsnap the top, right pocket of my utility jacket. I pull a grenade out into my free hand and grip its cold metal form. With my M-16 in my lap, I take the two prongs of the frag's pin that hold it to the spindle and straighten them out. I pull it for the feel of slight movement. It gives in a way that causes me to trust that it will be ready to continue all the way out if needed.

A radio check comes to us once again in Sergeant Matt's voice. "If there are any gooks in the bushes, give me two pushes, if there are none give me one."

I don't feel as if I should move, but I also know that if I don't answer, Matt will keep calling back, checking on us till he gets some sort of response. I inch my hand to the key grip and give it two squeezes. Then I wait for the response I know will accompany my confirmation. "I repeat, Charlie 2 Alpha, Charlie 2 Alpha, this is Charlie 2. If there are any gooks in the bushes give me two pushes, if there are none give me one."

Again, I squeeze the handset twice, and let it go. I grab the frag from my lap and pull it to my chest. My left forefinger slips through the pull-loop of the pin and I slide it a bit to make certain it remains loose and ready for a clean, swift jerk.

The rustling of flimsy material above my head precedes the sound of a wet flow and the patter of liquid on leaves. I move my eyes upward without flinching my body. A sandaled foot shows through the bottom of the undergrowth. The ammonia smell of urine tickles my nose as it falls through the tall grasses and leaves that hang over my head. I feel the wet splash of drops on my exposed face and hands.

With a firm grip on the frag's spring-handle, I pull the pin all the way out and wait for whatever it is that will follow the enemy's recognition of my presence. If there is a look downward, if Plant or Brice moves in their sleep, or if Sergeant Matt makes another call on the radio, the enemy will hear it from this close range. I wait.

Biting my lip, I feel the pain and taste the rust and iron of my own warm blood. Somehow this calms me. A concession to my fate prepares me to toss my armed frag onto the trail. I also aim my M-16 upward, ready to give a short burst toward the bulk of his body. I wait.

Not Plant, Brice, nor the radio makes a sound. More whispers and movement from the trail cause me to clench my teeth. But the gooks move onward and away from us in staggered spurts. I envision my enemy farther down the trail as he crouches in a shared fear. I know his uncertainty as he waits to cross the road that will carry him to the comforting lie of safety on the other side.

At some point, a last man in line passes us by. I stop hearing sounds from my left and front. Muffled rustlings to my right sound as the end of their patrol moves onward. I take the frag's pin and reinsert it through the open hole. Its prongs twist outward into a locked position. I put my hand on Brice's arm and signal a "shushing" motion with a finger to my lips. Plant gets the same gesture as I grab his head where it rests on my leg. I pull his face toward mine and give a slight shake of my head, mouthing the words, "Gooks...everywhere." I point to the trail and give an open-hand signal to indicate "don't move, don't move."

Into the radio mike I whisper, "Charlie 2, Charlie 2, this is Charlie 2 Alpha, over."

"This is Charlie 2, over," answers the voice of Sergeant Matt.

I cover the mike with my body and respond, "We had gooks on top of us. They're movin' parallel to the perimeter." I make my sentences short and crisp. "They're on the trail just west of OP-2. They've crossed the road now. They're moving away from the perimeter, over."

"Roger that. How many? Over?"

"Can't say." I wait for a moment to catch my breath, then add, "They were bunched—waitin' to cross the road. A squad of at least eight to ten. Maybe a few more. Couldn't see to make a count. Only heard their movement through the bush."

"Roger that," Sergeant Matt responds. "Stay on full alert with all men up until you hear from us, over."

"Roger that," I whisper. "Over."

Plant can be a crasher, but he isn't going to sleep tonight. Brice is almost as new in country as me, but I can tell by the size of his eyes that he will be wide awake till morning's light. The night drags onward with the endless pace of a Friday afternoon's last-period class. Our own lines are on full alert throughout the remainder of the night. But there is no contact after our report of enemy movement. First light filters through the thick foliage of our lair to announce the arrival of another day.

Finally, the word comes from the CP. "Charlie 2 Alpha, Charlie 2 Alpha, this is Charlie 2, do you read me? Over," calls Short Round on the radio.

Brice holds our radio. "This is Charlie 2 Alpha, we got ya," he replies.

"Bring it on in, Charlie 2 Alpha. Over," Short Round says.

"Roger that. Over," Brice replies.

We decide to take the same track the enemy patrol took several hours before. Brice walks point while I walk in the middle and carry the radio. Plant brings up the rear. When we hit the road, we see the lines through the open area and I holler, "Careful of booby traps, Brice. They coulda left somethin' behind on the road just to fuck with us."

"Got you, Red Man; thanks," Brice answers. "I'm so tired I'm not sharp."

"*No es un problemo*," I call back.

"The Mexican would kick your ass if he heard ya talkin' like that," Brice says.

We enter our lines at the same point where we left the night before. Sergeant Matt and Lieutenant Frost wait for us. They want me to come with them to the CP to give a report.

I'm too tired to try to read what they are thinking. I'm too wasted to explain the smell of fear intermixed with the urine that had wet my forehead. I don't tell them about getting pissed on. I just give the facts of what went on. When they finish with me, I go to our position in the lines, drop gear, and crash on the spot. Nobody fucks with me for the remainder of the morning. I feel bodies walk around me as the heat of day claims the morning's mist. But I choose to remain within the clutch of a daze.

Davie shakes me awake after several hours. I blink with the sun full in my face. I feel his concern. I also sense his anger.

"Fuck this shit, Red Man," he says. "It shoulda been me out there last night. It ain't right." He spits a wad of phlegm at a line of small red ants that cross between us. They look like cars with headlights lit in a funeral procession. Davie reaches out his foot and twists his boot in the middle of them. Then he drags his sole down the line, killing as many of them as possible. "Fucking Nam. This bitch can kiss my ass."

"Davie, we couldn't fight 'em," I say. "Hell, I did what you told me to do: think, then react. I didn't take the chance of wakin' Plant or Brice. I had my M-16 on semi-automatic and the pin pulled on a frag." I walk over and stand in front of him. "Hell, I even let a fucking gook piss on my damned, red head." I laugh at my own folly. "Can ya believe that shit?" Davie smiles and looks like he is trying to see the scene in his own head. "Now, I'm not kissin' your ass," I say. "But I remember thinking, 'what would Davie do?' No shit. Davie, you walked me through it." I reach over and place my hand on his shoulder. "You were there. I could hear your words. They guided me every step of the way."

He smiles, but his expression soon changes. I can tell he is gettin' angry. "Shit, Red, that's what I came here for. Now you, Plant, and Brice get laid down in the middle of it last night." He steps back and my hand falls from his shoulder. Pointing a finger at me he continues, "And what was I doin'?" He slides his boot back and forth again to squash some more of the scattering ants. "Hell, I was sittin' back here in the lines playin' with myself." He hollers, "Shit! I came here for the fight. And I missed it again, man. I missed it bigger 'n dog shit." He gives a solid hit with his right fist into his left palm. "Red Man, it's not your fault. But it still pisses me off. It just ain't right. No, it sure ain't the way it's supposed to go."

I now understand the clearest difference between Davie and me. Davie isn't afraid. He's in the Nam because he wants a piece of the action. Davie is "balls-out, let's get it on." I, on the other hand, am honest-to-God afraid. I've come to the Nam to prove that I'm not scared of the fight. But while Davie walks in his bravery, I live in constant fear of bringing shame to my sense of honor. I've come to this piece of hell to find out if I can face up to the big chill. I've taken care of this in my own eyes. But I still walk with a "catch of scare in my get-along," as Davie would say. I fight to prove to myself that I'm not a coward. Although I find ways to stand up to it, I continue to fear death. I can taste it near me with every damn, dry swallow.

However, Davie never blinks at the action we face. Not once. Standing up and spitting in the face of whatever devil dares to front him is the rush that drives him forward. It is who he is. I never see a trace of fear in his eyes. I can't even imagine he ever considers the possibility of death. He's too damn busy seeking out the adrenaline flow of a rumble. Not once does he imagine a fall. Davie never, ever sees a chance that anyone or anything can kick his ass. Death is just another bully that he can back down. There is no part of him that can imagine it has the nerve to ever fuck with his bad self.

I only see the inevitability of death. I make the leap beyond a fear of dying to an acceptance of it. I give up on fear and just keep going. I see the shadow of the reaper as he looks over my shoulder. And I feel his hot breath on my neck. The fucker scares the shit out of me. As I begin to understand the Nam, I fight, first and foremost, to save the lives of my brothers. Because "each other" is all we have. But I'm always uncertain of my complete trust in myself. I'm more driven by the shame of letting my brothers down and being viewed a coward in their eyes than I am of the death that stalks us.

I face combat's spiders and snakes by doing what the hell I am trained to do. I imagine that is what all small-arms warfare is about in the end. In the moments of unanswerable questions, grunts choose to react on the instincts of their training. I fight for the men of Charlie 2. I struggle to spit in the face of my demons of self-doubt. I fight to save face in the eyes of the men who sleep while I stand watch. I fight for the respect of Davie and O'Bie and all the others.

I feel a love for silly-assed Plant and a compassion for the forlorn eyes of Fontana. I've come to learn to trust the certain confidence of Thompson and to follow the "always forward" movement of The Mexican. Although I never seem to conquer it, I learn how to live through the fear and face this nasty bitch. I fight despite myself.

# Chapter Ten

## Incoming

**DATE: August 1969**

First squad takes the daytime patrol toward the south of the road and into several of the small hamlets of the Phu Locs. They radio back that they see some gooks running toward a tree line. Because the area to the south is not a free-fire zone like everything to the north of the road, they can't open up. By the time they receive the approval to fire, the enemy is long out of sight. We all know that they are not a happy group of campers.

Those of us left at the perimeter stand watch and attempt to rest for the remainder of the afternoon. Wearing the camouflaged gym shorts that we call tiger shorts and our sleeveless, soiled, green T-shirts, we hide in the false shade of poncho-snap tents. Lack of breeze turns our makeshift shelters into mini-ovens. My sweat bleeds the ink on the letter I try to write home to my sister. The words bead and swirl like a freak summer-storm puddle spinning a rainbow on a west Texas oil-topped road.

The images I attempt to translate into words home are lost in the transparency of their lies: "everything is fine—all is well—I'm okay—tell Mother not to worry." But I shudder at the pains that settle to the bottom of my soul. Remnants of last night's kills linger like dregs in a bottle of wine. An open wound, the memory festers and draws caldron flies to the jungle-rot scent borne on the decay of my innocence. I hear Satan's snicker magnified in their incessant buzzing.

His contempt assaults my sanity as he laughs at each sour drop of sweat that falls on my soiled writing paper.

First squad returns from their day's patrol in single file, dragging distress behind by a rope like a cow to a slaughterhouse. As they pass through our lines, their muttered protests mix and scatter, coming from all the tired grunts at once. Fatigue, frustration, and anger hover like a swarm of angry, feedlot horseflies over their heads. The smell of pissed-off sweat floats low and stinks of smoldering trash from a burn barrel.

"Holy shit, it is hotter than hell out there."

"Fuck me! I'm cooked clean through."

"Kiss my ass! Kiss my sorry, worthless ass!"

"This is bullshit, man. It's bullshit and there ain't a damn thing we can do about it."

"I had a fuckin' gook sighted-in, man," Davie says. "I coulda busted a cap on his ass bigger 'n Dallas. Then, Jay says to me, 'Not yet, Davie, not yet, Davie. Give it just a minute more, Davie.' Shit, back home, 'just a minute' will give a six-point buck time to get into a thicket and off the dinner table. I mean, these gooks were dead meat." Davie pokes his finger into my chest several times for emphasis. "And the rear don't let us shoot, man. They won't let me bring 'em down. I had 'em sighted in, brother." He raises his arms to the sky and looks upward to the heavens. "It was a miracle, no shit, a miracle. There were these damn dead gooks just trottin' away from us. Just like they owned the place."

"Davie, they do own the place," I said. I knew it would piss him off but couldn't let it go by. He hit me in the arm and I grimace at the pain. "Don't give me any of your commie crap, Red Man." Shaking his head, he adds, "Now, you tell me, what kind of bullshit is that? Tellin' me, 'Don't shoot the gooks.'" He takes the towel from his neck and wipes it across his face. Wet from sweat, it smears zebra stripes of dirt across his forehead and cheeks. "What the fuck are we here for, I ask you? Huh?"

He looks around at the others who stop to listen. "We kill their asses, or they kill us. It ain't no damn brain surgery, man. Just do the math." With his hands spread out and held to his front he weighs the justice of it all. He lifts his left palm and says, "Live gook." Then, raising his right hand higher, he adds, "Dead gook." A quick slap of his hands together creates a thunderclap. I jump back. He laughs. "I promise you the gooks ain't asking permission to cap our asses. No way." He looks from face to face, then asks, "Am I right, or am I right?" Sounding like a spoiled child whining to momma for candy in the checkout line, he mimics, "Sir, can we please shoot the gooks, sir? Pretty please, sir."

Davie takes the helmet off and slams it down. He turns away in anger. Arms held high to the sky once again, he yells loud enough for Ho Chi Minh's ears to turn south from his diddly-squat duck pond and bamboo hooch in Hanoi, "Fuuuuuuuuccccccccckkkkkkkk!"

Time ceases its circular crawl around the clock while we focus on Davie. We share as one his futile anger trapped in the echo of his scream. The sound settles like the last bit of stale breath from a deflating carnival balloon tangled in a thorn thicket waiting to die.

Time halts, restarts, and the rest of the squad go on by toward their positions in the lines. Davie walks along with me to my fighting hole. "Assholes. Shit, Red Man, they're assholes, every last one of 'em. We walked that chicken-shit patrol today. Gooks were runnin' all around us and we didn't get off a single round." When we reach my position in the lines, Davie stops and turns to face me.

His eyes focus on the tree line to the south where our group sprang the ambush last night. The intense look finally settles on me. "Y'all were just new meat out there. But y'all got ya some kills, man." His eyes focus back on the tree line. "Shit, I was back here in the lines, brother, not doin' squat. You were out there in the middle of it." Looking at me again he adds, "That ain't right. No, ain't the way it's supposed to go down."

Davie drops his gear and ammo and lets his flak jacket hit the ground in a burst of red dust. He takes off his shirt and tosses it down on top of it all. "You were in my first fire team, man. Fuck 'em and their 'we don't have enough grunts to make three squads anymore.' That shoulda been me as team leader with y'all last night. But, what was I doin'?" Davie opens his eyes wide for emphasis. "I was just sittin' back here watchin' it all fly by."

We drop to our knees and crawl into the poncho hooch, sliding our rifles in with us. We both lie on our backs and stare at the green ceiling that sags only a few feet above our heads. Davie starts up again where he left off. "Pop-ups, our mortar's illumination, and the higher rounds from An Hoa filling up the sky like a damn New Year's party. Their glows just floating to the ground on parachutes."

He reaches up and pops the droop like he's flicking paper field goals with the spring from his finger and thumb. "It seems like they were feathers on fire falling and circling on the wind."

Davie pulls his rifle from his side to let it rest on his chest. "Shit, Red Man, it drives me fuckin' nuts. I came here to fight and there y'all were out bustin' caps at the gooks. Kiss my Mississippi ass! Shit, me and my brothers back home ought to be out coon huntin'. Riding on some good ol' mules." He pauses and closes his eyes. A smile plays at the corner of his mouth with a small twitch at one side.

He continues, "Listenin' to the bayin' of the pack. Running them down and treeing them." His hand slides up, over and across the selector switch of his M-16. In slow motion, his thumb slips it from safety, to semi-, to full-automatic. He opens his eyes and winks at a face only he can see and eases the selector switch back to safety. After stroking his rifle several more times, he twists his body around and crawls out of the tent. Without another word to me, he picks up his gear and walks away.

We share the perimeter with Charlie 1. This night's ambushes and listening posts are theirs and we hold the positions in the lines. The afternoon furnace gives way to the minimal reduction of evening heat and we all begin the process of settling in for the night. We position our Claymore mines to our front and arrange our magazines and frags on the edge of our fighting hole.

With the sun's escape behind the crest of Charlie Ridge, the night's watch begins for Plant, Fontana, and me. I am newest in country, so I get stuck with third turn. With the end of light, first and second watch always seems to run together. They come at you before fatigue completely sinks its nasty teeth into you. But third watch is the real bitch. Third watch sucks. A sound sleep never has a chance to set in before a hand shakes you, and it's your turn on guard.

During my second round through, around 2:00 am, I see the flash and hear the enemy mortar's "bloops" from beyond our lines. They begin from the area north and to the east of our position. "Incoming!" I holler as loud as I can get it out. Several other men on watch from nearby fighting holes echo my call. Before the rounds start to hit, men are diving every which way for cover.

Their attack only lasts for several minutes. No assault on our lines by enemy soldiers follows the incoming rounds.

Thompson is running on adrenaline. You can see it in his eyes as they dart about. You can hear it in the quick, shaking sound of his voice. "I can't sleep, so I go over to shoot the shit with these two boys from mortars. I'm just killin' time till my turn on radio-watch for the Command Post comes around." Stopping to take a long swig of water from his canteen, he begins to choke. He coughs for a minute to clear his windpipe. "Anyway, we're sittin' there just bullshitting about fishin'." He shrugs his shoulders, shifting his weight from foot to foot, over and over again in a strange dance of disbelief. "Fishin', damn it—fishin'."

He starts to sit down but catches himself in the middle of the movement. It's as if he touches a hot coal and he quickly jerks back up. "So, there we are and we hear you guys holler out 'incoming.' Well, I grab the radio and dive away toward the outside of the brim of the pile of dirt they dug out for their pit. They roll to the other side and slide down into the hole for their cover." He stops and coughs a few more times. I can't seem to do anything but nod my head as he talks.

"Incoming rounds begin their movement across the compound," he continues. "Explosions and the whistle of shrapnel walk their way toward us. One of the rounds lands with a direct hit into the center of their small, circular, mortar pit. The flying fragments of metal reverberate within their shallow hole." Thompson covers his ears with his hands then shakes his head. "Hell, Red, I still can't hear much of anything. The ringing won't stop, either." His hands drop to his sides and he stands unmoving with his shoulders rounded forward. "Both of them die before the sound of the explosion coulda hit their ears."

His hands begin to shake. Looking away from me, he pauses to pull himself together. "A piece of an arm from the elbow down to the hand lands on my back," he continues. "I feel them hit my body while I lay there hugging the dirt." His expression changes. He seems to have closed a door behind him, and he begins to calm down. "I don't know how long it takes them to gather all the body pieces together. But you can be sure of this, The Man from Glad is gonna have a hell of a time sorting it all out back in Da Nang."

# Chapter Eleven

## Home-girl

**DATE: August 1969**

The next day Charlie 1 has the daytime patrols and we are to have the night operations. During the afternoon, Davie wanders over to our position. He can move like a ghost without making a sound as he floats along. I am the only one here and don't hear him approach.

He taps me on the shoulder and says, "What's goin' on, Red Man?" I jerk away in a surprise that sucks the air from my chest. I bend over and gasp to catch my lost breath. "Jesus, Davie, you scared the shit out of me," I say. "In fact, I better check it out right now to make sure." I turn my head, pull the backside of my trousers out, and make an exaggerated sniff of the air. Following a loud sigh of relief, I say, "Nope, okay this time, but Davie, give me a break. This is the only pair I got."

"Red Man, you smell like shit, anyway," he says. "Nobody would be able to tell the difference one way or the other." We sit down by the fighting hole and dangle our legs over the edge. In silence, we look out toward the rice fields to our front. The paddies are divided in a pattern of rectangles separated by an intertwined system of dikes. They remind me of an old tablecloth my Nana used to cover her kitchen table when I was a little kid.

"Davie," I say. "I'm just killin' time, man. Just tryin' to get this shit from last night straight in my head." He remains silent, then, and picks up a dirt clod and chunks it over the far edge of the closest

53

dike. He spits twice at a beetle on the ground and hits it both times. The bug struggles to right itself. "Listen, Red," he says, "I don't think any of this crap is meant to be lined up straight. Truth is, it's bent bad out of shape. There ain't no way you'll sort this shit out; so, don't even begin to try." He spits again and hits again, knocking the beetle back onto its legs. He smiles with pride and nods his head to an imaginary crowd. "Hell, Red Man, I don't have any idea why those mortar boys got it last night."

He reaches for another clod and tosses it several times into the air. Each time he catches it with ease. "They're gone, and you and me sit here side by side. We're left to bullshit and toss bits of dirt into rice paddies." He rears back and throws this clod further than the first. It disappears beyond the dike without a sound.

"Davie, I know you are more used to this killing-and-dying game we play," I say. "But me, I can't seem to get a grip on it." I smooth some dirt beside our hole and clear a chalkboard in the dust. With the tip of my finger I begin to draw random shapes in the dirt. "Those boys are dead—straight out. Won't be any 'take a shower and show up for practice tomorrow afternoon,' for them. This was their final toss of the dice." I drop to my feet to stand in the hole, then turn to face him. "They wouldn't set a priority on the Med-Evac choppers to carry 'em out last night. They just covered them up with ponchos." I reach over and wipe my slate in the dirt clean. Without thought, I draw a three-dimensional rectangular box. "They laid them out alone and in the dark. Their bodies remained on the hard ground until this morning.

"When the choppers came I walked over and saw them load 'em up." As I use more force to make my lines deeper in the dust, I notice the shape of the coffin I've created and quickly scrape my hand over the surface to erase the thought. "I watched the 'men from Glad' stuff them into the plastic bags. Zipped 'em up like winter suits for summer storage. Then laid 'em on stretchers and carted 'em off. They were in no hurry. Working at a steady, slow pace, they placed 'em on stretchers. They carried one out to the waitin' bird. Then they went back and brought the other."

I turn around to face away from Davie. I don't want him to see the pain. I look out to the far tree line and go over it again in my mind. I remember. The chopper boys didn't look at any of us. We just stood around with our hands in our pockets. Our M-16s felt like useless toys. As I watched them work, I remembered how the boys from the rear areas always looked so nice and clean in an abstract sort of a way. You could tell by their awkward diverted glances that we were an inverse reflection in their eyes. They seemed to view us as if we were the cast of a B-movie. It was like we were death-walking zombies to them. As if touching or talking to us might contaminate and doom them. Those boys just wanted to get their asses out of here and away from us. Hell, I can't blame them. It's like the way ball players avoid sitting beside an injured man on the bench. They acted as if acknowledging our situation in the bush might endanger them by association.

Two of the dead men's buddies from his squad followed the stretchers out to the chopper ramp. The boys were unashamed, crying. I couldn't hear them, but I could see the tracks of their tears snake their way through the red dirt on their faces. It clotted in the dust on the edge of their slacked jaws. The wash from the chopper blades whirled about them and flopped their utility trousers and soiled shirts. It bent them backward as they leaned into the force of the tormented morning air. As the chopper's engine increased power for lift-off, the sting of gravel caused them to turn away from the homeward ride of their cold and stiffened brothers.

The chopper took off before the ramp closed halfway back up, and the crew chief hopped on its edge. He dangled his feet over our heads like a Ferris-wheel rider on a hot summer's night. The awkward bird cut the sharp circles of a child's slinky toy as it worked its way higher and higher. It rose straight up above our position until it reached a height beyond the range of small-arms fire.

Two gunships, like angry wasps, buzzed low beyond our perimeter with their noses aimed downward and their cannon and rocket pods stinger ready. Then they were gone—vanished, as if it had all never happened. Like a morning dream that jolts you awake, it seemed so vivid. Yet, when you try to bring it back into focus, it slips just beyond the reach of your fingertips, forever lost. With their exit, the monotony began to seep in as water through the mildew of a cinderblock basement wall. And it all became the same once again. It was just another day in lovely Vietnam.

I still face outward toward the tree line. "Davie, I just stood there, alone, watching the choppers disappear toward Da Nang and whatever unknown processing awaits those boys," I say. "I didn't feel anything. I couldn't even remember their faces from the night before when I'd last seen 'em."

Dropping my head, I close my eyes. I can still see, sunspot burnt on my mind's memory, the plastic-wrapped packages of the two young Marines. They were just boys whose only mistake was to roll the wrong way in the casino crap shoot of the night at the sadistic last call of "incoming."

I look up to face Davie. He looks back at me, his eyes wet and red. Caught in an embarrassed, man-behind-the-curtain moment, he turns away when my gaze intrudes upon his sorrow. He fake coughs while he rubs his faded camo shirtsleeve across his much-too-wrinkled young face. Freckles that lay across the tops of his tanned cheeks, like splattered orange paint flung in a random splash of color, smear within the mixture of sweat, tears, and the flush of his embarrassment. For a moment he is once again the lonesome, lost boy of his early years.

"Aw shit, Red Man," he says. "I don't know about any of this. I'm just a dirt-poor hick from the cotton fields of Mississippi. Hell, I didn't never graduate from high school. School wasn't my thing. None of that shit ever came easy for me. I dropped out and joined the Corps because I didn't want to miss the fight, man." He draws the sleeve of his utility jacket across his face to wipe his running nose. "Hell, I've been fightin' all my damn life, and that's a fact." He kicks his boot at the edge of the fighting hole. A chunk breaks off and falls to the shadows below. "I couldn't let this big-un get away. Shit, it might be my only chance to be a part of somethin' important—a time to have me a piece of somethin' of value."

I pull myself up out of the hole and sit back at his side. He gives a short laugh, then continues, "I'm not a complete fool. I know what lies ahead for me after this damn thing is all over with."

He gives a sharp jab to my upper arm. I flinch. "Damn, Davie, that hurt," I tell him.

"Red Man, you are school smart and there is some sort of bigger shit waitin' for you back in the real world," he says. "That is, if I can just figure out a way to get your ass home to your momma in one piece." Time passes and neither of us say anything. The late afternoon shadows throw an awkward contrast between the angles of the paddy dikes and the sparkle of light that plays like broken glass floating on the sun-exposed surfaces that remain. The unexpected light show mesmerizes us both. Carried away in a brief escape, Davie begins to float back in time.

Following a long stretch of chunking dirt clods to see who can hit what, in a subdued tone he begins, "I never had any problem findin' me a willin' girl on a hot summer night. I can see it all now. She's a sweet young thing, eager and wantin' to ride in my patched-together old Ford pickup. The windows are down, and her bare feet are propped up on the dash. She tosses back her hair and lets out a laugh. She starts to smearin' the windshield with her candy-apple-red-painted toes." He whistles at the image that plays across his mind's eye. "She's switchin' through the AM stations on the radio lookin' for a twangin' kind of 'done me wrong' song to sing along with. The smell of honeysuckle and gardenias tickle the air. It mixes with the heavy smell of her JCPenney's perfume and sweet summer sweat.

"I've got my elbow hangin' out the window with one hand on the steerin' wheel and the other hung over her shoulder. Pulling her close, I feel the heat of her breath on my neck. My fingers start playin' with the buttons on her denim shirt. I sneak sideways glances at the creamy white between her tan line and the pretty little lace trim of her fire red bra. She's wearin' cut-off blue jean short-shorts of frayed and worn denim. Thin little white strings are climbin' all the way up to where the bottom of her soft cotton undies peek out a little. They are rolled and bunched in the elastic.

"I swear I can hear those panties cryin' to me now." Davie begins to whisper in a high voice, "'Come and get me, Davie. Slide me loose and set me free. Hell, boy, set us both free.' I find a place to pull over and we answer the call of the fire inside us. Neither of us knows for sure what we're doing. Me and her are just learnin' and practicin' as we go. Hell, we are both going to our own kinda night school." Davie laughs loud and clear. "I'm guessin' we're both gonna graduate with honors."

Davie is far away and gone now. He looks up toward a low-crawling gulf shore, white cloud a half a world away, rocking in the cradle of a memory. Like a small, nest-fallen mockingbird, child-rescued and returning upward to the sanctuary of its first home, he stares, wide-eyed in the innocence of his fond memories. He shakes his head. "Yeah, me—I'll do fine," he says to the now vanished cloud.

He places his left hand across his forehead as a visor against the sinking sun; he follows a low-flying bird as it skirts a few feet above the surface of the paddies. "Yeah, I'll be just fine when I get back home," he says. "I'll pick me one of them pretty little gearshift-straddlers from Magee or Mendenhall. We'll have us a couple curtain climbers. A mortgage and truck payments will find us making our way. I'll dig me up some good kinda honest work, like my daddy and his daddy before him."

He beats his foot against the wall of the fighting hole, keeping time to some country song in his head. "We'll live down the road from my brothers. One day our kids will play together just like we did. They'll do like me and Billy and Buck when we were invincible and full of piss 'n vinegar. Shit, it'll be a damn good life. Might not sound like much. But it's what I want more than anything." He has a big grin that lights up his face even under the bright Nam sun. "Yep, I can see it now. Hell, I can even touch it."

He reaches out his arm, grabs a handful of air, and squeezes it tight in his fist. Bringing his fist to his lips, he bites at his knuckle. His fist opens. His hand falls to his side. His large grin turns to an expressionless stare toward the toe of his scraped-and-worn boots.

# Chapter Twelve

## Knockdown

## DATE: August 1969

I think back to when my brother and I were in grade school, before we moved to Houston. We'd play like we were cowboys in the Saturday Westerns showing at the movie theaters down near the tracks in Tarentum, Pennsylvania. It was such a different world. In the back of our minds we would only think about the John Wayne kick-ass way of doing things.

Davie and I have towels laid out in front of us and are breaking down our M-16s for cleaning. Davie stops for a break. "Hell, Red, I don't mind the furnace we live in," he says. "I don't mind the mosquitoes sent by the devil to mess with us." He stands up and looks toward a child riding on the back of a water buffalo working a far rice paddy. "Man, I can handle the physical pain of my exhausted body. Hand-in-your-face rain, boot-sucking monsoon mud, and jungle-rot gook sores are just a part of the program. I don't pay no mind to the damn leeches we cigarette-burn off our bodies with each rice paddy and blue-line crossing of the streams and rivers." He walks around a bit, shaking his legs to get the blood flowing again. He looks back at me. "Even lack of sleep that numbs my senses and the endless hours of boredom don't push me over the edge."

A group of choppers flies high above us with a pack of gunships skirting around as their escort. Two of the cobras drop low and angle their noses toward the ground. They fire several rockets into the distant tree line that runs along the river. We watch them work. Davie moves back and sits down by the towel and the separated pieces of his weapon.

"Davie, let me use some of that gun oil you got there."

He picks it up and tosses it over to me. "No, I can't say I like any of it," he continues. "But it ain't shit to me, neither. None of it is shit to me. I can take anything they got. Always could and always will." He reaches over and pokes his index finger into my chest with exaggerated force. I feel the shock of anger in his touch. His voice rises in volume, "I'd already showed every one of 'em back home. Showed 'em I was badder than the baddest of 'em all."

I start to give him some shit for poking at me, but I just look at him instead. Without saying a word, I go back to rubbing oil on the pieces of my M-16. Davie talks while wiping the oil from each cleaned piece. "Red, they were most all bigger 'n me. Yes sir, every damn one of 'em. But they'd all back off when they came to know that I'd never step aside. They learned I'd never step back, no matter how badass they thought they were."

He looks up, then throws his cleaning towel at me. "Here, use this one. I'm done with it," he says. He begins to put his weapon back together and continues his story. "Shit, I'm only five-eight in combat boots and no more than 140 pounds dripping wet. But when those big dumbasses looked in my eyes, we'd be on level ground. That's a fact. You know why they was scared of me?" I pause my cleaning and look up at him. He is smiling at me now. "It's because I was never scared of 'em, and they knew it," he says. "Red Man, weren't a one of 'em who'd fuck with me. And you could be damn sure there wasn't a one of 'em that would mess with one a my little brothers. Oh sure, I got my ass whipped more than once. But I'd keep comin' back and keep comin' back. Each time, I'd get me in some licks. Each time I'd make it harder on 'em." He laughs and we both look down and continue our work. "Word got 'round that I couldn't be worn down. I'd win in the end. If not this time, then the next time, or the one after that. But they all knew I wasn't ever gonna quit. Shit, the more those big boys dared to mess with my crazy ass, the harder I fought back."

I hear him slap his weapon and look up to find him packing up his cleaning gear. "Here, catch," I say and toss the cleaning fluid back to him. "Thanks, I ran out and they haven't sent any out from the rear lately."

He catches it and rolls it up in his cleaning towel with the rest of his gear. After he stashes it away in his backpack, he leans back and goes on with his story. "Red, I came to the Nam to kick some butt and mix it up. Ya see, fightin' is all I got. It's all I ever had that made me feel I wasn't invisible. Made me feel that I was alive inside. See, that's why I was so pissed the other night when you all got to bustin' caps and I missed it."

He sits up and crosses his legs. "But ya know, I didn't never think about them killin' us. I didn't count on no other boys gettin' carried out on the birds to Da Nang." Like it's a security blanket, he grabs his rifle and lays it across his knees. "Man from Glad, my ass. Fuck that pansy, Hollywood, son of a bitch anyway. He and that prissy Marlboro drugstore cowboy can sneak their pretty-boy candy asses out in the bushes. They can have them a little one-on-one 'boom-boom' session for all I care."

I finish putting my rifle back together and start to pack away my own gear. "Hell, it wasn't what I'd call fun, Davie," I say. "I know that stuff gets you going. But me, I'm still dealing with the shakes. No shit."

Davie holds his M-16 up and sights in on some unseen enemy in the tree line. He squints his eye, lets out a breath, and says, "Pop." The rifle shines in the sun's light reflecting off its freshly cleaned surface. He pulls it down and rests it in his lap again. "Red, I don't have this gnawin', deep desire to go and kill anybody," he explains. "Not even the damn gooks that hit us last night. Shit, they was just doin' their thing. They was jumpin' for the man, just like us. But they are on the other side of the line of scrimmage, brother. That's all it comes down to in the long run. They square up against me and they are going down." He pauses for a second while he gets up off the ground.

"Aw hell, that's bullshit," he adds. "You and me both know it, too. I want those fuckin' gooks to go down, and to go down hard. I've seen the blood on my brothers. Those gooks can kiss my ass. They're the enemy, my friend. They're the bad guys. They are out to kill our sorry asses, big time. They are tryin' to elimi-fuckin'-nate us. There ain't no ifs, ands, or kiss my butts to any of it. It's them or us, Red Man. That's the only one rule that counts in this game."

I put away my cleaning gear and rise to stand in front of him. "Davie, I don't know. It doesn't seem like I know anything anymore."

The muscles in Davie's face tighten. We stand face-to-face on our small piece of high ground. Caught in the middle of the bone-dry dirt and the wet mud and the shit stinking rice paddies. "Fuck you for sheddin' tears over those gooks ya been killin'. Right now is all that counts. You get to thinkin' on what mighta been and we're in trouble. You get to dreamin' about shit like that and we are all fucked." He takes a step closer to me. I can feel his breath as he talks. "Your head has got to be here, Red Man, right here.

"You are my brother. You have been my responsibility from the get-go. They cut out a third squad when our numbers fell again. Said we only had enough grunts for two squads. So, they go and split up my fire team, and that's okay. But, Red Man, you are still in it with me as far as I'm concerned." His head angles to the side. A slight smile turns the bottom edge of his lips upward. "Like my Pawpaw used to say, 'It's just the way the cow ate the cabbage,' Red Man. Ya got that?"

I stare at my feet and tap my boots toe-to-toe, causing the dust to rise like greenwood campfire smoke. "Red, look at me." Davie reaches out with both hands and shakes me by the shoulders. "Hey, shit face, look at me. I said, look at me!" I'm aware of his voice as some sort of echo, but I am still caught in a purgatory of rotor backwash and body parts in plastic bags. He looks into my eyes, then glances down to stare at his own scuffed boots in the powder-puff-dry August dirt.

I don't see his right arm move from his side before I feel my head jerk to the right. His fist hits my chin and I stagger to catch balance. The force of the blow stuns me. I turn back to face him again just in time to catch the cuff of his left hand on my right cheek. I follow the force of the second blow around. It twists my body down toward the ground. My left shoulder hits the dirt hard and my forehead bounces on the red soil. Davie's outline towers over me with his legs spread over my prone body.

He looks down on me. "Way I see it, there are gonna be hungry choppers with Glad boys for the rest of our tour," he says. "They're just waitin' back in Da Nang. Their crews'll be watchin' stateside movies and chasin' nurses. Puttin' some stale dip-shit moves on their

EM-club massage girls and their baby-oil hand jobs. Playin' around like they was on some kinda summer vacation." He steps back two paces but continues to look down on me. "Well, I say they can all just kiss my ass. Brother, my 'give-a-shitter' has been broke damn near all my life. Now ain't no fuckin' time to be worryin' 'bout fixin' it."

Davie begins to calm down, his voice softer and more direct. "Only ones gonna keep us alive is just us," he explains. "It'll take you and me, and every last swingin' dick in Charlie 2 to do it together. I got a better chance of stayin' alive if I can teach you to get your shit together. Your best chance is me coverin' your ass."

He scans the horizon around us in all directions. "All of this shit, all this bull-fucking-shit is bundled up in one package. There ain't no damn guarantees, neither. We still can just roll the wrong way into a ditch and end it all. Like those two good ol' boys last night, we'd be takin' that long, last ride." He points his finger down at me. "This means killin' as many of those sons a bitches as we can. Don't you never let that thumb on your selector switch hesitate for even the smallest eye-blink of a second."

His face turns ice cold and still as a deer caught in middle-of-the-road headlights. "This shit is over," he says. "No second guessing my ass now, neither. My life depends on your reflexes. I need you ready to react without thinkin'. Ya got that? Are we on the same page in the hymnal here, my born-again killer?" His head jerks to emphasize that this is a statement and not a question. "I'm not dyin' 'cause you blink twice thinkin' about those homeward-bound boys on the chopper. I'm not goin' down 'cause those damn gooks get their asses blown away and you feel bad about it. Hell, Red Man, when ya walk with the enemy, ya are the enemy." He spits to the side then tightens his lips and squints his eyes. "I'm gonna start boot kickin' next," he snarls. "You're gonna feel your damn nuts in your throat if you don't start noddin' your head right this minute."

I sit up and begin to wave my hands above my head. "Davie, I've seen the light," I sing out. "You're preaching to the choir, Brother Dave. I'm a back-pew Baptist. I've just been born again." I laugh a bit, and Davie's frozen intensity thaws. He dusts his hands on his pants and begins to smile along with me. "Davie, I'm a shit-load more scared of your Mississippi badass than I am of any fuckin' tourniquet-strapped gook sappers in the wires crawling in through the lines. I'm straight. It's all good."

Davie gives a deep-down, right-with-God, pure laugh. He reaches out to offer his hand and pulls me to my feet. "Red Man, it's okay to hurt inside," he says. "It's all right to shed your tears for all the boys they carry home. But it is not okay to let the weight of that shit cause you to flinch. Not even for a selector-switch thumb tick in a firefight." He turns, picks up his pack, then grabs his rifle again. Looking back, he adds, "If you ever want to see round-eyed women again, you can trust that I'll be there for you. And if I ever even hope to hold denim-and-lace sweet things close to my heart again, I need you and everybody else here to keep their shit together. Are you gonna be here for me or not? Red Man! I said, are you gonna be here or not?"

"I'm here, Davie," I say. "I'll never doubt it of myself again, nor should you. I'm here now. And I'll be here tomorrow and the day after that."

Davie stands before me and nods his head twice up and down. "That's good then," he says. "You get done mournin' those boys and those kills, and then put it away. I imagine you will have plenty of old-man time some day to think on it all. Then if you still want to, you can sit with a shit pile of death stink on your clothes. Some day when you're fat and bald and full of middle-of-the-night memories, you can go there. But for the here and now I need you, one hundred percent, to cover my back."

I answer again, "I'm here. I'm here." Shaking my head with a first communion conviction, I repeat for emphasis, "I'm here, and I'm now."

# Chapter Thirteen

## Ambush

**DATE: August 1969**

Our seven-man ambush follows the warped, corduroy road toward the firebase at An Hoa. We leave the ruts of the road to the north and take to the high ground near OP-2. Moving slowly across the old graveyard, we choose a position above the same trail the enemy took the night before. Plant and I drop our gear and smooth out a space in the dirt and gravel to our front. With our entrenchment-tools, we scrape at the dirt and build a bit of a mound to hide behind. Fontana walks two Claymores to the edge of the trail and sets them in, facing at angles to the path. He makes certain that their back-blasts will not rebound into our own faces, then meanders the wires back to our position. He lays their hand-keys to either end of our small claim of earth.

We pull off our hot, heavy helmets and put on canvas jungle covers for some sort of relief from the humidity and heat. Not in total darkness yet, we just sit in silence and arrange our bandoliers of magazines for easy access. Old dogs moving round-and-about in circles, we form a nest in which to settle our weary bones.

We sit whispering our order-of-watch when Brice's eyes, like melted watches in a Dali painting, grow wide and skewed. Fontana and I follow his frightened stare toward the trail where we see a spread-out line of enemy soldiers. They walk at a calm pace and must believe they are moving too early to be caught in one of our night actions.

Fontana pushes his body as tight to the ground as possible and whispers, "Oh, fuck me." He brings his M-16 to his side and I watch him flick the selector switch from safety to semi-automatic. Brice follows with, "This is the real shit. Oh, fuck me, too." He seems to melt into the rough ground. His belly flattens as he tries to escape into the dirt beneath him. I just say, "Fuck," and remain upright as I watch it all unfold. They move at the easy pace of a walk between school classes.

I feel strangely calm and view the scene as if I'm not even here; as if I see it all unfold from a center-row seat at a cinema of the absurd. I reach for the hand-key to the Claymore on my left and squeeze it with an adrenaline rush hard enough to wring the life from a chicken's neck. The ensuing blast throws dust and gravel back and upward. It blinds my view of the trail like a blanket left to dry on a sagging clothesline. I reach for the other hand-key and blow the second Claymore with a strange, cool confidence I don't expect that calls, "Fuck it. Let's get it on."

Between the two explosions, Plant spends his magazine on full-automatic. He sprays it all in a single burst from their front man toward their rear. Fontana keeps his rifle on semi-automatic, shoots in short bursts, and covers the outward funnel of our field of fire with cold, calculated precision.

There is a split-second moment of silence when the great "All" stops. Everything freezes, and I look around at each statue on the high ground and notice that expressions, odors, and leaves stop on the wind. I feel as if I could walk amongst them and stare into their eyes and they would remain without motion. Then I flinch at the "whoosh" of a handheld, pop-up illumination that Fontana sends skyward, and the world catches up in a fast-forward rush. The cracking of AK-47 fire from our front and center drives me downward for cover. I begin to feel the slow motion of fever-dreams from childhood sicknesses: those where I try, and I try to run, but my slow-motion steps slip and slide beneath me and I feel lost to the boogieman clawing at my heels. As hard as I try, I can't take even one step forward.

Soon the clouds of dust and gun smoke settle into a waking reality. Through the clearing fog, I see a man's face rise from behind the bulk of a lifeless, shattered body on the trail. He looks into my eyes with a stare of intense concentration tainted with a trace of fear. I watch as my enemy changes his focus and moves, molasses smooth, pulling the muzzle of his rifle toward my exposed body. I register every frame as if a slide show of my life's end projects onto a cinema screen of bamboo stalks and elephant grass.

My M-16 is at the ready, shouldered with its selector switch thumb-clicked upward to semi-automatic. Death must see within the depth of my eyes the self-same fear I see within his. In those stilled moments, I also see his resignation of recognition that I am sighted-in first. A slight smile crosses his face. I squeeze the trigger and fire into the acceptance of his stare that anticipates certain death. I watch as his awkward smile explodes into a thousand pieces of jigsaw-puzzle destruction. Bile rises to burn my throat. I have crossed over.

Fontana has the radio and calls in for illumination from the mortars back at our perimeter. The area around us glimmers with an eerie glow of flares that drop from hanging lines on toy-soldier parachutes. He also calls in for mortar rounds of fire to blanket farther down the trail toward An Hoa and outward beyond our position to cover their anticipated route of retreat.

The enemy responds with a rocket-propelled grenade that hits beyond us. I feel gravel on my neck, but no shrapnel. They also fire a shit-load of rounds at us in a randomness that indicates panic on their part. They are firing in retreat, in hope of keeping us down for a few moments of stolen safety. We shoot after them in short bursts, trying to anticipate their path of retreat, aiming at a guess into the darkness.

The sky lights up with 155-rounds of illumination from An Hoa, and the firefight ends in the same still silence in which it began. It once again becomes a night of "perhaps," "maybes," "what ifs," and "fuck mes." I look upward to the small shiver of a new moon. It's a crescent, snide smile that accuses me of unforgivable sins. I nod back at him and mouth the title from a children's book, *Goodnight Moon*.

This night, with a look into another man's eyes, I end his life. The "he'd have done the same thing to me" argument carries no weight whatsoever. I know that I did what I had to do to stay alive and to protect the lives of my brothers, yet the reality of death hangs in the air about me like stink on shit. It is a smell that I am certain will never, ever wash away. Its snide smile accuses me of unforgivable sins.

# Chapter Fourteen

## Nurses

### DATE: August 1969

The night passes without a whisper of sleep to comfort us. Artillery from An Hoa continues to offer intervals of illumination that cast a distorted haze through the glow of floating parachutes. We can hear rustlings in the brush to our front. Facing outward from our cover-your-back defense, we try to convince ourselves that combat has ceased for us, at least for this night.

Sunrise brings a radio call from the Command Post. They instruct us to wait on a squad that is coming out to us. Their instructions are to search the ambush's kill zone for any weapons, bodies, or random evidence of our enemy that might remain behind following the night's firefight. While we sit, adrenaline plays with our nerves. We avoid speech and lie in the gravel and pray for the full light of day.

When First Squad arrives, we move toward the trail in an on-line sweep. We find the field of fire picked clean of any ordinance, wounded VC, or dead bodies that the enemy could drag away. Although we saw more enemy bodies fall in our brief firefight's trade of rounds, all that remains of our night's visit to a deeper hell lies to our direct front in the portion of the trail where I blew the two Claymores.

Two intertwined bodies wait at rest in patient silence. Their forms pose in the awkward sprawl of the rigor of death. Fly swarms begin their feast and the stench of death covers the ground upon which their wasted bodies lie. Their loose pajama tops and formless pants billow like River Styx sails in the morning breeze. Straw hats remain tied to their chins. Their misshapen, childlike bodies rest as lifeless limbs stick out beyond the covering of the soiled, silken material of their death shrouds. The lack of realism seems almost comical.

They lie in death just a few feet apart, thrown several yards beyond the trail's center by the force of the Claymores. One's misshapen arm held captive beneath the other's swollen ankle and broken leg fuse the bodies into one unit. The bodies resemble alien caricatures dropped from space in some sort of cosmic joke without a punch line. The Claymore mines leave hundreds of small, machine-rounded and polished balls behind as reminders of their destructive power. Worms and beetles slither in and out of jagged wounds while winged monsters circle and dive for their share of the bounty.

An ice-pick stab of numb reality freezes my bloodstained hands as the realization slips under the locked door of my conscience. Like a primal cockroach squeezes flat through an impossible razor-thin opening, the naked truth enters my mind and calls to me from these two broken forms in the dust. It stares back at me and smiles. Once vibrant, young women trapped within my enemy's shoes, these Viet Cong nurses with their sling-packs of bandages and primitive medicines at their sides lie as still as rag dolls. The mines' blasts stripped some of the fragile clothes from their altered forms and exposed their flesh to the eyes of the morning's light. Their naked vulnerability shocks me, the image burnt forever on my mind's retina. Unable to move, I stand and stare at the broken forms. I cannot divert my eyes. Bile rises to my throat and I bend forward and throw up on my own boots. Others walk around me as if I am not here. No one says a word. I turn and walk away from the final testament on the trail.

Time stops again for me: in a fog of denial, I feel the earth cease to rotate while I, white-knuckled, pray that gravity will defy Newton and release me to float skyward and leave this unthinkable truth. If I can undo the reality of the bodies on the trail's edge, I will trade my place in line for theirs. As it stands, lost high above the reach of the grasping hands of honesty, I pray that I gain permission to float, ever upward, into a forgiving, accepting, transforming heaven for balloons—and refuge for buffoons like me.

Looking downward, I feel my dream slip and the brief spell of unaccountability breaks. I see that my dust-covered boots remain on the powdered earth. I accept the reality of the young female corpses, their faces frozen in silent screams, last breaths, and unaccepting disbelief that their own patrol this past night was a final act. Their forward motion forever ceases while my own nightmares begin in earnest. I know that this moment will linger within my forever-lost soul.

The remainder of this day's opera blurs for me. At some point Lieutenant Frost tells me that an attached ARVN (Army of the Republic of Vietnam) Ranger Scout comes out from Liberty Bridge to check the enemy bodies. I learn that he found a hand-scrawled map hidden within the desecrated body cavity of one of the women. The information contains, with meticulous accuracy, the detailed gun emplacement locations for our firebase at An Hoa. I flinch in shock as I am backslapped and congratulated for the kills and for the lives the information potentially saved. It is good news/bad news bullshit, no doubt. I know I took more than the lives of two nurses this night.

# Chapter Fifteen

## Swing

**DATE: April 2010**

In the late summer of 1969, two days following a nighttime ambush on a nameless hillside near a grouping of small hamlets identified as the An Bangs on our combat maps, our second checkpoint in the day's patrol brings us the all-too-familiar stench of rotting death. We soon come across the body of a Viet Cong soldier. Here lies a young man who crawled for several hundred meters through rice paddies, over dikes, across intermittent high ground from the site of the original firefight to the end of his personal war. For fear of the body being booby trapped, we loop a rope around an outstretched arm and pull him over to lie on his back facing the blistering mid-day heat, eyeless sockets staring up at endless blue silence in the mid-day heat.

The smell of his decaying body in the humid heat of Vietnam remains with me to this day. I still gag at the memory. Like stale cigarette smoke in a cheap honky-tonk lingers on a soft cotton shirt, the odor lurks unfaded, remaining more vivid than any snapshot image aging in a locked, bottom-drawer photo album, and more distinct than the half-remembered cracking sound of the toy-like AK-47 Russian-made rifles spitting fire into the crypt-dark surrounding night. Even now, I can rub my finger and thumb together and feel as if its slick texture remains—and taste the terrible slaughterhouse stink. That smell envelops me with its stark salutation of death and its pointed finger that is an inescapable accusation of guilt in the mist.

I search, blind, for a dangling light chain in a windowless cell and look to the heavens for solace. The time-tired light from stars long dead casts muted shadows on my lost soul. Its glow reminds me of false facades from grade-B Westerns that filled the Saturday matinees of my Roy Rogers youth. My soul forever wades knee deep and mud drenched alongside those fire-deserted stars. It lives as a brother to their cold, dark, demolished backdrops. It lies hidden by the blinding truth of their cosmic deception. This falsehood guides me as I stumble through the sickle-carved maze of my farsighted memory's eye. I see through a distorted fisheye peephole that I am the long dead star lurking on the other side of a locked door. Weighted and weary, I stagger in endless hallways like a lost melody seeking tip-of-tongue forgotten lyrics.

Two score and more years fade in a backward glance since the loss of my essence in jungle firefights. I realize the compromise of my worth made amid the dripping ooze that whispers with the final gasp of random bodies that hide in elephant grass, bamboo thickets, and rice paddies. Forty-plus years, yet silent booby traps; dung-smeared, sharpened bamboo; and dust-covered land mines still quicken my pulse and shorten my breath. The weary corners of my eyes show the wrinkles of crow's feet, and the weight of time sags my jowls and compresses my height.

**\*\*\*\*\*\*\*\*\*\***

Tonight, I find myself trapped within an old man's body I no longer recognize. An early spring's light breeze interrupts the quiet. I watch as the toes of her canvas shoes darken and become wetter with each step across the dampening, dew-shrouded lawn. The soft mist parts as she crosses in hesitant steps toward the wooden swing that hangs with an angle from a low-sagging limb of an ancient post oak. She pauses, then coughs twice into the cold of her hands so as not to take me by surprise and stir what she knows would be my reflexive response of ducking low for cover. She sits by my side, then turns to look at the outline of my face while I continue to stare upward toward the cold, star-sparkled sky.

Without altering my gaze, I say to her and the eavesdropping night, "I didn't think you would come back, not this time. I felt you were gone for certain. I thought this really was the last of the very last times."

She must smell the almond-sweet taste rising from the bottle of Chardonnay I hold between crossed legs. She must also feel the warmth of my body where her thigh rests against mine, side-by-side, separate yet together, like matching pieces of luggage on a porter's dolly awaiting destination ticketing.

"I thought so, too," she replies. "I was packed and on my way, to being on my way."

I respond with a sudden shivering that causes the swing to shudder in a zigzag against the whispers on a breeze that carries the faint echo of voices from each night's sleepless journey. Rustlings of shadows in the clouds drift, now and again, between the fireflies of a universe that hovers beyond the reach of our lives.

I don't look toward her. "I couldn't breathe when you walked out," I say. A low branch droops in the wind to brush my hair. I reach and pluck a leaf, like a berry from a bush. "I found myself on this floating chair unable to move. I don't know how I got here." The leaf provides a diversion for my eyes. I rub it and find a green stain paints my forefinger and thumb. "Apparently I passed the wine rack and found a corkscrew on my way. It was an involuntary movement, I guess."

"I know," she whispers. Taking my hand, she pulls it to her lips and offers it several silent butterfly kisses. She turns, smiles, and holds my fingertips close to her cheek like a warm memory. It is as if a child's rag doll, long missing and forgotten, appears once again by random chance, wedged behind the cushions of an old chair.

"I had no intention of hurting you," I say. "I would never do anything to cause you more pain." She reaches out and touches my face with the tips of her fingers. I look up and see within the sadness of her eyes a slight blink of confirmation. Her lips curl inward like a frustrated child challenging my convenient rationalization. I take her hand within mine. "I believe I am going crazy." I speak to the gentle concern in the crease across her brow. "No, more than that, I now know with certainty that the 'going' part has been at work for a long, long time. The 'crazy' part has just recently begun to run the show."

She recognizes the serious depth of honesty in my tired eyes and pulls her hand from mine. "I don't want to hear you talk like this. It isn't you." A sigh passes from her lips and floats in the back-and-forth swing of a pendulum, toward the wet ground at our feet.

I pause. "No, I've gone all the way crazy," I add. "I know now that I've lost whatever 'it' is and I can't find a handle to a false concept of vacant sanity any longer. I don't know where or when reality escaped, but it is not in the locked box any longer. Perhaps 'it' stole away in a helium mist from a misshapen birthday balloon. It was just fine while free-floating near the ceiling, trailing a rainbow-ridged ribbon. Then somehow, after playing pin the tail on the donkey and blind-man's bluff in the backyard of my 'used to bes,' I look to find it lying at the feet of my rational self. All reality leaks away while my back turns and the 'bugga-bugga-bugga' of the night breaks down walls and doors to take its place."

She lowers her head and speaks to the cold damp at her feet. "Why do you do this to yourself? Why do you insist on beating the same old horse to death over and over and over, again and again, and then again?" Tears form at the swollen edges of her eyes. She pulls her hand from mine and reaches to wipe a loose shirtsleeve across her face. She draws her tongue over chapped lips and tastes the salt of my slow-dying sorrow.

I turn away from the sting of her pain and begin to talk in a monotone. "There was a time when it was all so very clear—a time when flash images born on the shutter's eye of my plastic-wrapped instamatic camera were exact and precise, developed and returned with month and year stenciled on a thin border of white. There was a day when the glossy, forever-young, frozen faces grew soiled by smudged fingerprints of sharing friends attempting to avoid the destruction of last smiles, lost limbs, and final gasping in the indifferent fields of fire.

"That past has become a stranger to me. Like late-afternoon shadows that turn to face a deadening dusk, I am lost. Its clear-color outlines now bleed, to fading stonewashed madras. Once-distinct sounds mute into distant thunder from the crashing lie of heat-lightning, and cloud-formed shapes diffuse in wayward winds. Frozen and red, the touch of the wind becomes numb."

I turn to meet the face of my love, take her hand in mine once again, and continue. Guilt cuts deep and true as I sense the pain in her eyes. I look to the sky in search of adequate words. "I reach for sleep. I plead for silence," I say. Clouds cross the moon and leave a path of smoke and dust in their wake. I lower my face into my hands and rub at an ache that settles into my eyes. "I beg for any form of solitude. I plead for some soft moment in time to offer the release of momentary sanctuary."

Her eyes burn into the top of my head and I look up and see her pain. "Shit, Cindy, I understand that, in an existence of accountability, I am without justification." I reach up once again to the branch above my head and slide my hand down a thin twig. The movement scrapes several leaves into my clenched fist. Like a ball of crumpled paper, I throw them at her wet shoes. She steps back half a pace as if great pain accompanies their fragile collision with her foot. My voice rises with lack of control. "Don't you see that I am bleeding to death here? Hell, Cindy, I will always march in pace with the unforgiven." My knees feel the blow of both my hands as I slap them down in unison. I wish to scream at the bowels of darkness in a Lon Chaney, red-moon howl. I stop talking. Worn tired and short of breath, I sag like sheets on a clothesline caught in an unexpected spring shower.

A nod of her head calms me. "It is going to be all right," she says. "You know that, don't you?" She senses that I am back with her once again and she knows I traveled full cycle and returned from the unseen dark side of the lonely moon.

I grin in return. "Yes, I think so, at least for the time being," I say. "Perhaps 'maintainable' is a better descriptor. Yes, 'maintainable' will do for now, for this moment, for this night alone with you." I pull her close to my side. My arm surrounds her shoulder and we are one, once again. I shake my head side to side.

Turning away, I look upward toward the silent shouting stars and add, "Oh, I forget. Did I tell you? Did I remember to tell you—that I think I'm going crazy?"

# Chapter Sixteen

## Killer Team

**DATE: August 1969**

Davie wants to take out a four-man "killer team" the next night. He talks Dutch, Caruso, and Tiny into volunteering along with him. Always looking for a fight, Dutch can't back down when Davie challenges him with the idea.

"Why the fuck not?" Caruso tells Davie. "I'm bored shitless. Hell, I got nothin' better to do. Let's boogie."

"It beats the shit out of standing lines," Tiny says. "Count me in."

Dutch and Davie go to the CP to talk Lieutenant Frost into letting them break up their fire teams for the night. They want to convince him that the site of the daytime Observation Post 2 will be a good place to start the night. The area just beyond the graveyard where we ambushed the enemy and killed the nurses three nights before is what they have in mind.

When the lieutenant tells them that he thinks it is still too hot out there for them to take the chance, Davie answers, "Lieutenant, no disrespect, but that is what the hell we are here for, ain't it, sir?"

The lieutenant shakes his head. "Yeah, but I just don't know whether this one's a good idea or not," he says. "I know you men want the fight, but I'm not real comfortable with this idea. Let me think about it for a while."

Dutch watches him for a minute. "Lieutenant Frost, they are runnin' around all over the place," he states. Rubbing his hands together like he's trying to generate even more heat into the already-scorching day, he adds, "They're movin' at night and lyin' low durin' the day. It's the way they've been doing it since day one. It's time to do war, not play at it, Frostie." The knuckles of his right hand begin to pop as he works them over one after another. "We can't just sit around with our thumbs up our asses waitin' for them to zero their mortars in on us." He shakes his head and scratches the back of his neck. "Not again like they did the other night. If we don't take it to them, they are going to bring it to us."

Lieutenant Frost rises and paces back and forth. "Shit, Dutch. Davie here is so wired up he can't see straight," he explains. "But you've been here a long time and damn well know what's out there."

Dutch now begins to crack his knuckles. "Yes, sir," he says, "I do. I surely do. And it's off your head. We are the ones askin' permission to go, sir."

The lieutenant starts to respond, then hesitates. He reaches into his pack and pulls out a combat map. With it already folded to show the area we are operating in, he studies it. He scratches a line of mosquito bites on his left forearm. Blood seeps from the furrows his nails cut in the skin. He wipes his hand on his shirt, then looks up at Davie and Dutch.

"Okay," he says. "Make sure there are men to cover each of your positions in our lines." He starts to add something else but stops short, takes a deep breath and continues, "Well, get your shit together if you are going. Take extra frags and magazines." He reaches out and grabs Dutch by the arm. "Dutch, I don't want to write any more letters home to mommas. Do you hear me? I'm tired of all this shit and I'm not up to it anymore." Dutch and Davie face each other and slap hands. Together they give an, "Oooh Rah."

As they leave, Lieutenant Frost calls after them, "Marines, kick ass and take names. But for God's sake, be careful out there." He stands in place and watches them hustle off. In a soft whisper he adds, "God, I hate this fuckin' war."

Davie stops by our position and tells us what is up. He asks if we have any extra camouflage paint sticks he can use. Fontana has two fairly new ones of the only two colors that exist for us: dark green and light green. "Davie, sit down for a minute and I'll help you with it," I offer. He up ends his helmet, lays it on the ground, and squats on the round rocker seat it provides. I mark a dark line under one of his eyes and a light one under the other, then take my fingers and spread the paint gel around. I dab my green fingers here and there across his face. Dots like freckles on a redheaded kid at the beach merge as I smear the colors together. I cover the back of his neck from his hairline to his collar and from under his chin to the top of his buttoned shirtfront. Even in the stifling heat of the near-fallen sun, I button his shirtsleeves and put camouflage on the backs of his hands and wrists.

"Davie, you look good enough to take home and meet the family," Plant says as he giggles, caught in the excitement of the moment.

Davie replies, "Plant, how the hell would you know?"

"Now stand up, Davie, and put your helmet on," I tell him.

Each of us has an inch-wide slice of rubber inner tube snapped around the outside of the cloth that camouflages our helmets. We each keep a bandage package tucked in the back for the corpsmen to access in a hurry if needed. I pull some scrub grass and weeds from the side of our position and stick them in the helmet band to break the straight lines of its silhouette against the darkening sky.

"Davie, I hate to admit it," I say, "but Plant is right. You look pretty enough to take to an indoor movie."

"Fuck you both. Y'all just stay back here and play with yourselves while I take care of Mr. Victor Charles for all of ya. That stands for VC, Plant. That's the gooks, the bad guys, in case you can't figure this shit out." Davie winks at me. "Be cool, brother," he says. "Thanks for the makeover. My momma would be jealous."

A quick jab to my shoulder from Davie knocks me backward and off balance. I stumble and fall to the ground. As I begin to rise, he feigns a left hook to my head; in reflex I raise my right arm to block. "Got ya, Red Man," he says as he pulls me back up. "Just want to keep you on your toes, my brother."

"Shit, Davie, aren't you ever going to cut me some slack?" I ask.

"You ain't ready yet, boot," he replies.

I hold open his flak jacket for him to slide into, then hand him his rifle and magazines. As he distributes six frags in his pockets, he says, "When you hear the caps goin' off and the shit hits the fan, you'll know it's us. I got a good feelin' we are gonna get us some bad boys tonight, Red Man."

With a shit-eating grin etched on his face, he turns and walks toward the center of the perimeter to meet up with Dutch, Caruso, and Tiny. I can't help but laugh at his bantam-rooster strut: his head high as he walks straight and proud.

"You are a piece of work, Davie. A piece of work," I holler out to his back as he walks away. He raises his right fist, and without turning back, shoots his middle finger skyward in defiance.

Plant shakes his head. "That damn Davie, he is one bad ass, Red Man. One very bad ass," he says.

"Plant, learn some manners," I reply. "Just say he's a good Marine and leave it at that. I know it might not mean shit to you. But I also know it means the world to him. Yes, I know for certain that it does to him." As I watch Davie walk toward the center of the perimeter to meet up with the others, I smile at the confidence he shows. He passes each group of men with a greeting and a wave. "Come on, Plant, let's put out our Claymores and get ready for another night in lovely, fun-filled Viet-fuckin'-nam."

We each put out a mine and walk the wires back to our position and set several frags out on the side edges of our fighting hole within easy reach. When everything is set up, we begin to bullshit about bullshit while we wait for Fontana to return from the CP. He will report any new information we might need to know. Yet, it always seems that the gossip of scuttlebutt moves much faster than real-time orders.

By the time Fontana shows up, day is now dusk and a little beyond. He tells us what we already know: there is a killer team going out to our south to the area of OP-2. He adds that gooks are all over the place, and that according to the intelligence boys at An Hoa, we should expect to get hit tonight.

"Right, Fontana," I say. "So what else is new on the 'getting hit tonight' bullshit list? It's a broken record, man."

"Red's right, they tell us this crap every fuckin' night. It gets old, man," adds Plant.

"I know, I know, but this is supposed to be true scoop," Fontana responds. "No shit, they are everywhere out there, and you all know it. We are outnumbered bigger than your momma's love for me, Plant." He laughs when Plant shoots him the finger. "I don't know why the hell Dutch agreed to help with this killer team tonight.

Dutch is fuckin' crazy, and Davie is damn near as bad when it comes to a fight."

Fontana sits down beside us and checks his M-16. "Caruso and Tiny are both just bored to death," he says. "They are ready for anything that will break the monotony of the Nam. Boredom is a tickle-your-ass bitch, and you better believe it. It is one dangerous whore, too. It'll seduce you into some bad choices. This night scares the hell out of me."

In a few minutes the word passes on down our side of the lines from position to position: "The killer team is going out. Hold your fire. They are leaving the lines now. Hold your fire."

# Chapter Seventeen

## Assault

**DATE: August 1969**

"Crack, crack, crack, crack, crack." The obscene toy-gun sound of an AK-47 spitting out rounds on full-automatic breaks the false quiet of dusk like pine branches snapping in a deep winter ice storm. Plant and I sit on the side of our fighting hole and slide into its protection at the all-too-familiar sound of enemy fire. Fontana runs from the poncho hooch a few yards behind our position and dives in on top of us headfirst. We are so cramped in the small confines that it is difficult to untangle ourselves. We wiggle around enough to untie our knotted limbs and rise above the hole's edge with our rifles shouldered at the ready, then scan outward to cover our designated field of fire. I pull the hand-keys to the Claymore mines closer toward us as we wait to identify the area from where the shots originate.

The explosion of two frags blowing close together follows more M-16 fire on semi-automatic. The ripping sound of a complete magazine on full-auto trails in quick succession. Illumination from a pop-up lights the area OP-2 occupies during the day. We see the bare gravel of the high ground in red haze beneath the small parachute that drifts downward at a slight angle on a weak breeze. We watch flashes from several AK-47s on the far side of the rise and hear frags explode in a random, offbeat improvisation. Shouted out and passed down the line from position to position is the order, "Don't fire. Our boys are out there, too. Hold your fire! Hold your fire!"

The sound of more frags exploding and additional M-16 and AK-47 fire continues to bore angry holes into the once-silent night. A "whoosh" from the center of our perimeter sends two quick mortar rounds of illumination skyward to explode above OP-2, a good deal higher than the shallow, bottle-rocket height of the hand-held, pop-up flare. Soon after, much higher rounds of illumination from the 155s at An Hoa bring an eerie, rose-filtered daylight over the entire area. It lights us up like Bourbon Street strippers on stage.

I feel a slap on the backside of my helmet and turn to see O'Bie crouching behind me. "Red, you come with me," he says. "Fontana, you and Plant stay here. Look for them to hit our lines anywhere, anytime. That shit out there now might just be a distraction to misdirect our attention. Keep your profiles low." I stand and climb out of the hole. I feel the rush of blood through my veins and my heart begins to beat faster. "Red, grab your frags and a bandolier of magazines, and get ready to haul ass. Stay low, stay alert, and follow me," orders O'Bie.

We move down the line from position to position and stop at each fighting hole to get enough men to put together a relief group. We pick up Frenchie at one hole, the Mexican at another, then Jay and Oklahoma at the last two stops. O'Bie gives each of them the same instructions he gave me.

When we reach the road that divides our section of the perimeter from Charlie 1, we squat down together. "I don't know much, but here it is," O'Bie explains. "The killer team was hit as they were going out. There are some men down. We need to get our asses out there and help them." He looks at each of us. "Any questions?" We all shake our heads, no. O'Bie nods. "Okay, we are going straight to them, right down the road," he says. "There are casualties out there, so we'll be taking Doc Love with us."

Sweat rolls from my forehead into my eyes. The sting causes me to squint, then wipe my face with the sleeve of my jacket. "The gooks are all around, but they've stopped firing back at the killer team. They have either withdrawn or they are sitting there waiting to draw us into a trap. It really doesn't make a shit bit of difference. We're going to the aid of our brothers and that's a done deal. We will not leave them out there on their own."

We all move closer in toward O'Bie. "As you move, spread out, but not too far apart," he cautions. "Weave back and forth across the road and hit the dirt every now and then. It's all we can do to make us harder to hit under this damn lit-up sky. We can fire to either side, but not to our front or to our rear. We're going to be caught between our lines and the killer team. Remember, none of our guys can be cleared to offer us any support. But fuck that. Don't think about it. We're just going to do it."

Sergeant Matt is at Charlie 2's last position, closest to the road, and meets us. "Give us just a minute to pass the word that you are going out," he says. Frank is here with us, and O'Bie tells him to spread the word. He turns to make his way down our lines to let our men know what is going on. A squad leader from Charlie 1 is also with us, and he leaves to cross the road and inform their positions, too.

Holding the radio, Short Round follows beside Sergeant Matt. When the word comes back through Short Round that all is clear, O'Bie turns to us and says, "Oklahoma, you're point. You go first. I want you to head straight to OP-2. Mexican, you go next, then Doc, then me, then you, Red. Frenchie, you are tail-end-Charlie." He takes the time to look into each of our faces and gives a slight nod of encouragement as his gaze passes from man to man. He claps his hands together, then adds, "It's the real deal. Now, let's do it."

Oklahoma says, "Ain't no need to wait no more. I'm out of here." He rises and runs about fifteen meters down the road, then dives forward onto his belly. He waits to catch his breath, then gets up and heads forward again while angling toward the right side of the road in a bent shuffle-step of a run.

O'Bie hits the Mexican on the shoulder and says, "Go!" The Mexican shoots up and follows Oklahoma's footsteps. After he reaches the spot where Oklahoma hit the ground, O'Bie sends Doc to follow them. He begins to get ready to head out himself. Before he leaves, O'Bie turns to Frenchie and me and says, "This is what it is all about. Lives are on the line. Do it right. Do you hear me? I said, 'Do it right!'"

O'Bie hustles out, his M-16 at the ready. I wait until he dives for the ground, rolls one turn to his right, then rises and begins moving at an angle on down the road. I take a quick look over my shoulder at Frenchie and see his tight, determined expression. He gives me a quick nod and then pushes me on the back to get me going. I damn near fall forward on my face. Righting myself with a second step, I am on my way.

My chest pounds and the rhythm of blood echoes in my ears as it pulses through my temples. I think, *so this is what it is like to die.* I find myself waiting for an impact of some sort to assault my body. I continue to run, dive, roll, then rise and run some more.

The sour taste of the bug juice I wiped across my face earlier in the evening mixes with soiled sweat as it filters through my mustache and curls over my upper lip. The chemicals and salt burn my tongue and catch in my throat. I cough and spit to my front as I run. The spray is thrown back onto my cheeks and into my eyes. It runs down my chin to form droplets that catch like melting ice cream from a carnival cone before they take a final dive down my stained shirt.

I squint my eyes against the intrusive burning and keep running and weaving, dropping and rising, squinting and spitting. The sounds of gunfire and explosions assault my ears with the indignant slap of a pious maiden. Hidden within the thunder, there is a quiet eye that watches us all from a distance and calms me as I run. My movements seem to become more fluid and natural, and my fatigued muscles lose the cramps that have been gnawing at them like unfed guard dogs. I feel as if I am outside the confines of the sand box in my Papa's backyard, looking down upon the green, plastic-molded soldiers my brother and I maneuvered from upturned, bucket castles, to hand-scooped trenches as we played at combat. I can hear our make-believe "rat a tat tats" and "ka-pows" bark louder in my ears than the firefight of the here and now. The two games of war melt together like wax.

When I reach the grouping of men at the slope of the small piece of high ground at OP-2, O'Bie motions for me to stop and squat beside him for cover. I am soaking wet from the exertion of the assault as I gasp for breath.

"I think the gooks are gone," OBie says. "If they are anywhere around, they will be on the far side of the OP. They might wait near the site of the ambush from the other night and try to hit us one more time before they're through. We are going to get on line, rush across the rise, and spread out to make a rough perimeter for a Med-Evac chopper to land. First, there will be prep-by-fire for support. I want you to stay low and wait until you hear me give the word to go."

Beyond O'Bie I see Doc Love bending over a body on the ground. I can tell he is working on someone but can't make out who it is. Beside Doc, someone leans over a second body, but neither the form on the ground nor the shape above it moves.

"This has got to be fast," O'Bie instructs. "Take off down the ridge and spread out as you go. We've done this shit before. You all know what to do. Now do it. Go! Go!"

We rise and begin moving along the lower edge of the high ground. As I pass Doc, I see that he is working on Dutch's shoulder. I look down into Dutch's eyes and he gives a blank stare back up into mine. There is no emotion in his face. His cold look bores through my heart, and I feel a chill like winter's first frost at the back of my neck.

Crossing beyond Dutch, I see it is Caruso who is bent over the next body. Caruso doesn't look up. The flak jacket has been removed from the form on the ground and is laid over its upper chest to cover the face. Neither Caruso nor the body at his knees move. Nothing seems real. Gunfire ceases, and only the hissing song of the falling flares play above our heads with the incessant defiance of escaping air from a punctured tire on a long, dark, country road.

I keep moving until I reach the place where I am to stop along the line. I lie flat and wait for our artillery to throw their rounds into the other side of the rise and begin a rain of shrapnel and tossed gravel. I hear whistling over my head as the mortars from our perimeter at the Alamo begin to pepper the far tree line. Explosions walk nearer and nearer toward us as the gunners adjust their fire. Then the thunder from the 155s at An Hoa begins to rain down upon the same area with much greater intensity. I feel the earth beneath my prone body dance a shimmy-and-shake with each round's coin-drop into the high ground's juke.

I feel numbness, if anything. There is a separation between the force of the explosions and the depth of my emotional disconnection. Even as all of my senses were acutely alive just minutes before, while we assaulted the high ground, they are now nullified in this wrinkle of time. There is only a blank as I wonder, again, what it will feel like beyond the pain at the moment of the final dirt nap.

I look inward and see only a bottomless dark hole where my soul must once have resided: No sight, no smell, and no sense of touch. A great void sleeps like an ocean's depth within my chest and reaches beyond my inner self. I know it is one of our own men on the hard ground just a few meters away from where I lay, waiting for the barrage to cease, but I can't get it right in my head. I can't remain within the lines and make the paint-by-numbers picture take form. There is a brother, and there is death, and as if caught between different dimensions, the two refuse to mesh. I feel as if I've opened the door to a fun house at the fair and found a room with walls of wrinkled mirrors that distort everything within. A troupe of white-gloved performers with pancake-powdered makeup mime "surprise" while cameras click in the dark but fail to flash. They all seem to know who I am, but I don't recognize a one of them, not a one.

There are candles burning on tables throughout the room. As I move my gaze from face to face, searching for some point of reference, the flames rise higher and higher. Fire jumps from wick to wick and unites in a Fantasia dance of animated magic. Their white heat marries in a coupling of light, and the room explodes in a phosphorous glow of bright red. Sparks like lost moonbeams seeking shelter from dawn's overpowering triumph over night hide beneath the shadow of Nam's sneer, and the light blinds me.

# Chapter Eighteen

## It's Time

**DATE: November 2011**

It's time.

I've been skirting this damn thing for beyond too long now. I've tried to sneak up to it in a cat's game of pouncing on yarn, but every time I've gotten close, every time I've worked my nerve up to dive into these icy waters, I've created justifications to avoid the plunge. Somewhere, hiding in the depths of my self-delusional diversion, lies the truth.

Soon. Soon.

Up to this point I've elected to wear blinders into the starting gate and avoid even peripheral eye contact with the devil's handlers. I've followed the pathway that leads to my self-made castle of cards. I've felt the breath of the wolf on my neck as he has huffed and puffed at my shelters of sticks and straw. I've walked the darkened hallways and opened all doors, save one. I've heard the prowlers of the night murmur my name in hushed, diluted tones. I've ignored all final-phone-call pleas for clemency.

The cock has crowed past dawn, and I've denied, and denied, and denied again. I've felt the silk-fine, spider-web tangle of fear slide with a feather's touch over my eyelids, catch on the tip of my mustache, and slip across my dry lips like the razor cut of a straight-edged blade over wrists in a bath of lukewarm water.

Yet I continue to return to this point in time. I keep coming to this place, to this slap in the face, which moves me nearer to the white tip of the flame. Its heated condemnation blisters my soul and singes the hairs on my shamed-and-bowed head. Still, every time, with every afforded opportunity, I've balked and shied away from the snake in the road, refusing to cross over.

It is time.

My pen, a frozen blade, shivers in my numbed fingers. My hand refuses to respond as I stare at the black-ice tablet of empty lines. The slick page laughs back at me in contempt like a schoolyard bully, encouraged by the scent of my fear. I wish to write it down and confront the words, but I instead sit and stare at the sunset of another day with a second glass of cheap house wine at the ready.

Tomorrow is the Marine Corps birthday, and the day beyond that is Veterans Day. My conscience, my wife, who has shown only love and encouragement through all the rationalizations and nightmares, waits patiently for the ink to begin its flow. The words hang on my heart's skipped beats like falling snow balanced on thin, winter branches. It is time to let him go. It is time to ease him downward with a delicate care onto a bed of soft grass. I've carried this moment with me for over four decades. I've self-medicated on a regular basis to muffle the voice of reason and drown its echo. It is all now held together with sleight-of-hand and magician's-assistant diversion. It is selfish, self-centered, and indulgent of me to demand that his soul remain suspended in a purgatory just for me.

It is time to lose Davie.

I bite my lip and taste the iron-red rust of my own blood. I need the spark of pain to reconfirm my own existence within the odyssey.

It is time.

The third glass of wine has taken hold, and I say to the northwest wind in my face and to the ever-present eyes gazing over my shoulder, "Shit, Davie, what do you want to do? I'm not going to let you go. I won't leave you behind. I swore to you that I would always have your back. It's all right. I'll give it the best words I've got and throw them to their ears like breadcrumbs to beach gulls.

"Wait, not yet; no, not yet. I'm not about to listen to my own bullshit. I won't buy it. My ears are forever deaf to any talk of submission. I'll tell the damn story, Davie. I'll let them know how it went down. But they can all kiss my ass; I'm not letting you go. No fucking way. You live and breathe so long as I live and breathe. For as long as my 'always' might be, you are present in my here-and-now. You will exist in a forever day-before-yesterday."

No, wait…there I go again.

It is time.

It is time to lose Davie.

"Crack, crack, crack, crack, crack." The unmistakable sound of an AK-47 spitting out rounds on full-automatic breaks the soft early quiet like heat-lightning thunderclaps…

# Chapter Nineteen

## The Man from Glad

**DATE: August 1969**

When the mortars from our perimeter and the artillery fire from An Hoa cease, O'Bie hollers, "Let's go!" We cross a flat portion of the high ground to an area where several grave markers stand like sentries on eternal guard duty.

O'Bie tells us to spread out and form a circle, linking up back where the killer team remains. "Make enough room for a chopper to land," he says. "There is no place for cover up here. Just lie flat and hug the ground facing outward. Choppers should be here any minute."

Silence indicates that no fighting goes on back at the Alamo. We're not taking any incoming fire, so it seems the enemy got the hell away to escape an expected response on our part. If they were still around they'd be capping at our asses while we've been so vulnerable crossing the high ground.

I hear the distant roar of choppers in the night's sky. Two Cobra gunships cross treetop-low over our heads, and I flinch as they make a sharp bank to our left to rise upward like angry wasps. O'Bie throws a smoke canister into our center to mark the small perimeter. It spits yellow waves that flatten and dance in the turbulence from the Cobra's wake.

Searching outward into the darkness to cover my field of fire, I feel the downward force of swirling air. It presses me into the earth

91

so that my clothing ripples in the artificial gale like red storm-warning flags. Debris and gravel pepper my body and sting my exposed hands and neck. I squint my eyes into thin slits and turn to see the Med-Evac chopper touch down. Its rear ramp drops to the ground and three men emerge from the rear of the beast.

I turn back and face outward to maintain the security of our defensive position. Forcing myself to block out the reality behind me, I concentrate on the shadows and half-truths to my front. The elephant grass and banana leaves beyond us bump and sway like last-call dancers at closing time. Each twisted shape takes the possible form of an enemy soldier sighting-in on us. I fight the urge to fire at the lie of shade changes that go from gray to black and back again.

I sneak another look back toward the chopper and the hailstorm of gravel that continues to pepper my body. I identify Dutch, running low with his arm in a sling, led by a chopper crewmember with a rifle at his side. Behind them come two men carrying a stretcher. On the canvas between them lies a motionless form, covered by a dark green material. It whips like a clothesline sheet caught in the mechanical whirlwind of the rotor's wash.

The rippled dancing shroud holds its form. I know, without doubt, that it is a tight, zippered, body bag they carry. The sound of the beating blades becomes a rhythmic jackass's "hee haw." I know the laughter comes from the never-sated Man from Glad as he embraces the body on the stretcher. I see the son-of-a-bitch's smile in the folds of the body bag and watch him lick his lips in a French kiss of death. Disgust at my own fear shames me.

I fight the mesmerizing urge to watch the scene unfold and return to my responsibility of defending the perimeter. The gunships circling low around the high ground add volume to the Med-Evac's constant din. One Cobra slows and angles its sharp nose downward. Back-blasts shoot fire to its rear as rockets race from the pods beneath its small frame.

The ground to my front and left erupts in fire. I feel a concussion that equals the pulsing rotation of the Med-Evac's blades. After releasing its arsenal of death, the Cobra's nose pulls upward, and the gunship jumps forward and away in a sharp banking motion.

The force of the wash on my back grows more powerful. The pressure pushes me downward while the assault of angry gravel insults my exposed flesh once again. The wind and roar begin to decrease. I steal another peek over my shoulder to catch sight of the chopper's climb in a helix-curve above our perimeter. It circles upward until it disappears into the night's ebony void.

The Med-Evac chopper and the buzzing gunships vanish. The Man from Glad pulls off another flyaway, and only dull vibrations remain in his wake. I hear the taunt of his laughter fading within the last echoes of the Da Nang-bound hearse.

O'Bie's voice cuts through the oppressive quiet. "Get your asses back to me now." I look over my shoulder to see him squatting down with an outstretched arm waving back and forth. "Every one of you, straight back here. Now!" he adds.

We gather, and O'Bie gives instructions as to how we will set up and defend ourselves for the remainder of the night. We settle in and wait for morning light. No thunder from An Hoa sounds again to light the night. More illumination will just serve to highlight our vulnerability at this point. Only darkness and silence remain to redefine the long hours till dawn.

The rest of the night passes without further event. Morning shows its face, and our return to the perimeter becomes a blur to me. As we come through the lines, Sergeant Matt tells us to return to our original fire team positions. I find Fontana and Plant waiting for me.

"Red Man, what's going on?" asks Plant. "No one ever tells me shit. What the fuck is happening?" I walk past him without giving a response. He calls to my back, "Red Man, Red Man, what's the scoop, brother?"

"Shut the fuck up, Plant," Fontana says. "Leave it alone."

I go straight to the poncho tent, drop my weapons, and crawl inside. Everything around me seems to stop. My breath stills, and my thoughts are without form. Sleep refuses to visit my wasted eyes. I stare at the ponchos above my head. They devour me within their olive-green veil.

Events of the night replay over and over in vivid exactness up to the point where we reach the high ground. Then it all seems to merge in a blur of double-exposed photographs. Images bleed together like moisture running down a steam-clouded mirror to form an awkward smile in a puddle of melted-wax disfigurement. I just can't get it to sit right in my head. The harder I try to focus, the more blurred and disjointed the memory becomes.

Each time I restart the slide show it becomes less precise. A polluted wind erodes the memory and covers me like a blanket of rush-hour smog. My eyes begin to water, and my dry throat turns to a bed of hot embers when I attempt to swallow.

There is a tugging at my boots and a voice cuts through the haze, "Red, it's me, Doc. Red, come out of there. I've got to talk with you."

I hear the voice but don't respond. Wanting only to be alone, I feel that if I ignore everything around me I will be able to erase it all and break the back of the memory. Perhaps I can eliminate its presence if I can close my eyes, hold my ears, waggle my tongue, and chant, "Na, na, na, na, na, na, na, na…" long enough. Maybe then it will all go away.

My back begins to burn as someone grabs both my ankles and drags me out of the hooch and into the early morning sun. Bouncing on the hard earth, my head rattles and aches, but I refuse to respond. I believe that if I can hold on to the darkness and ignore the light, I will be able to destroy the evidence of the night before.

"Red, open your eyes, damn it. It's me, Doc. I don't have time for this shit. This is fucking Nam and you are not any kind of special case. Get your shit together, now!" I open my eyes and sit upright. Looking to my front, I try to avoid direct eye contact with the voice that challenges me.

I recognize Doc Love's outline in the glare. "Shit, Doc," I say. "I'm sorry, man. I can't do this. Let me be. Please, just let me alone. I can't do this. No, I can't do this."

He squats beside me and reaches out to hold me by my shoulders. He turns my body to face his. "Red, look at me," he commands. "Do you know what went down? Do you know what happened?"

"It just won't come together and make any sense to me, Doc," I say. "I know what we did, but at the same time I don't know just what happened."

"Red, you saw it. You just blocked it out," he explains.

"No, Doc," I respond. "I didn't see shit. I didn't see anything at all. Everything is just shadows moving together. It's muddy water, man. It's all shit-colored, rice-paddy crap." Rubbing my eyes, I try to see the thoughts within me. "Doc, I keep seeing it, yet not seeing it. There is a painting underneath a painting. The two flash back and forth, overlapping each other again and again."

94

"Red, it's time to get it right," he says.

"Doc, leave me alone," I tell him. "Go away. Don't do this. It never happened, Doc. Let it be." I look at his face and see him shaking his head at me. "It didn't happen," I say. "Please, Doc, just leave it alone."

"Red, Davie is dead," he says in a calm voice. "He was walking point. He stepped up over the rise to the flat top of the high ground. The AK-47 automatic burst started at his gut and the recoil pulled more rounds up his chest." Doc drops his head into his hands and rubs his face as if trying to erase the pain that burns him like acid. He looks back at me. "It damn near split him in half," he says. "He never knew what hit him, Red. There was nothing for him to feel. I promise you, Davie never even knew he died."

I shake my head back and forth. "No," I say. "Wait a minute. Wait just a minute." I turn away from him and whisper, "No."

"There couldn't have even been any time for pain, Red. There is no doubt about that in my mind. But, Red, it is real, and it did happen. Davie is gone. We've got no choice to make. He's gone." Grabbing his weapon from the ground at his feet, he plays with the magazine. Pushing the release button, it drops loose. He holds it in his hand and checks it out, then slams it back in the opening. Looking away from me and talking to the rice paddies to our front, he says, "We are here. The gooks are still out there. The beat goes on, my brother, the beat goes on."

He begins to stand up and slaps me on my leg as he rises. "Red, I'm going around our lines and telling the rest of the men what went down. You take whatever pulling-together time you need. I'll get back here in about thirty minutes." After taking a few steps he pauses and turns back toward me. In a voice void of emotion, he adds, "I expect you to have your shit together by then."

I stare at him, look down, then rub my legs up and back. My head seems to shake back and forth of its own volition. "I don't know what to say to you, Doc."

"Red, listen to me," he says. "You owe Davie that much. He never quit. You can't quit now. It wouldn't be what he would want. You know it for a fact. Stay to yourself. Pull yourself together. I'll be back later."

Doc walks away and leaves me sitting like a broken tin soldier propped half-upright in the dirt with both legs spread straight out in front of me. I pull my knees to my chest and roll over into a ball. The side of my head lies flat against the dry red dirt. Dust rises into my ears and I hear the faint roar of a distant ocean. Cold sweat chills my body and I begin to shake without control. Gasping for air, I taste burning bile in my throat. There is wetness on my cheek and I feel the tracks of tears on the tip of my jaw. Eyes swollen and face to the ground, I remain motionless and cry like a child lost in the woods with the sun going down on day as darkness falls.

# Chapter Twenty

## The Child

**DATE: November 1969**

Tiny enters the hut first. Frenchie and Fontana rush in at his heels.

"Don't shoot! Don't shoot!" Fontana hollers. Moments later he follows Frenchie out of the hut.

"What the fuck is goin' on?" asks Lieutenant Frost.

"Lieutenant, I didn't...I didn't know what to do," Fontana says. "We...we saw this bundle on the floor by the far wall. When it started to move, Frenchie turned toward it and was about to bust caps. Tiny was closest to it and he reached over—reached and pushed down the barrel of Frenchie's weapon. It was Tiny—Tiny did it. It was him that shut it all down, Lieutenant."

Tiny bends his head forward to fit through the small opening and step out into the sun. As he straightens up we see that he holds a small bundle of rumpled cloth like a sack of loose, dirty laundry in his huge hands. He turns to look at Lieutenant Frost and a bone-thin arm falls out from the sack and hangs over Tiny's muscled forearm. Two little doll legs drop from the front edge of the bundle and dangle like damp socks hung out to dry.

"What the fuck you got there, Tiny?" asks Lieutenant Frost.

"It's a kid, La'tennit. I don't know if it be dead or not. It ain't movin' now, that's fer shur. I couldn't see in there so I brung 'em out to the light."

"Tiny, you know you shouldn't have done that," adds the lieutenant. "The damn thing could have been booby trapped and blown all three of your asses up. Shit, use your damn head, boy."

Tiny steps closer to Lieutenant Frost and towers over him by at least a foot. He twists his head from side to side as if to free a hitch in it. "La'tennit, it's jus' a fuckin' kid," he says. "Hell, I got a li'l brother back home—Billy Joe. He ain't no bigger 'en this pile of nothin' here. All I seen was li'l Billy Joe's face when I lookt down on 'im. I didn' think 'bout any of that other shit." Tiny pulls his bundle tighter to his chest and looks down with the eyes of a Madonna on its skeletal form. He scans the bundle's short length several times back and forth. Tears begin to show in his eyes. He attempts to wipe them on his shoulder, but his massive breadth makes this impossible. His attention moves from the child to the lieutenant. Anger enters his voice and, like a knife thrown true, he challenges, "It's a kid—a damn kid."

Tiny looks around at those of us who surround the conversation to find some confirmation of his feelings. Eyes drop to the ground and faces turn away. His gaze returns to Lieutenant Frost, where it remains without a blink for several heartbeats. Tiny pulls himself up straight and stands even taller above the lieutenant. "I weren't gonna leave him there in the dark," he continues with conviction. "That weren't gonna happen, and God knows that for a fact. Shit, the kid be in there all 'lone, La'tennit—jus' this li'l piece a nothin' by hisself in that black hole. My li'l Billy Joe, he's skeered of the dark. I couldn't do nothin' but pick this 'un up and get 'im into tha day...into the light. Weren't no other way of choosin' on my part, La'tennit. Write me up if ya need ta do it, Sir, but I had me no choosin' ta do with this 'un."

"Doc Love, get your ass over here and check this shit out," Lieutenant Frost hollers. He shakes his head and looks around for his corpsman.

Doc Love runs over. When he reaches our group he asks, "What's up, Lieutenant?"

The doc looks over at Tiny and recognizes a child's form in the bundle he carries. He walks over to them in silence and reaches with arms outstretched like an image of Christ calling for a gathering of his children. Tiny allows the bundle to settle like a soft feather pillow into the cradle of Doc's waiting arms. Soiled cloth falls away and the small head of the child comes into view for all of us to see. Doc moves to the side of the hooch that offers some shade. He kneels to lay the child on the powdery, red dirt. Tiny takes the green towel he always carries hanging from his neck, folds it over itself, then places it under the small head as a pillow.

Doc lifts a canteen from his webbed belt, unscrews the plastic top, and brings water to the child's mouth. He tips it enough to allow a small flow to wash over its parched lips. The child's tongue crawls in a labored, licking movement toward the moisture. Arms too weak to hold the canteen, he opens his mouth wide, as a baby chick does waiting for food. The doc pours some water over his towel and wipes the child's face. Its eyelids fight to open, and for a moment two small dots of deep black give a frozen stare back into the doc's baby blues. Doc Love's calloused hands cup the fragile head with a warmth and grace of a da Vinci statue.

Scabs and open sores cover the child's exposed legs. One foot, an obscene shade of green, smells like rotten eggs. I turn away in disgust. Like knots on a hickory tree, the bones of the toddler's body poke outward at sharp angles from joints. His starved and bloated stomach rises as an over-inflated balloon, contradicting his skeletal outline like twigs of stacked kindling.

Doc Love shifts the weight of the child in his arms. He looks to Tiny and then to the lieutenant. "Frostie, this child is hurt bad—far worse than I have the ability to deal with out here. We've got to get some help." He glances down to the child, then back up to the lieutenant and adds, "Sir, we don't have a whole lot of time to play with."

Lieutenant Frost paces to his left, then his right. He checks the magazine in his M-16 to see that it is in place. An attempt to spit at the ground to his front causes a small amount of spittle to dribble onto his boots. "Doc, what in the hell do you expect me to do about it?" he asks. Then he wipes a string of saliva from his lips with his sleeve.

Doc Love responds with fire in his eyes. "Frostie, I expect you to get a fuckin' chopper in to Med-Evac this child out of here. I don't think he has a chance in hell of making it, but who the hell are we if we don't try to save his life?" The doc lifts the child and moves it farther into the shade of the hooch where he sets it like an expensive piece of crystal on the dry earth. "We have lost it all—Frostie, look at me—we have lost all we have that is good if we leave this child behind."

Lieutenant Frost stares at Doc Love and the doc stares right back. The lieutenant's eyes break away first. "Short Round—Short Round, get the CO on the horn!" he hollers.

Short Round works on his radio for a few moments. "Sir, I've got Captain Collins for you," he responds. "He ain't a happy camper, Lieutenant." He turns his back to Lieutenant Frost and hands the mike and headset back over his shoulder.

"Sir, this is Charlie 2, we've got a—well, we got a situation here," says the lieutenant. "We've found a child left behind in the ville. There isn't anybody else here but this beat up kid. He looks like death warmed over, Sir." He looks over at the doc, bent over and working on the kid. Shaking his head from side to side, he says, "Doc Love wants a Med-Evac for him. Please advise, over."

Only Lieutenant Frost can hear the other end of the conversation, but we can all tell by his face that he is getting his ass chewed out. He begins to respond, "But, Sir—" then stops and stares at his feet. After another few minutes he tries once again, "But, Sir—" then he returns to his downward, silent stare. The one-sided conversation comes to an end when the lieutenant gives a sharp, "Yes, Sir."

Handing the mike and headset back to Short Round, Lieutenant Frost walks over to where Doc Love crouches beside the child rubbing salve on the sores that cover its broken body. "Doc, the CO says that this ain't what we're here for," says the lieutenant in a low voice. "He told me, 'This is a fuckin' free-fire zone and anything we find out here is the enemy.' He also said, 'I don't give a shit how big or how small it is: In the bush, a gook, is a gook, is a gook.'" The lieutenant takes a deep breath. "He ordered us to move on out toward Check Point-3."

Lieutenant Frost can't hold eye contact with Doc Love. "We are way too vulnerable out here in the fuckin' open," he announces to the rest of us. "We are fixin' to get our asses in a sling any minute now if we don't move on." He pulls on his flak jacket and continues with a louder voice of authority. "Get your shit together, Charlie 2. Let's get our sorry asses the hell gone."

The Doc challenges, "But, Frostie—" He looks around at the rest of us for a sign of support. No one speaks up in return. "Lieutenant, this kid's gonna die if we leave him behind. That's the pure, damn truth of it, Sir. It is guaranteed death before dark if we walk away from him right now."

"Well, we are all dead if we stick around here any longer," Lieutenant Frost responds. "Charlie 1's patrol to the south took fire this morning." He reaches out both arms and gestures to the area all around us. "The fuckin' gooks are all over the place while here we piddly-ass around bitchin' and moanin'. We're just waiting to get our asses blown away. Hell, this baby-san was probably left behind as bait." He points an accusing finger at the child. "If they gave any kind of a shit about this kid they wouldn't have left him here in the first place."

Standing off to the side, Tiny doesn't move. He turns and faces Lieutenant Frost. He begins to say something, then just shrugs his shoulders and looks down to Doc Love for some sort of guidance. We are Marines and can't question Lieutenant Frost's orders, but the doc is a Navy corpsman. He has the authority to stand up to the lieutenant in matters of the platoons' health.

"Doc, just leave the little booby trapper here and the gooks will come get him," orders the lieutenant. "Put him back in the hooch. Then we can get our asses out of this turkey shoot we're sitting in. Fuck it."

# Chapter Twenty-One

## Redemption

**DATE: November 1969**

Lieutenant Frost looks straight at me, then moves his gaze from man to man in our small group. Eyes of darkness on faces of stone in this sun-scorched day mirror his expression in return. Pulling the M-16 from his shoulder, he calls out, "Saddle up, men. Let's get the fuck out of here." He spits a wad of thick moisture to the ground. It raises a cloud from the dust and a small crater forms where it displaces the dirt at his feet. He turns to me and begins, "Red, put that kid back in the hooch and—"

I feel nothing within my heart. Without sensation, I stand here lost in a winter's storm and shiver within the sweltering heat of the Nam. My body lies. I am cold and feel goose bumps on the back of my neck while fine hairs on my forearms stand at attention. All I see is my friend Davie, gut-split by enemy rounds, and Tater with a hollow look in his eyes as he sits by the old train-track path, shaking in a torn body wet with blood and rain. My mind's eye zooms to Smittie's leg where it lies at the side of the trail. Only grays, blacks, and shadows survive inside—there is no color whatsoever in my field of vision. Sweat pours down my face and drops to the soiled-and-stiff T-shirt that clings to my body like a second skin. A garter snake through playground grass, it crawls downward in meandering curves.

Doc Love jumps between the lieutenant and me. "What the fuck is wrong with you two?" Doc asks. "We can't let this happen. We

102

can't become animals in this jungle. I won't allow it." Lieutenant Frost looks away from Doc and checks to see if everyone is getting their shit together. The doc yells at the back of the lieutenant's head, "Frostie, do you hear me? I won't let you do this to this child. Hell, more than that, I won't let you do this to yourself."

With the snap of an over-wound watch, time breaks and stands still. The doc looks at the lieutenant. "Frostie, you're all gonna destroy whatever's left inside of us. Everything, damn it! You must see that we all die if we don't try to save this kid. I won't allow that to happen to my Marines." The lieutenant stops but doesn't turn around. "Do you hear me, Frostie?" Doc says. "It ain't gonna go down this way. Not on my watch. No, no fuckin' way."

Doc walks back over to the side of the hooch and picks up his gear. Along with one bandoleer of magazines, two more bandoleers of his field dressings, and his medical kit, he slings his M-16 over the thick shoulder of his flak jacket. Tenderness shows in his large hands. He scoops the motionless bundle from the dirt and cradles it close to his chest as if it were a newborn. "Let's get on with it," he says in a tone lacking doubt. "I'm as ready now as I'll ever be." He moves his shoulders from side to side to settle the load on his body. "Let's do it."

Lieutenant Frost turns and glares at Doc. He appears ready to offer an argument, but after a few tense moments gives none. He shakes his head and turns away. "Saddle up!" he yells. "Pass the word we're movin' out." He looks back at the Doc and asks, "Love, are you fuckin' with me?"

"Frostie, I'm not doing anything more than I'm required to do," Doc says. "Hell, I love you guys." His shoulders fall, and he takes a deep breath. "But I can't live with myself if I leave this life behind." He lowers his gaze to the bundle in his arms, smiles at it for a few moments, then looks back up at the lieutenant. "There is something else here, Frostie. It has to be about more than just keeping each other alive. I believe there is a meaning that goes beyond us and it's right here." He nods to the bundle in his arms. "This little one is gonna die—there is little doubt about it. But if we don't attempt to give our all to save it—well, then, we all cease to exist along with it." Doc begins to walk toward the lieutenant. Lieutenant Frost turns and walks away to join his place in the patrol. Doc stops to wait for his spot in line.

The word passes, and the line of our patrol moves out. Footsteps copy those of the man to the front in constant avoidance of booby traps and punji pits. Doc Love carries the child and acts as if the weight is as natural as an extra Claymore or a shoulder pack of M-60 ammo. Our line of men passes through the clearing of the small ville, then moves into the deep green brush and cane stands of higher ground. The further into the green blanket we slip, the more intensely the heat and humidity enclose around us.

Doc follows behind Short Round within the order of our patrol. He stops for a moment to reposition the child against his chest. We push on through the thick elephant grass. Dense undergrowth and fatigue cause the doc to stumble and trip forward. As he falls, he twists to his side and rolls to his back before he hits the ground with the immobile child cushioned on his front. Exhausted, Doc stares up at the sky while the patrol to his front continues onward.

Tiny follows behind Doc Love in the order of the patrol. "Slow it up for just a minute," he hollers to Short Round. He reaches down to the doc to explain, "It's my time—it's my turn." He places his hand on Doc's shoulder and gives it a soft shake. "Are you gonna make it all right on your own?"

Doc smiles. "Love ya, Tiny."

Tiny winks and smiles back. "Don't be sayin' that too loud, my brother," he says. "The guys'll begin to wonder 'bout us." He pulls the child from Doc's arms up into his own.

The doc rolls over, rises to his knees, then stands once again. He turns his head to the side. "Move it out!" he hollers. "We're ready."

Tiny carries the load with the same degree of care shown by Doc Love. He cradles it in his arms and holds it close to his heart. We drop down into an area of rice paddies again. The mud of the flooded field causes Tiny to tire faster than he expects. By the time he reaches the third dike and begins to crawl up its side, the fatigue shows in each of his labored steps. "Tiny, sit tight till I get there," Fontana calls up to him. "It's my time on watch, brother. I got your back."

As the day wears on, the child passes from one man to the next until the bundle reaches the last man in line. The child then goes back up through the sequence again as each man struggles to carry his share of the load. Heat and the weight of our weapons and gear begin to take their toll. The time for carrying the extra load begins to last for shorter and shorter intervals.

The second time the child passes forward, Short Round can only take its added weight for a brief time. The heft of the radio, along with his other gear, kicks his ass all on its own. Doc calls up to him, "Pass the kid on back, Short Round. We'll work him toward the end another time." Short Round hesitates and wants to continue. "It's gonna be all right, brother," Doc tells him. "Your best is all you can give, and you have given more than that."

Ahead of Short Round is Lieutenant Frost. He turns back and says, "Give it to me, dammit." He then looks beyond Short Round to the Doc. "It's still my damn platoon, Love," the lieutenant says. "Can you hear that, you fuckin' Squid?"

"Sir, yes sir," Doc answers. Their eyes meet over the distance. "You are a damn good man in spite of yourself, Frostie."

The lieutenant carries the child for longer than the others before him. But after a while he also begins to falter. I walk to the front of the lieutenant. So the child can reach me, I stop along the trail and wait for them.

"Lieutenant Frost, please let me take the kid?" I plead. My voice catches in my dry throat. "I feel like I'm some kinda monster, and—" I stare down at the mud at my feet and kick one boot against the other. Unable to go on, I slap at mosquitoes that feast at the back of my neck. I pull myself together, look back up, and continue, "I don't have any expectation of making it back to the world again." I take off my helmet and run my hand through my wet hair. "Lieutenant, at least allow me to do one decent thing this day."

He looks at me and shakes his head in confirmation. "I know how you feel, Red Man," he says. "I know. God forgive me, but I know." I take the still-unmoving body and move on without further words. Within a trance, footstep follows footstep through the mud.

We are near the end of the patrol. I see the positions that mark our perimeter in the distance. The child is my load to bear for the remainder of the way in—hell, for the remainder of time. As Company Guide, O'Brien meets us where we enter the lines. "Red Man, give me the kid and you keep out of this," he says. "The shit is about to hit the fan."

"O'Bie, let me see this thing through," I say, then walk over to the side where our patrol's first fire teams rest. My flak jacket and gear fall to the ground while I shift the bundle from arm to arm. I pull the child to my shoulder and cradle my arm beneath its bottom. The unsteady head lies secure above my neck. The child hasn't moved since I first picked him up. I can barely hear his breath even as his mouth and nose press against my ear. I pray for some sound. There is a rasp, like the squeezing of a deflating air mattress, from its lips. I hear nothing other than these fragile whispers of life. Loose in my arms, the child remains still upon my chest.

I feel the soft touch of its forehead against my cheek like a late-morning dream. Sweet sweat mixes with mine as its small skull slides across my wet skin. A soft pulse pumps like the rise and fall of an unfaithful lover's promise. My beating heart begins to sync with the faint pumping of the child's. For a moment, on this small piece of high ground, we are the only two lives in the garden. The remainder of the patrol follows through the lines, unloads the weight of their individual arsenals, then collapses in exhaustion. Lieutenant Frost passes by and heads straight to the Command Post. Doc Love approaches to meet me. "Red, follow me. Let's see what we can do for him," he says.

Behind Lieutenant Frost we make our way to the Command Post. Doc Murph and two more corpsmen from Charlie 1 wait for us. I release the broken body to Doc Love, then back away. Other corpsmen begin to surround the child, blocking him from my view.

I stare off into the distance and understand that, due to my responses, I looked into the face of the devil this day and saw that his is the image I will see in whatever mirrors remain till the end of my time. Even after these forty-plus years, when my eyes close at night and seek the shelter of sleep, I see, with the clarity of a blink in time, the broken form of that child in the dust. I will always taste the sweat from its brow on my lips. I will forever feel the fragile beating of his heart against my chest.

# Chapter Twenty-Two

## And the Rain Falls

**DATE: August 1990**

The rain falls with a patter like the echo of squirrels playing tag on the tin roof of a wooden shed. I stand on the small porch off our bedroom and stare into the darkness. Every few moments a gust of wind blows droplets sideways into the thin-wire screening. The moisture splatters into a fine mist that floats on the wind and wets my face like tear drops. Flashes of lightning to the northeast expose the tree line that runs along the small creek behind our storage lean-to. Trunks and limbs become backlit like silhouettes on a window shade as each fresh flash gives the breath of life to new images. Their brief existence plays out in a melodrama of a millisecond.

Crooked hands with long-knuckled fingers point at me. Skeletal faces of Halloween pumpkins held high by headless horsemen accuse and taunt me. False smiles tempt my trust, darkness erases their forms, and the blink of an eye sends them all back to the depths of their inferno. They are banished till the next flash, the next cinema in the sky.

An explosion of light freezes and the stick figures stand together within this theater of the absurd. Abstract forms merge into the smooth lines of photo album, time-travel characters, and the shadows of blurred memories become distinct, individual, young lions at the ready. Flash—one thousand one, one thousand two, one thousand three—then thunder explodes in a volley that shakes the windows

107

behind me. They shimmy in their frames like dominoes mixed for the next hand of forty-two, their chorus sung by wrinkled hands of old men who gathered under the shade of the giant oak in front of Matthews Feed Store. Men long ago passed over to the other side, now called upon to play one more game. A loud clap slaps worn, dotted rectangles down hard on a Formica-topped wooden table. Is the sound that of the worn ivories as they collide, or are they the clicks of misfitted dentures chewing tobacco? I don't know.

The slaps trigger my reflexes to duck, cover my head, and wait for shrapnel and gunfire. It's the same with each loud noise that carries the unwanted promise of a last glimpse backward. An uncomfortable lull in the storm lies like a forgotten name on the tip of a tongue. I stand alone and wait for the next mortar round's "whoosh" and the death-warning call of "incoming!"

I feel a hand reach across time and touch on my shoulder with the softness of cottonwood fluff in flight on a spring breeze. I jerk downward and turn to my left. The reflex comes like the twitch of a dissected frog's leg that frightens freshmen in the formaldehyde-scent of a high school science lab.

My wife stands before me. I have a mental picture of a dot in the center of a "V" sighted in on her forehead. Her eyes carry the lost and worried look of time's eternal war brides. It is not one of fear; rather, it is one of concern and sadness. She reaches out and touches my face. The warmth from her hand and the sadness in her eyes bring me back. She says, "Another stormy night?" I am embarrassed, ashamed that I have, once again, pulled her love into the darkened pit of my ghosts in the night. I know all too well that it is her goodness and affection that lead her to step much too close to my flame.

I take her hand, feeling all that should be ours snaking away from me like the shadow of a cloud rolling across new-mown pastures. "I'm sorry, I didn't mean to wake you," I say and shrug. "I couldn't sleep. I needed some fresh air."

She squeezes my fingers, shakes her head. "I know where you've gone," she says. "I know where you've been for the past hour." I start to pull my hand from hers, but she holds tight and refuses to let go.

She says, "I've been watching you through the window. I've seen you duck and jerk to each shout of the storm. I know what it is that calls to you."

"I'm all right," I say. "Really. The thunder and lightning seem to talk to me at times, that's all. It's like they are trying to tell me something, but I just can't seem to make out the words. I'm okay. It's just the storm. I know where I am. I do. Honest. Don't worry about me." I pull her close and hold her against my body. She buries her face in my neck. She kisses my damp skin with soft, cool lips. I feel small bumps rise on my neck and shake in their false chill.

Her head rests on my shoulder, speaking to the falling rain. "I hate that damn bitch. You and I have been together for fifteen years and that slut has shared our bed and your dreams every single night. If she were a woman, I'd know what to do. I'd bitch-slap the hell out of her. I'd put a gun to her head and a knife to her throat. I'd break both her knees with a ball bat if she'd ever dare to come out into the open for a fair fight."

She breaks away and holds me out to arm's length. "There is nothing I can do to that damned mistress of yours. I can't stand her; she mocks and offends me. I hate her for the games she plays with you. I despise her for the intimate time she cheats from us in barking lies like a carnival conman."

I pull her close to my chest—to my heart—and say, "I'm sorry. I know that is not enough, but it is all I have to say." I kiss her cheek and add, "Always know I love you."

I see the tears grow, flooding her eyes. She says, "I know...I know." She pauses and looks down and shakes her head with a false chuckle. "No, I don't know. I don't understand, not really."

We stand in silence for a few moments, then another flash of fire lights the porch. My body tenses. One thousand one, one thousand two—thunder! The house shakes like a frightened child. My body jerks and we begin to sway back and forth: two ships rocking in a gale.

She says, "Come with me. Let's go back to bed. We've got to get up early in the morning. It's time to rest. Please." The rain starts to come down harder than it has all night, as if some unseen master valve opened to capacity.

I release her hand and say, "You go on ahead. Go get some sleep. I'll be in in a few minutes. I'm just going to stay out here for a little while longer. Just a little while longer."

She turns and walks back into the bedroom. I turn and face the rain that once again begins to blow through the porch screen into my already-moist eyes.

# Chapter Twenty-Three

## A Package from Home

**DATE: December 1969**

The choppers arrive early to Phu Loc-6 on the morning run. The sun works its way through the lazy haze from the Song Fu Bong River, fights the low-lying clouds for a share of the eastern horizon, and rises from the depths of the South China Sea like a fire from hell. It paints its presence with flames of blood red and sparks of orange before it establishes dominance and reclaims the high ground from the night.

"Brown, ya got a package, big boy," Frank says as he squats in the center of second squad with our share of the mail sack. Each Marine's silent prayer that Frank will call his name hovers in the air like the smoke from raked autumn leaves above a curbside burning.

Frank tosses a package in an underhanded lob that Brown snags with the grace of a natural athlete. "Nice catch, big boy," Frank says as he continues to deliver the remainder of the squad's letters from home. Lucky recipients peel off to devour, with great hunger, words of sustenance from "the world." The rest of us descend upon Brown like vultures circling over road-kill drawn by the stale aroma of broken cookies and melted chocolate. Brown sits down and crosses his legs in the dirt. He appears to take great pleasure in his game of unwrapping the box with the deliberate moves of a seasoned San Clemente stripper. His coy prize reveals a treasure chest of hard candy, Kool-Aid packets, and assorted junk foods. Here's the gift of gifts: a care package from home.

"Hey, Brown, don't forget your homies, man," calls Fontana from the rear of the small group that congregates to watch the unveiling. The bottom of the box reveals a small stack of multi-colored envelopes, bound by a thick ribbon of purple and tied in a flattened bow with frayed and curled edges. "How many babes ya got back in 'the world,' Brown?" says Short Round. "That's a shit-load of letters, brother."

Without response, Brown tears the flap from the top card. Thigpen spies over his shoulder a "Happy Birthday" greeting stenciled in blue on a field of red and yellow flowers. Charlie Brown and Lucy, surrounded by balloons, stand beside little Linus, who clings tightly to his security blanket. Brown smiles as he reads the inscription: "We love you, big brother" followed by three signatures of George, Sally, and Kiki. "He's been holdin' out on us, men," Thigpen says. "Hey, Brown, is today your birthday?"

"Nah, well, not today," he responds. "It was a week or so ago. I guess my momma didn't get it posted in time." He looks up at those of us forming a corral around him. "You all know this damn mail takes forever to get to us out here in the bush." He looks back down at the cache of booty nestled in his lap. "What's the date today? Does anybody know?"

"Shit, I don't have a clue, man," says Plant.

"We all know that, Plant," Fontana adds. "But Brown asked you what the date is." Everyone laughs at his play on words.

Plant pulls his helmet off and throws it down on the hard ground. "Fuck you, Fontana! Get off my ass!" We continue laughing as Plant puffs his thin chest out in mock defiance.

"It's January somethin', that's all I know," Gino says. "I guess that means we should be expecting some snow soon."

"Well, my birthday was last week," Brown announces, then adds, "Does anybody have any idea what day of the week it is?"

We look around at each other like back-of-the-classroom commandos once again caught without their homework. No one speaks until Fontana pipes up. "Hell, who knows, and what damn difference does it make anyway?" he says. "All I know is that we're one day shorter in the Nam." He pulls his green T-shirt up and over his head and sticks a portion of it within the back of his utility trousers to keep track of it. "We're one day closer to our rotation dates and the big silver bird that'll fly us away. Other than that, it's just another day in sunny Vietnam—beautiful mistress of the South China Sea." He moves his right hand upward and creates the soaring sound of an imagined jet engine taking off. "We are closer to being gone, brothers. And that's all that makes a shit."

Brown seems to change before our eyes. Like wax slips from the lip of a burning candle, the smile on his face makes a slow fall down the sides of his cheeks. He asks in a subdued voice void of emotion, "Hey guys, how about letting me be by myself for just a little while? I promise I'll share this shit with you later. But for now, how about backing off a bit? I need some space for a little time alone, okay?"

The Mexican says, *"No problemo, mi amigo."*

Everyone starts to walk away except Plant. Frank grabs him by the arm and drags him along with us. Plant turns to holler back over his shoulder, "Hey, Brown, don't forget your buds, man." Frank slaps Plant on the back of the head in a Three Stooges wakeup call. Plant yells, "Ouch, what the hell was that for? I didn't do shit."

"That's right, Plant," Frank says. "That's what your problem always is. You never do shit."

The morning crawls along like a milk-stop freight train while I sit nearby and clean my M-16 and magazines with a toothbrush and gun oil. I glance over at Brown several times to catch him reading, and re-reading, each one of his long bridges to home. With great care he replaces each card and letter back into its envelope before he moves on to the next offering of love and escape that spans from here to half-way around the world.

Time drags on at oxcart pace in the monotony of another day in the Nam. Morning's long shadow crawls toward noon and mocks our boredom with the silent laughter of the unrelenting sun. Frank calls, "Saddle up!" and we begin to make our way toward the bottom of the hill where the platoon is forming for the day's patrol.

Sergeant Matt says, "All right, men, let's get ready to move out."

Brown's fire team will walk point, so he, O'Bie, and Gino move toward the front of the squad. As he passes me, Brown stops and turns to get my attention, "Red, it's not right today," he says in a quiet tone. "Something is—out of balance. Something ain't right, brother."

"Brown, stop this shit," I respond. "You're only working yourself up. Why don't you let the Mexican walk point first? He likes gung-ho crap. Let him start it all out today." I notice an unusual, faraway look in his eyes. It's like he is somewhere else. "You don't have your head on right, Brown. No shit, let the Mexican take it. Come on, man, you can take it over after the first check point if you think you need to."

He shrugs his shoulders and begins to walk away, then stops. He scratches the back of his neck and spits into the dirt at his feet. Then he turns back to face me. "Red, if anything happens, if anything goes wrong out there today, you get that box of mine. I want you to split my shit up with the squad.

"I don't care how you do it, but I want you to be sure to let Plant get the foil-wrapped slice of chocolate cake." Brown shakes his head and looks to the sky as he searches for some sort of way to explain our own lost boy. "You know, he takes so much shit from everyone else. And well, I know he is a royal fuck-up. But sometimes I guess I just feel sorry for the little guy. Granny Brown would say, 'Seems like he always gets the part that goes over the fence last.'" I laugh, shaking my head in agreement. Brown laughs along with me, then continues. "Anyway, just this once, let him have the best part. Let him be a winner. Even if only for this one fuckin' time."

"Brown, you're scaring me, man," I say. "Stop this bullshit. It's not funny anymore. We've all got each other's backs. We're going to make it just fine today."

He looks into my eyes for a moment longer than usual and his distant gaze turns to a tired grin that fails to fill his face. He winks and says, "Shit, I was just fuckin' with you, Red Man. It's no biggie."

"Well that's more like it, Brown," I say. "You had me worried there for a minute. No shit. I'm not used to negative crap like this from you." He slaps me on the shoulder, turns, and takes a few more steps away. He stops once again to look back with his certain, shit-eatin' grin, and laughs. "You get the shoestring potatoes, Red Man. I don't think anyone else will eat that shit but you." He points an accusing finger at me. "Not even fuckin' Plant."

The patrol forms, leaves the perimeter, and moves south along the river's edge. We soon turn inland through dense undergrowth with Brown in the lead. He directs us toward the first checkpoint beyond a little hamlet set on a small piece of high ground. He takes us on a meandering trek across the thick mud and tainted water of the paddies. We avoid the high dikes as much as possible, where the booby traps lie in wait with their indiscriminate letter-home promise of torn limbs and death at the ready.

We walk, spaced at a frag's kill-radius apart, through the weight of strained breath and rising heat. We each step in the footprints of the man before us, trying to avoid the traps their footfalls miss. The sun sneaks through the bush toward high noon and bakes our worn bodies without thought of mercy. It sneers at the weight of weaponry and ammo we carry. With each step, our jungle boots press deeper into the gumbo that grabs at our feet like Dante's hands reaching upward from the depths of his inferno.

The Nam is ninety-five percent nothing going on, so the greatest challenge often becomes the strain to remain alert for the five percent that can jump out like a bus-ride pervert and grab you by the ass at any moment. The monotony of this day's endless patrol settles in. We each know we must remain alert to stay alive, yet the step, after step, after step—and the effort required to pull each new movement upward out of the mire—creates a rhythm of sameness. Yesterdays collide with yesterdays and they all intertwine with each of the lost days before that.

Gino holds up his hand, and the signal passes back for us to halt. We crouch down, alternate our directions, and aim outward in a defensive position to watch and wait. The word reaches us, "Brown hit a tripwire. It was a dud. It didn't go off! Pass it on. Pass it on!"

"That lucky shit," Plant blurts out. "Birthday Boy, my ass. They'll bring his fire team back and put O'Bie's team on point now in this bad-assed shit. It's the Brown's day. Way to go, Brown. Way to go." Brown earns the semi-sanctuary near the center of the patrol. On alert, we wait for the switch in our order to take place.

"We're moving out, get your shit together," Gino says. "Let's get a move on." The patrol continues. We approach a small stream that runs through a maze of banana trees and bamboo. I hear the distinct "crack" of an AK-47 enemy rifle ahead. Once again, we drop to face alternate sides. Low in the mud, we wait at the ready for more of the ambush to hit us. An electric static hangs in the air like a jokester's bucket of water balanced over a partially opened door. But no other sounds of enemy fire disturb the lie of silence.

A call reaches Gino to bring second squad up through the line. We rise as one and rush past the men to our front until we make it to the small clearing where Doc Myrt is bent over a body lying on the trail. Sergeant Matt and the Platoon's new commander, Lieutenant Galyean, also kneel beside the motionless form. Short Round's antenna stands high above us like a ladder to the clouds, and I hear him calling for a Med-Evac.

"Take second squad and move to the open piece of high ground across the blue line and to our right," Sergeant Matt tells Gino. "Secure a perimeter for a chopper to land." He grabs Gino's elbow to halt him for a moment. "And Gino, make it quick, and make it good. There is no leeway to play with here. We're damn near all out of time."

Everything begins to move in the awkward slow motion of the dream where you try to run but you can't make any forward movement. It's the nightmare where you can't escape the chase of the boogieman. I look toward the group to the side of the path and see Brown propped against the stream's embankment. I watch as Sergeant Matt hands Doc Myrt his ballpoint pen. Doc takes it, unscrews the center, and removes the ink cartridge and spring from the top portion. He inserts the remaining half of the tube into the front of Brown's neck where he has cut a small slit through the flesh for a tracheotomy. I hear the "hiss" of air through the makeshift tube. Looking higher, I see the bottom part of Brown's face. His jaw is gone and only the top portions of his teeth remain beneath the raw, torn skin of his twisted nose. His eyes cling to life like bloodied fingertips grasping at a cliff's edge. His face is ashen gray, making a slow turn to an even more washed and faded shade of pale.

Sergeant Matt looks up to find that I stopped on the trail to stare. I'm unable to move. My feet are frozen within the cement of time and I am without ability to respond. "Red, get your ass in gear. Now! Now!" he yells.

I look at Brown. His eyes make a slow, pained crawl upward toward mine, to stare a last dance of recognition. I watch as a light glows within the spark of a freak breeze upon waning embers, then fades away. Gino grabs my arm and gives a quick tug. I respond on instinct. I run behind him and begin to take care of my responsibilities to maintain the squad's security.

We find open ground, spread out, and wait for the choppers to arrive. There is no follow-up attack by the enemy. I search for the movement of straight lines within the random twists of the natural irregularity that surround us, but there is none. The act of a lone sniper, the fight for this day's victory ends. No other rounds fire.

The Med-Evac chopper lands in our center and the corpsmen rush out of its bloated belly. They hurry to avoid the danger of their snake-strike vulnerability on the ground. From the trees a stretcher appears with Doc Myrt and Sergeant Matt following the chopper's crew of corpsmen. A rushed sense of urgency no longer appears in their calculated trot to the chopper. The lone form on the stretcher lies within the dark, zippered bag of the omnipresent Man from Glad.

The chopper's ramp goes up, and the awkward machine moves skyward in the circular pattern of a frightened whirlwind. Upon reaching a predetermined height of safety, the chopper joins its accompaniment of gunships that provide support cover. They head northeastward toward the coast, the hospital, and the morgue in Da Nang.

"Saddle up, we are moving out!" Sergeant Matt hollers. "Gino, your squad's got point. This shit may not be over yet. Be ready for anything."

"Fontana, your fire team's got the front," Gino yells. "Move it out."

"Oklahoma, you got first shift at point," Fontana says. "Watch your ass. Here, let me show you where you'll locate Check Point-2." He pulls his map out and points to a small piece of high ground beyond a wide stretch of rice paddies ahead of us. "Watch yourself, Okie. This is not a good place. No, this is not a good place at all." He grabs him by his shoulders and looks into his eyes. "Are you alright, my brother?"

"No, I'm all fucked up, Fontana," Okie says. "I am a crazy man through and through." He puts his thumbs in his ears and wiggles his fingers at him. "But I can still take care of my shit. Don't worry, I've got it together. Let's do it. Let's go get us some."

Oklahoma walks his time at point until we reach our second checkpoint, then Frank takes the following stint at our front. We make it back to our perimeter without further incident. Evening arrives like a stranger in dark clothes seen through the fisheye of a hotel-room peephole. To Sergeant Matt, I give Brown's soiled letters to send back home to be washed by the tears of those who love him. I take his box of gifts around to the men who mourn his loss and pass out individual items to each member of the squad. Everyone receives some little thing. I make certain Plant gets the chocolate cake he craves. He cries without shame when I hand it to him. I keep the tube of shoestring potatoes.

Taking a seat on the ground in front of our poncho hooch, I open the tin-topped can. I think of the stiff sticks with their once-crisp crunch and feel an overpowering sense of loss and despair within their salted taste. I realize that I failed to even acknowledge my friend's birthday. With no tears left to shed, I sigh and say, alone and lost, to the waning light of day, "Happy Birthday, Brown—Happy Birthday, my brother."

# Chapter Twenty-Four

## A Visit

**DATE: July 2011**

It is a Thursday afternoon. I sit with my old friend, Russell Brown, on a peaceful spot overlooking the Pacific. I talk with him in the warmth of the sun and the comfort of a cool breeze that blows in over the cold water below. There is a gentle slope that ends at a chain-link fence before falling into the sea. To our left are several bent pines; to our right front is a weathered tree with orange balls of string-blossoms. The lawn is thick and freshly mown. It smells of picnics and backyard parties.

I sit with my legs crossed. I bend forward and play with the individual blades of grass and rip one from its runner. Placing it between my thumbs, I blow into the makeshift reed and am rewarded with the shrill whistle of the summers of my childhood. I dig my fingers through to the dirt and find a tiny skeleton, grown white with time, of a small roly-poly bug still curled in a tight ball. I pick it up for a closer look and see it disintegrate between my thumb and forefinger.

At first words refuse me. I don't know what to say. It has been so long since we were together that I feel more strangers than friends. I stand up in the awkward silence and turn from his side to look down upon him, then begin to talk. At the start, I ramble as only the briefest of statements come to me. But, after a while, more meaningful thoughts begin to form with a natural flow that serves to wash away the cobwebs of forty-two years.

I sit back down at his side and watch the white caps play far out to sea and begin to melt like crayons in the sun into the indistinguishable colors of the horizon. Within the distant haze I can see the outline of a navy vessel. I watch a series of military choppers work their way from shore toward the dark outline. Kites without strings, gulls float beneath our strategic position over the cliff and soar on unseen currents. I point these mundane observations out to him and laugh at the magic of their insignificance.

Brown, I don't understand any of this. Even after all these years, the incredible lack of fairness still confuses and haunts me. It cuts with the thrust of a knife. Damn, it still hurts beyond explanation. I carry no visible wound; no physiological damage exists; no scar remains to mark a point of entry. Yet, I bleed. The pain is alive, always present. I feel it under the surface of my damp skin. It flows through my veins; it is the shock of the electric jump of synapse from nerve cell to nerve cell. It shimmies and shakes throughout me without regard to biological roadmaps, a deep sorrow in the bottomless pit of my breast. Guilt without hope of absolution, it races the infinite figure eight around and around, again and again. But I don't tell this to Brown. He doesn't deserve yet another load to carry. It is not his to bear.

Instead, I talk about the view and the beautiful day. I tell him about our mutual friends from Charlie Company. I give him a rundown on what I know of their lives. I remind him that they all send their best regards. I tell him about my family and the joy their love brings me. My wife and my children, my brother and sisters take form and sit beside us upon the grassy hillside. I share with him the loss of my mother five years before and describe the hole in my heart where love still leaks out like water from a shattered pipe in a deep winter's freeze.

I tell him about walks in the pasture with my dog, and the simple pleasure of watching him chase squirrels and rabbits and dig in earnest futility for moles that laugh their way through rear exits of escape. I explain evenings spent stargazing with my wife while I hold her hand. I attempt to describe the comfort of a silence that has no need for words.

My wife returns to us. She asks if I have had enough time with my friend, then adds, "Are you all right?" I say, "No, but it has been good. I guess I have said what I have wanted to say for all these years. Yes, it's been good after all. It has been a good thing to do." I take her hand and say, "I told Brown about you and the kids. He knows you are the only one who keeps the ends tied together." I look back down to the grass at my feet. "It's okay, we can go now."

"I'd like to say a prayer for your friend if you will permit me to do so," she says, then begins to speak. But words catch in her throat and tears begin to wet her eyes and slip a slow trail down her cheeks. We continue with our silent prayers until Cindy squeezes my hand and says, "Amen." Before we turn to leave, I say, "Brown, you are not forgotten."

# Chapter Twenty-Five

## Shoestrings

**DATE: July 2011**

I sit here on the side of a mound overlooking a small park and the beach in Santa Monica. A child of four or five runs down the side of the hill and her father scoops her up in an outstretched embrace of pure love. She screams with glee as he falls over backwards with her arms squeezed securely about his neck.

A young woman in her twenties lies back against the slope and turns the pages of a paperback novel while her small white dog sprawls on his side and sleeps. There is a rabbit-chasing twitch to his hind legs. The movement scratches her side. The girl shows beautiful white teeth in her smile of affection, then returns to reading while the dog chases onward through his rabbit dream.

On a walk this morning I found an Albertson's grocery store on the corner of Lincoln and Ocean Park. I searched the aisles up and back several times through without success. Neither the cashier nor two different stock clerks had ever heard of shoestring potatoes. A reality check suggested that there was a good chance they no longer even made the damn things, or that they at least didn't exist in the health-food haven of southern California. I decided to begin a search for something that might come close to matching its taste and texture and came across a cardboard tube, tin-topped replica of the shoestring container I remembered from a time when junk food was junk food, at the best of its worst, and bought a similar container of

122

French-fried onions. I also bought a large bottle of a low-end Pinot Grigio.

I pour a large amount of the wine into a used Starbucks coffee cup with a plastic top to protect the sunbathers from viewing my sin of alcohol in the park. I open the fried onions and propose a toast to my friend. With a sip of wine and a greasy handful of fried onions I call his name, but my voice fades in the strong wind that rises from the beach. The wine is cheap but goes down well enough.

The onions taste nasty and greasy and perfect in their decadence—just the sort of over-seasoned good shit from so many years ago that we'd find wedged into care packages from home. "Here's to you, Brown," I say. "Here's to the young man you were." I take another sip of the wine. "To the young man you will always be."

A young couple sets up an umbrella nearby with cloth sections of multi-colored pastels. The mother holds a newborn in her arms while the father takes pictures to capture this moment when all things are possible. They place the baby in a seat beneath the shade of the umbrella. The father takes out a guitar, lies on his back in the sun, and begins to strum out a tune. His wife smiles at him and reaches out a hand to caress their child. The breeze from the ocean carries his music away from me. Its melody becomes every song. I choose to tap my foot against the palm tree in a Beach Boys' "Good Vibrations" remembrance. Why not? It's my hill, it's Brown's hill, too, so Beach Boys it is. "...they're giving me good vibrations."

Out on the water, sail boats cross in the wind, paddle boarders fight to maintain an awkward balance, and surfers look out to sea in search of the perfect wave. Young girls walk by with a confidence that eyes follow, and their hours spent in quest of the perfect tan are not in vain. Young boys on bikes fly down the mound while joggers and skateboarders zigzag out of their way. Shirtless, teenaged boys in baggy shorts play a pick-up game of basketball at championship intensity. With the wonderful, deep growl of power and money, a Ferrari passes on the street below. I think about Brown as he floats through my mind on the wings of non-specific memories.

A World War II vintage fighter passes overhead. Another couple further down the mound embraces. The woman leans back against her partner's side, and he reaches his hand to her lips and crosses them with a soft brush of his fingertips. Their two dogs watch the intimacy with indifference and wait for the toss of a red Frisbee. She lifts a leg over his, and I look away to allow them their imagined privacy. I eat my fried onions, sip my wine, and think of Brown.

The afternoon sun begins to throw reflections of silver and diamonds against the waves. Its brightness causes me to squint as I look toward the beach umbrellas and tarps that line the shore. The mistresses of the Los Angeles freeways continue to arrive in the parking lot between street and sand. I turn to look at the twin high-rise condos behind me and see three homeless men asleep beneath trees offering sparse shade. Each shadow wears a heavy jacket and leans back against plastic bags of bare necessities. Saddened by the contrast between the opulent Ferrari that passed a few moments ago and these men who have, for whatever reason, chosen to surrender to the game, I sit here, mourn lost souls, drink wine, eat pseudo-shoestring potatoes, and think about Brown.

A single-engine plane passes overhead, trailing a banner I am unable to read. A young girl with short blonde hair, short shorts, tiny bikini top, and a pair of cowboy boots runs by and jumps into the arms of a boy in a ball cap with bill turned backward. He lifts her off the ground and slaps her on the ass. She shouts in delight and kisses his cheek and neck.

A kite rises from the sand and dives up and back to the directions of a trained master. The plane trailing the banner flies back by, closer this time, and I read the words that instruct me, "Miller is the beer that loves you back." I sit here, drink my wine, eat my shoestring onions, listen to Miles Davis on my iPod, question Miller Beer's affection for me, and think about Brown.

The sound of helicopter blades causes me to jerk. I look up into the sun, blinded by the light. Following the noise, I find a Coast Guard chopper patrolling the beach. So many years ago, so many days in the sun gone by—yet it remains as today; forever and always, today. The memory of my friend squeezes on my heart as a string tied round my finger, reminding me never to forget. I sit here and drink wine, eat shoestrings, listen to Miles, question Miller's sincerity, remember the chopper that carried the plastic bag to our landing zone near a small stream in the Nam, and think about Brown.

I'm not clear what I believe. I've lost so much faith with the passing of the years. There was a time when I knew the why. I understood the becauses. But now, I just float amid the maybes, what ifs, and perhaps that inhabit the uncertainty of the certainty that I don't know shit. I thought age would bring me wisdom. Like an uninvited guest who shapes balloons, entertains with jokes and jingles, and becomes the life of the party, I believed wisdom would remain after all others went home. I thought we would then sit on the couch and drink the good stuff in the liquor cabinet. He would laugh, and I would laugh, and he would reveal truth. Instead of truth, the years only brought to me a partial-understanding of jaded curiosity. I imagined that one day I would know at least a portion of the why that wanders through each of my cloudless, starry nights. Instead, clouds roll by at inopportune moments while stars disappear and die on their voyage through time and space.

With these thoughts I become angry. It infuriates me that I do not have some sort of inner wisdom. Annoyed that the price we paid with our youth continues to return with a stamp of "insufficient funds," I reply, "Fuck you. What more do you dare ask of me? 'I gave at the damn office' and 'the check is in the mail.'" But shit, I've earned the right to view the answer to whatever the correct question might be: to glimpse a "truth"—at least once. Shit yes, I have.

I will forever ask, "Why Brown?" I understand the explanations of "survivors' syndrome," those clean and clear definitions that state, "They died, you didn't. Enough said." Well, that isn't enough for me. I live on as a survivor, but from Brown's view of "Why the fuck me?" it is not enough. I may not deserve an explanation of the "why" but, fuck it all, he does. Damn it, he does.

There is a granite stone with Russell Lee Brown's carved name that watches the end of each evening over California's golden Pacific Coast. In deep-etched letters and numbers, it weathers the assault of time. I sat with Brown and watched the sun move lower in the western sky only a few days ago. The God of the universe, or the damn, false wizard behind the curtain, or something or someone owes him an answer of some sort. His sacrifice warrants that much.

I pray, "My Lord, please grant me a truth to pass on to my friend, Brown. Explain to me so that I can sit by his side and explain to him why. Shouldn't religion be a two-way street? Shouldn't we expect in return an explanation of some sort?" But then, shit, what do I know? I'm just a grunt, a life-long grunt, a wader through the mud. What the fuck does a grunt know?

I do suppose these damn unquestionable truths: my friend Brown existed; he walked bad-assed point in the Nam; he got fucked by the random, beyond any sense of fairness and justice, fickle middle finger of fate. There is a part of me that begs for a "why?" Just give me some inkling. If I am unable to explain Brown's death, then I am unable to explain my life. If Brown's death was just random bullshit, then my life has been nothing more than random bullshit as well.

I sit here, watch life go on around me, sip cheap wine, eat my version of shoestring potatoes, listen to Miles Davis, question my God...and I think about Brown.

# Chapter Twenty-Six

## One-on-One

**DATE: August 2008**

"How are you doing?" She touches my shoulder and gives it a soft squeeze of affection, not knowing just who the hell I might be this day. Walking around the porch bench, she sits by my side, curls both feet beneath her bent legs, reaches for a large pillow, and pulls it onto her lap. It cushions her body as she moves in closer to me. I can feel the rise and fall of her breathing as she leans against my arm. Within the shelter of her love I feel privileged and affirmed.

She begins to scratch the back of my neck and twirl the ends of my hair with her fingers. The scent of cut onions, tomatoes, and peppers linger on her hands, along with the lemon she squeezed on the avocados to keep them fresh. A bit of lavender floats from her fresh-washed hair. I am intoxicated by the gift of her presence, and I feel lightheaded.

"Not so good today," I respond, continuing to look out the window. Two young squirrels play a game of chase in the closing shadows of day between the trunks and lower branches of our backyard oaks. Their diversion allows me to avoid her eyes, which hold too many questions. Her stare contains too much information to let it go. I search for an explanation. "It all seems to be weighing down on me again. It closes in and my head shudders within a silent scream while I search for an exit."

"You know it's going to be all right, don't you?" She lays her head on my shoulder and remains still for several minutes. "This one has been coming on for some time, hasn't it? I thought when you met with your friends in Mississippi this year it helped you." She intertwines her hands and pushes them outward, away from her body. "Since then, you have appeared to be happy and easy, and at some sense of peace." Her fingers tangle into a strained here-is-the-church, here-is-the-steeple design. She unties them and allows them to drop softly into her lap. "Your dreams haven't seemed so intense," she continues. "Your tossing and turning and mumblings haven't stolen entire nights of rest and respite from the storms, or have they?"

"I don't know, I thought so too," I half-whisper. My neck feels wet where her eyes press against my skin. She lifts her head from my shoulder and I sense her gaze touch the side of my face. My old mixed-breed hound, Burke, enters the backyard. The squirrels take their game to higher branches, taunting and teasing him, yet he shows a Vegas dealer's lack of interest in their excitement. Walking on over to the roots of one of the oaks, he scratches some new ruts in the dry dirt, then circles several times before settling down into an evening's easy slumber. I remember days gone by and the times when my old friend would chase critters all summer in a younger dog's body of quicker reflexes and greater energy. "That's okay, Burke. Chip and Dale just believe they see a dog. Those silly squirrels don't know anything about the heart of a lion that beats within your chest."

The sun sinks behind the trees, and the sky weaves streaks of soft purple mixed with pink and a trace of yellow to mark its fall. I can hear the clear song of mockingbirds coming to rest for the night and the familiarity of a whippoorwill's call on the wind. Cindy watches Burke's indifference and laughs as his tail moves from side to side through the dust and dry leaves. He rests in the certain knowledge that he stole our hearts, his life complete in its trust and consistency. She takes my hand within both of hers and caresses it with the soft embrace of satin on silk.

"But it was good last night," she says in a whisper. "It was very good last night. You woke me, and I could feel the desire in your touch. Even within your need you were slow and gentle." She looks away and watches the growing darkness settle like a thick smoke over the yard. "You have always been a considerate lover. Thank you."

She gives a slight tug to my hair. I don't respond, and she gives a stronger, playful pull.

I smile at the openness of her compliment. "Thank you, too," I say. She needs confirmation and I need to explain. "You are my only love, in all ways and for always. With you I am alive. Everything else is empty space in between. Time with you is my time on the wire."

She reaches over and picks up a pinecone from the ground. "As we became one I could sense that this time together was about me, it was for me," she says. "You did all the special little things you understand about my desires, as if you made a shopping list of my appetites." She begins to pull the open scales from the cone. As they come loose she stacks them in her lap. "I could feel you going up and down the aisles of my body, marking checks as you filled my cart. I was complete and significant. I felt your permission to be released from constraints and the freedom to share myself with you. The beat of your heart on my chest provided a pace for my own and we were one body, one soul, and one beating pulse." She reaches the end of the cone. Without scales it looks like a thin pole over its base. Tossing the naked pole and the pile of scales, she then stops to brush the dirt from her hands. "I sensed your need and knew the effort you were making to hold back," she continues. "I prayed for a little longer, for just a little bit longer, please. Then I was at the magic place of 'there.' It was wonderful. It was perfect."

She moves her soft hand toward me, grasps my jaw, and turns my face toward her. "But I knew, even then, when I looked into your eyes, I knew that not all of you was there with me. Even as we continued, as you joined me in the height of our passion, I could feel you pulling away from me once again. I knew that I was losing you to your night. Like those squirrels in the branches, the demons that lurk and linger in the shadows had come to play." She gives a half laugh that carries all the blue chords of sad songs within its resignation. "I knew then that the Bitch was back in town."

I join her laugh with my own, but it is awkward and staged like a bow at the end of a rehearsed curtain call. She slaps my arm with a bit more force than play. "She is a damn addiction I cannot control," I complain. "There's no rehab center for this Bitch. She's a self-induced, continuous, worse-than-heroin fix that flows through my veins. I can feel her slip and slide with each beat of my heart. Then she stops to plan renewed assaults of needles and pins before continuing within the ensuing beat of the 'down.' Her song plays, again and again, and it goes on, and it goes on, and it goes on."

Cindy does not smile any longer. Not a bit. "There is not a damn thing funny about this shit, not one damn thing," she says.

"I know," I respond. "It is unkind of me to make light of any of this. I try. Honest to God, I try. I try my damnedest. She just won't let go." I stand and turn to look down at her. "I think she is gone," I continue. "She doesn't show herself for days and weeks at a time. Then she appears and teases me with the allure of her lies."

I close my eyes and remember: The rush is there throughout my body, and it is sweet, and it is pure and true. It steals my breath and my heart races within my chest. I become so high that when I look down and see myself, there is nothing left to view. The "me" means nothing at all.

Then I think, what arrogance it takes to find excitement within pain and suffering. What a sorry excuse for a man I am to hunger for this high.

I sit back down beside her; she adjusts her position and gives me a look of doubt and pent-up anger. "Look at me closer," she insists. "I'm telling you it is all bullshit. Pure crap. You know that, don't you—don't you?"

I face away from her. The sun sets, and darkness wins its fight against late-evening shadows. "You are all the way right," I tell her. "I'm sorry, I really am. No shit. It's okay. I just allow myself to wander along and get lost at times." I pull her closer and kiss the top of her head. "When I lose my way, I reach for you. That is an unfair load to ask you to bear; I apologize forever for that."

With her hand on my leg, she rubs her palm in small circles over the bend in my knee. She gives me a tender tap then pulls away. "I don't believe the Bitch has gone anywhere," she says. "You're just feeding me crap so I will let it be. You want me to step back so you can be alone within your firefights, ambushes, and shadows in the dark. Then it can be the way you want it to be: one-on-one." She slaps my leg with force. "That's right, isn't it?"

I squeeze her hand and look away. A bittersweet-tasting smile of truth and irony crosses my lips. I pause to reflect for a moment. Looking into her eyes, I prepare to throw a knife-show dagger as her spinning form goes round-and-round, shackled to the circular target. Those faint of heart hide their faces. I pull the blindfold down over my own eyes and draw the blade back and above my shoulders in preparation for a daredevil's toss. The crowd sounds a chorus of "oohs" and "aahs."

"Yep, that's it," I say. "There are times when that is the truth of it all."

# Chapter Twenty-Seven

## The Good Grunt

### DATE: March 1970

"Lead us not into temptation but deliver us from evil." My rotation date (the date to mark the end of my thirteen-month tour in Nam) is getting near. A short-timer, I have had enough, not only because I'm sneaking up on the end of my time here, but also because I am done with death. Not needing to prove anything to myself or to anyone else, I just want to survive. I want the men with me to make it out, too, so I'm looking for all the help I can get.

Before each patrol or ambush I repeat the Lord's Prayer several times. Is this sacrilegious? I don't know. I really don't. At times it is more of a robotic chant than an act of meditative communication with my God. I am ashamed for this sin of omission. Nonetheless, I fix a strong sense of immediacy to the "temptation" and "deliverance" message of "let it be."

Reaching the part where I ask the Lord to please "Lead us not into temptation," I add my own interpretation with a disclaimer of "I don't want to kill anyone else, Lord. Honest to You, I don't. Please, just keep them out of my way. That's all I ask, because if we do run into them, Lord, I will take care of my business. I will do whatever I need to do to keep my friends alive. I know that means taking the enemy down. You see, I'm committed to this rifleman thing. I am the 'good grunt,' Lord. No better way of protecting ourselves exists than to kick ass, take names, and get rid of the Cong. A fact, without doubt. So again, I just am asking you to keep them out of our way, Lord; to please 'lead us not into temptation.'"

After getting this plea as clear as I can seem to get it, I move on to "And deliver us from evil." I just ask, "Lord, don't let them get any of us. I beg You to please guide our point man around all the booby traps and walk us beyond the range of spider-hole snipers and hit-and-run ambushes. To my limited way of thinking, a good deal, Lord. We don't kill any of them, and they don't kill any of us—everybody makes it through one more day. That ought to be a 'win-win' situation for us all, Lord. Just one day at a time. No killing for just one damn day at a time.

"By this part in my tour, it sure sounds like a good deal to me. I've lived through my gung-ho moments of 'let's get some.' I've made it beyond the 'kick ass and take names' crap. All that doesn't mean a damn thing other than boot camp bullshit. Sorry for the language, Lord, but I am done with the game of it all. There is no more adventure tied to the chase. Hell, no joy exists in killing and no joy in dying, either. There is no more 'man's man' lure of acceptance anywhere near here. I just want my boys alive and unharmed, and I don't give a rat's ass about contact and body counts.

"There aren't any rules in war, no argument about playing fair, one way or the other. Now, don't get me wrong, Lord, I will always continue to do what I am told to do. A 'good grunt,' I am a Marine and proud of it. It is my sworn oath that I will stand my watch to the very end. I will always aim to kill when the time comes. I learned my responsibilities well but reached the point where I would just as soon not make the choice any longer—not in this war. We keep dying while they keep trying to find a way to wind it down. And all the while, Lord, we keep losing the best of the best.

"I don't look for shit anymore. But if the shit chooses to show up, Lord, I will do whatever it takes to cover my boys' backs. I am the 'good grunt.' I know that the only sure way of keeping the gooks from killing us is to kill as many of them as possible, so that is what we do. But the little fuckers keep coming back like mosquitoes after a rain.

"We do sweeps and follow pre-planned objectives of the operations they devise in the rear for us to find more gooks. We grunts never know what in the hell is going on. We just keep moving from checkpoint to checkpoint. We are the 'good grunts,' Lord. We'll clear one ville, destroy food caches, uncover their hidden weapons, and then move on. We run our night ambushes and they run theirs. We catch them out in the open or they catch us, and day after day is the same damn thing. But we are the 'good grunts,' so we keep pushing forward.

"We win damn near every encounter. We kill many more of them than they do of us. And they keep coming back. Our enemy must know they have won the battle back in the world. They just need to make certain that they keep some sort of line-up of body bags on the six o'clock news. It's good press for the 'talking heads,' and Nielsen ratings are the only count of import in our war.

"I still believe that doing our jobs will work it through to some sort of end to it all. Perhaps I can just barter with General Dynamics, US Steel, and the other war factories for our ticket home to the real world. If the profit margin reaches some kind of 'enough is enough,' there might come a point where it will have hurt us long enough that the pain will either give up and go away, or we will grow frustrated enough with it all to limp our way home like Walter Brennan in *The Real McCoys*.

"They can fly us into El Toro Air Base in California after dark, and no one will see a one of us get off the plane and walk away, alone. We can make it back home and leave the Nam in our rear-view mirrors. It will fade into a cloud of country road dust. Yeah, well, that's a Loony Tunes lie of 'That's all, Folks!' proportion. It won't happen, will it, Lord? Not even to the 'good grunts.'

"They should never have taken the very best. I do love you, Lord, but you shouldn't have let that happen. I know that talking to you like this is fire-and-brimstone blasphemy, but I earned my way into hell soon after you landed my ass in the Nam, anyway. Souls die a quick death in the Nam. Don't they, Lord?—Even those of the 'good grunts.'"

# Chapter Twenty-Eight

## The Long Flight

**DATE: June 1970**

Military personnel fly home by commercial jet from the airport in Da Nang. I can't remember much about this day at all. I walk forty yards across hot cement and a beautiful girl greets me at the top of the loading steps for the aircraft. She wears a civilian flight attendant's uniform and looks so good—so damn good. She smells like honeysuckle after a spring rain, and there is a taste of lilac on the breeze that follows her as she moves about the cabin.

She welcomes me aboard, but I only nod and mumble some sort of awkward, "Thank you, Ma'am," in return. I respond as if I've never seen a filled-out woman before, one with breasts that press tight against the thin material constraints of her official hostess jacket. I move my hands down in front of me to hide my growing interest in the curves of her charms.

The jet races down the runway and jumps into the sky. The shoreline and the straw hooches, and the rice paddies and the kick-your-ass mountains disappear in a haze behind us. The Nam remains behind on the ground. It is over and done. The flight to Okinawa doesn't seem to be a long one, but my head is elsewhere. Not certain of anything at all, I find myself lost and confused where I should have felt the elation of going home at last.

A ringing in my ears and a pounding at my temples fight, like cats in an alley, my attempt to rest. When I close my eyes I still see the

Nam in a thousand shades of green. I hurry to open them again and find the cushioned seats and soft lights of the freedom bird surround me. As the involuntary motion of blinking wipes my eyes, I slip back and forth from Barbie doll stewardesses to barbed wire and sandbagged bunkers. I cannot seem to get my head around any of it, lost in these damn clouds. Out the small window I see a much younger self, sitting on the wing dangling his feet over the edge. I blink again and the boy fishes on a wooden pier at Nana and Papa's little shack up the Allegheny River. I see myself looking into the water, looking at myself, looking back at me.

I reach out my hand and rest it on the face of the double-paned glass. I touch all the shapes in the clouds as we fly by them. I feel myself grab on to their Thanksgiving-parade balloon forms and taste the sugar in their cotton-candy fluff. The blown and twisted fibers melt in my mouth and disappear, along with the image of my youth that fades into the changing clouds. A twelve-year-old version of myself turns and gives me a playful wink, then slips away. I am in here alone with all these men, yet I am also out there, somewhere, watching the jet grow smaller in the distance as it flies away home with a part of me back there. I never really believed that I would get all of myself out of that place. It held so much of who I am, for so long.

I don't know the name of the base where we stay in Okinawa. I believe we are here for three days, but this time is also a blur. There is a damn nice NCO club with cute Japanese bar girls and a lot of slot-machine-type games with little steel balls and hand-flipper controls. Their sounds of dings and dongs ring through the room like a riverboat casino. I drink too much beer and vomit on the way back to the barracks. I crawl to lie within the cover of neatly trimmed shrubs to hide from the Military Police, looking up at the stars and worrying about who is supposed to be standing watch tonight back in the Nam.

At some point I walk up different steps that put me on another commercial jet. A beautiful clone of the first flight attendant in a seam-strained little uniform top with short, matching skirt greets me with a practiced smile for which her daddy must have paid a shitload of cash. I trip on myself, confronting another loss for words, irritated when faced with the reality that all the attendants are making much more fuss over the officers seated in the front rows than to us enlisted men in the bleacher seats further back in the plane. Welcome home, grunts! Everyone around me wears the thousand-yard stare with deer-in-the-headlight eyes that look frozen and lost in the middle of this lonely highway home.

As the strangeness of riding on this freedom bird home begins to wear off, I feel myself slipping into a sense of lost songs on an imagined jukebox playing in some honky-tonk in the back of my head. Caught between realities, I laugh at my own folly. I taste stale beer and smell cheap perfume. I watch truck drivers slide their hands down and around tired waitresses who laugh at even more tired jokes. I push a button and expect to hear Elton John play "Goodbye Yellow Brick Road" for me. Instead, the Stones steal the machine and explain to me that, "I can't always get what I want."

I referred to the States for the past thirteen months as the 'real world,' but the truth is, a transition took place. The Nam is now the 'real world' and the States are my fantasyland. I remember when I was four or five years old and would walk in my sleep. Waking up at any hour in any room, one night I found myself in the darkest part of the basement of our house, near the furnace room. All the lights were out, and the furnace was making creaking sounds like wandering ghosts dragging coils of chains. Lost and alone, I had no way out, nothing left to do but yell without hope of being heard. I screamed not for help, but just to hear myself and reconfirm that I was alive.

Going home today frightens me the same way fear shook that small boy in the basement. Life lately scares the living shit out of me and I wish to scream even louder than before, "I am still here!" I don't have a clue what I am going to do when I get back, and the thought of disconnection terrifies me. My high school friends have no place in my life. Good men, they nonetheless are light years away from me now. I ask myself, "Who am I?" and I can't find any answer. Lost in that damn basement again with ghosts of the Nam circling me with their chains rattling, I know that hollering won't do any good at all. So, I'll just whisper it for now: "I do exist. I am still here."

It is night outside. I don't know how long we are in the air. The plane's window is darkness and stars, and the lights within the cabin are low. It feels as if I am the only one alive on this plane, caught in a Twilight Zone episode with Rod Serling pointing out my "next stop" predicament. I notice that the jet is descending. Clouds beneath us crawl closer and closer toward our falling wings. We soon make it into and through their sporadic white wholeness. The moon shines bright and sparkling on our thin metallic wings while ocean waves rise up to summon us as they grow nearer and nearer still.

I'm concerned that there appears to be no sense of panic and there is no call of alarm from the captain. The plane drops, and drops, and drops. The great Pacific reaches up to snatch us from the sky like mighty, lost-in-love King Kong holding Faye Wray in one hand while swatting at toy planes with the other. I sit up in my seat and look out both sides of the plane to see water, water everywhere, and think it is certain we are going into the drink. Is anybody else here? What the hell is going on? It can't end like this—not unresolved, with all these questions left unanswered.

I hear a rumble and feel a great shake of the plane beneath my seat. Here goes the Lord's Prayer again, at double time, over and over, again and again. "Can you hear me, Lord?" I even throw in as much of "The Twenty-Third Psalm," as I can remember on such short notice. I am a grunt. I am much too proud to scream for help, but it sure feels like it's nearing time to take drastic measures. I feel a bump, then a sense of something solid beneath us. I wait for the walls to start closing in and the water to rise from below, grab my ankles, and take me under while I gasp and swallow. I know at this point that we must be on the ground and not in the deep blue sea, but my mind can't come to terms with the contradictory signals it receives.

There is a back-thrust of the jet's massive engines. By now everyone around me is awake and joins me in my "what in the hell is this shit" moment. The jet makes a slight turn, and land comes into view out my window. "Thank you, Lord, thank you, Lord, thank you, Lord," slips out through my chewed lips. I taste my own blood as I experience yet another religion-in-the-foxhole moment of, "Okay, no more drinking, no more sex, no more 'any of that stuff.' Lord, I have seen the light."

The pilot comes on the speaker to tell us we landed on Midway, or some damn airstrip atoll, and that we will be here for an hour or so while they refuel. *Thanks a shit-load for that news, Sky King*, I think. I could have used that little nugget of information about ten minutes ago—before you stuck me with all these damn promises I'll end up breaking and feeling so damn guilty about.

A voice tells us to keep our seatbelts fastened while in the air. Apparently military flights don't warrant the same landing checks that civilian flights do. It seems we just dropped out of the night sky without notice. Who knows? Maybe I was dozing in-and-out of dreams and am the only one who missed the call. All I do know is that I rush straight to the restroom in the small air terminal building. It's good to stretch my legs and arms for thirty minutes.

A loudspeaker calls us back onto the plane and we take off over waves and up into a sea of darkness. The pilot gives a nice little explanation this time that we will be landing in Hawaii for another refueling stop. The layover in Hawaii is short. Although we disembark from the plane, the pilot tells us to stay close and not to wander around. I'm not exactly sure who in the hell they think might give a damn about talking to us.

My knowledge of Hawaii is an airport terminal where small fish swim amongst lily pads under a wooden bridge that spans some clear water. I'm sure it is beautiful, but my anxieties are rebuilding. I have lost my feel for the esthetics in life. I should understand a concept of "beauty," but I forgot it during the last thirteen months. There aren't any pretty little Hawaiian girls to place strings of flowers around our necks and kiss our cheeks. Arriving tourists in flowered shirts and Panama hats get such appreciation. I guess the Honolulu Chamber of Commerce thinks there aren't enough leis to go around.

We soon re-board our plane for the final leg of our trip to California. Another long flight through darkness awaits us. Having spent thirteen months on shifts of one-hour-up and two-hours-down, the first two hours of sleep is the best I can hold onto. Then there is darkness, and darkness, and hours awake staring at more darkness. Just like in the Nam, I search the night and look for unexpected movements and unexplained straight lines that might mark my enemy's mistake in the bush.

I don't know whether it is coincidence or planning, but during the middle of the night we land at El Toro Marine Air Station near Los Angeles. With mixed feelings, we step onto the solid land of the continental United States. The earth feels so wonderful and so sweet—so very sweet. A place called "home" once again. I feel, perhaps, even more alone and lost than ever before as I disembark, back in the "real world" again.

I stand here along with the great majority of the young enlisted men and watch the officers and older Non-Commissioned Officers as their families greet them. The tears and hugs and pure joy that accompany each reunited grouping of embraces become a catch in my throat. I feel both a sincere happiness and sorrow in watching their "high," while not sharing their joy. A welcome-home-rush teases me as I walk past these expressions of love and reunion. I look to my front and try not to intrude upon their special moments.

Most of these men, away for as long as I, certainly deserve these gifts of shared ecstasy. At a moment when I should feel extreme gratitude for being home again, I find myself in the dark of night surrounded like black-on-black and the wet dew that clings to our seats at the far end of the terminal's final statement of "last call." I am lonely. I miss, more than anything else, those whom I have come to love and depend upon: the men of Charlie Company. Feeling deserted by a greeting that scoffs, "so what, you're back," I also feel as if I deserted these men I left behind. Hell, I feel like shit. I damn those who should be greeting us. Nothing at El Toro makes me sense any kind of "welcome home and thank you, Marine" within this moment of return. Like used coffee grounds tossed into the wet trash under the sink, I shiver at the cold waste and laugh at my sorry predicament. However, I do feel grateful that I did make it back. I am very aware that I owe a sincere, "Thank you, my Lord."

Duty Officers rush us through a mini-customs station in the terminal area. Then they direct those of us without any other greeters than these stateside Marines, who are obviously unhappy about late night duty, to go outside. Dark green Marine transportation buses wait for us in the empty lot like we're cold crates of vegetables in transit from farm to market. I am one of a group headed to the Marine Corps Recruit Depot in San Diego where they will process us out of the Corps.

I guess they see no damn, worthy reason to put out a red carpet for grunts on the way out. Well, they can kiss my sweet ass. Someone owes us some sort of greeting. I don't give a shit how late at night we land, or whether we are just "end of the line" grunts on our way to being processed out. No shit. Fuck those in charge of who decided to say to us, through their lack of recognition, "Welcome home, my ass." I know, I know. Quit your whining. You are a Marine and this is what Marines do. I understand that. But it doesn't make it right, and the injustice is unacceptable.

# Chapter Twenty-Nine

## The Bug

**DATE: June 1970**

The old green bus waits for those of us without anywhere else to go. The driver, in regular green stateside utilities, gets behind the wheel. Someone with a roster calls out our names in loud shouts to the silent night. After the usual period of hurry up and wait, the green transport bus pulls out of the empty lot, half-full of lonely shits caught in the same loss of significance that I am feeling. We head down the freeway toward the Marine Corps Recruit Depot in San Diego, about ninety miles south.

The highway is almost empty in both directions. It must be around three in the morning because there is no glitz and little neon. Only moon shadows and darkness in great sections of southern California greet us at this late hour. We don't know each other, so conversation falters even though we are now all wide awake from the short stop at El Toro and are excited and anxious about whatever this "home" in California might represent.

A yellow Volkswagen bug drives up from our rear. The little car is obviously not a racing machine, so any attempt to pass us takes a good deal of effort on their part. As the VW nears the back of our bus, word passes up that the VW has three girls inside: two in the front and one in the back. How much more information is necessary? Our green, piece-of-shit, Marine-transport bus is only half-full and the right-hand side empties of riders to lean over those of us on the left, passing-lane side. Our windows are down for a breath of June breeze from the coast. The sound of our bus strains against its overstressed shocks and accompanies groans of, "Oh, my God." Lust. We remember now. These young women represent all we missed and dreamed of for the past thirteen months. They breathe life into us merely by existing at our side.

At top speed, the VW creeps up the side of our bus. The driver lets off the gas to help the bug's progress. Smiling with teeth that reflect moonlight, the girls wave with the energy of a queen and her court in a homecoming parade. They offer a little bit of hope, in a small promise of potential love that might exist within our tomorrows. The girl riding shotgun and the lone girl directly behind her roll down their windows and wave up at us. Their young smiles are worth much more to us than gold. Their greetings hold pure welcome and warmth with so much more truth than damn El Toro held for our touchdown a little more than an hour before.

The girls blow kisses that fly like rose petals in our direction. These young maidens of the lonely highway throw "welcome back" to our lost and forgotten selves and we are eating-up every morsel of it with our deepest appreciation. If our olive-green bus and their yellow Volkswagen beetle are our "Welcome Home" parade, then so be it.

The VW begins to fall back from our side and drops out of the passing lane to follow behind us. Slowly, it falls farther and farther behind. The men on the right side of the bus lose their reason for standing. They retake their seats and settle back into the monotony of the ride south. A bit further down the open highway the VW begins to pull back up toward the rear of the bus again. As it approaches nearer and nearer to our rear, those Marines not giving up hope of potential "anything" begin to shout, "They're coming back. The girls are coming back." We all yell to the driver, "Slow down, damn it. Slow this damn green piece of shit down."

The refrain of, "Oh, shit, the ladies are back," echoes from the rear of the bus and reverberates off the metal sides, ceiling, and floor of our cheap ride to San Diego. Once again, the weight of the bus shifts from the right side to the left. The VW moves up beside us until it reaches our mid-section. At this point we all squeeze our faces into the open bus windows and scream an indistinguishable mixture of "We love you!" "Marry me." "Have my children." "I need you so, so bad, Darlin'."

Then the two girls on the right side of the VW lift their tops up to reveal their bras and their restrained, compressed cleavage in a "V" for victory. I have not even the slightest idea of who these young ladies are or where they might come from. I have no memory of what color their bras reflect within the night or what sort of strapped tops blow in the breeze of this southern California night. But I will, forever and forever, know what they say in their partial nakedness because they shout to our busload of lonesome grunts: "Welcome home. Welcome home. Welcome home." At least, this is what I choose to hear, and I will hang onto it with all strength possible.

The big green bus swerves a bit from side to side with the shift in weight from the boys leaning to the windows on the left. There is frantic waving and silly smiles, then a slow falling back movement of the VW until it falls in behind the bus once more. When the VW drops farther back still, the experience of a serendipitous welcome home fades behind us into the darkness of the night. All shades of lost shadows leave me without hope of what the real world might hold—must hold.

Everyone from the other side of the bus moves back over to resettle into the tedious non-comfort of their straight-backed bench seats. Two fellows in the last row continue to maintain a vigil of optimistic fervor that the yellow bug will miraculously reappear on the dark highway. After ten minutes or so, one of the two gives up and begins rubbing his neck. The other Marine refuses to stand down from his watch. Someone else near him laughs and says, "Hey, buddy, are you gonna stand watch the whole damn way to San Diego?"

Without turning his head from his backward view, the Marine on rear guard says, "You got that straight. I've stood watch for thirteen sorry-assed months, every damn night, for a shit-load less chance of any positive return than this." As if the Nam reached across the ocean to shake anger into him, he stops to calm down and pull himself together. With a slap of his palm to his forehead, he fights against the intrusion.

"One more night of frustration can't hurt," he says. "And this one carries the thrill of potential for what might just happen. My good Uncle Patrick, God rest his soul, taught me that long shots pay off, at least some of the time." He turns toward us for a quick bit of advice. "You gotta believe, men. You gotta believe it will happen before the saints will even consider allowing you the glory of a long shot." Most of us laugh along with him, and then he returns to his dedicated watch.

After about five more minutes we hear a loud, "Praise the Lord," from the last seat, followed by, "They are coming back, men. I told you, by God. You just have to believe hard enough." Damn near everyone on the bus looks back, and sure enough, headlights are gaining on us. They appear to be the small bug-eyes of a Volkswagen. There is no way to tell if it is the same one that came along side of us fifteen minutes before, but it sure as hell looks like it. As the car crawls closer to the back of our bus, we yell to the driver. "Slow down, damn it, slow down!"

He lets off on the gas a bit and the VW gets right up behind us. Lo and behold, Uncle Patrick must be looking down on us from above. Here's the same yellow beetle, with the same three smiling girls as before. We all move to the back of the bus again, wave and shout like school children, and pledge our everlasting love for the girls in the yellow VW. Our driver hollers for control and demands that we get back into our seats. Not a one of us listens to a damn thing he has to say. His orders have no significance whatsoever.

The VW begins to let up and fall back once more, and our driver seems to give the old green bus a little additional pedal as this third brush with the strange reality of the night appears to have run its course. Even old back-window-Charlie turns around in his seat and faces the front with a satisfied smile on his face for his, and his Uncle Pat's, partial victory. It doesn't take long for the bus to become quiet and still once again within the early-morning hours of cool June darkness and isolation on this lost highway to San Diego.

Another fifteen minutes pass. The quiet breaks once again with a loud shout of "Oh, shit. Oh, shit. Uncle Pat, would you look at that?" The shouts grow louder as the girls in the yellow VW near the rear of the bus once again. However, this time the shouts are of a "Can you believe this shit?" nature of disbelief. Beside us now ride the driver and the two passengers of the yellow bug. All three girls have their blouses off, their bras discarded, stripped naked to the waist. The two girls riding in the side seats are very much hanging out the window now, giving the best shaking moves they can put together for us.

The entire left-side riders cram against whatever small portion of our windows provide some sort of view downward toward the much lower VW bug. This great shift in weight causes the driver to fight like hell to maintain control of the bus. It seems about to tilt onto only those wheels that carry the left side of the vehicle. The frightened driver, but only he, gives a damn. He keeps hollering for order, but nobody pays attention. There is nothing for him to do but slow down as quickly as he can to regain some of his stolen control. Along with his loss of speed comes the assumed encouragement to the young ladies that their mission meets approval of the US Marine Corps at the highest levels of Green Bus Authority. "Sir, yes Sir!"

Why the hell not? The girls are having fun and I know in that moment that they are the greatest of beauties to ever ride the lonely nighttime Marine route between El Toro and San Diego. No movie star or Hefner foldout ever, ever looked better than our ladies of mercy. I have no way of knowing what sort of men these girls will wind up with later in life. However, I am certain that they will not come to their marriage beds with any men more desirous of their love, nor more appreciative of their physical gifts, than any one of us with whom they shared a light-hearted laugh, a harmless tease, and a welcome, welcome home this night on the dark and lonely highway of southern California.

As the bus slows down, the VW gains speed and forges on beyond us. I look into the reflection from my window at the guys from the other side of the bus who are up and over us, struggling for their share of the view. Along with the show of swaying breasts, waving hands, and sworn oaths of "I'll love you forever, and forever more," I am able to focus my line of sight upon my own reflection in the glass.

For a moment, lost and puzzled again, I don't recognize the smiling face looking back at me. These eyes of mine are older than I ever remember. Wrinkles now exist where there were none. The hazel with sparkles of reflected light now seems dull and without luster. More than anything else, they stare back at me, tired and worn. They remind me of the eyes of Tijuana whores who smile for show in the broken light of border bars, their loss of dignity hidden behind the banter of give-and-take, the thrill long gone.

I angle my look higher up into the reflection of the images at my back and see the laughs and jeers and slaps on backs that accompany our fluke run-in with the highway bandits who stole our hearts. I don't know any of these men on this bus, but the sameness of our circumstances unites us. After all these months, trapped so far from home, we are just a bunch of lonely kids. The elation of being back in the States rolls off our backs in a slow drip onto the hard, vinyl seatbacks of a big green bus, dampening our spirits. Then the wonderful wake-up call from three silly girls out on a joy ride who, for whatever their reasons are, choose to play a harmless game of tag with a green bus. The girls know it is a false embrace of jacking around with poor horny boys who can do nothing about it but hoot and holler and notch a memory for an old man's reflection one day. It is all just one big tease, no doubt at all. But everything else aside, they save our homecoming night for us and turn disappointment and shit into a lasting memory of "it's good to be home after all."

The VW is at the front by this point, and our driver has a big smile on his face in addition to having the big old bus under control once more. I look once again at the reflected faces of the men behind me. A little farther back, looking over those directly behind me, is a group of men less animated, but with smiles of good times etched on their faces nonetheless.

Davie stands there in the glass with the confidence that always accompanies his laughter and indifferent smile. Brown squeezes in beside him with just a thin grin, almost of boredom, but with a trace of a real smile playing at the corners of his mouth. Big Al, the tallest of them all, grins only with his eyes while the rest of his face, as always, holds stoic nobility. And then I see them all: my friends from Charlie Company. They flash like frames in a photo album through the reflection in the smeared glass. Every man I served with in the Nam laughs from behind me, along with the shouts of those I don't know on this wild, leaning, green bus on the LA freeway.

At last, under these bizarre circumstances of jiggling breasts, smiling young women, and joy rising from nowhere other than Uncle Pat's belief in long shots, I have this one, final chance to say goodbye to them all.

This is the welcome home of welcome homes for tired and torn old grunts like us. Flesh and bare breasts with nipple points stiff and hard in the cool night's breeze, Marines greeted by no one at all following a touchdown on a lonely runway in the middle of the night, and an uncomfortable bus ride down a long, lonely highway. And my boys from Charlie Company briefly alive, together, and in one piece here with me. It all makes for a "not so bad" ride home after all. Hell, much more than that, I'm pretty damn certain it is the best ride home of them all.

# Chapter Thirty

### Telephone Line

**DATE: June 1992**

"Hey, Daddy, a man is on the phone. He asked me if my father was home." My five-year-old son unwraps the phone cord from the tangles it has wound around his arm. "'Are you the 'Leonard Reese, from Vietnam?' I don't know. Are you that man, Daddy?" A cold chill starts at the back of my neck and works its way down my spine. "He asked me if you were a Marine. I don't know that, either, Daddy. I said, 'Sir, I don't know.' Did I do right, Daddy?"

"You did just fine, Son." I get up and reach for him. "Give your daddy a big hug." I rise from my rocking chair on the back porch and put the newspaper down on the end table. My son runs from the door and jumps up into my open arms. I smell peanut butter and Cheetos and feel the heartbeat of love in his tight squeeze about my neck. "Downs, you are getting stronger and stronger every day." He laughs with the joy of young innocence, gives me an even tighter hug.

"I love you, Daddy," he says.

I squeeze him back. "I love you too, Son," I promise. Pausing for a moment longer, I enjoy the heat from his warm arms about my neck. "Here, let me put you down so I can catch my breath and go talk to this man. You did real good answering the phone that way, Son. Thank you."

I lower him to the ground, reach down, and run my fingers through his short hair, the color of baled hay in late summer. "I'd like

149

you to go back to your room and play for a while," I say. "When I'm done talking to this man I'll come back and we'll read together. How does that sound?"

"That would be really good, Daddy, I'd like that a lot," he says, then runs over to his mother who is sitting in the chair beside mine. He gives her a hug. "I love you, too, Mom," he says, then scoots back into the house, throwing the door shut behind him. Energy radiates from his movements like heat ripples off a tar-topped country road. The porch window shakes along with a loud "boom" that shares the slamming of the door.

With an instinct born from incoming rounds, I start to squat down and throw my arms over my head, catch myself between the 'now' and 'then,' and straighten up again. I look over at Cindy. She has a concerned frown on her face. Married for seventeen years, I have never talked to her about my time in Vietnam. Not once has she put any pressure on me, knowing only that I was in the Marine Corps, that I fought in the war, and that someday, maybe, we will share this talk.

Such a good woman, my wife is strong enough to never challenge the beast and to let it lie all these years. Like a camper standing back from a hot fire, she gives me the space I need to keep that part of my life from burning us both. "Would you go and check on Elizabeth?" I ask. "She's in her room reading a book. I'd like for you to keep them back in their part of the house until I take care of this." She shakes her head and begins to say something, but I speak before she can start. "Don't worry, honey, it's going to be all right." I bend down and give her a kiss on the cheek. She reaches up with both hands and turns my face so our lips can touch. I taste the salt from the peanuts she's been munching on. It lingers on my tongue as I turn and go into the house.

In the kitchen I pick up the phone from the counter, step into the pantry, and close the door behind me. I've a good idea where I'm heading. It frightens me as if I were a small animal with a pack of hounds at my heels. My heart beats faster and my hands shake. My mouth is too dry to draw spit. "This is Leonard Reese," I answer. "What can I do for you?" From the other end of the line I hear an accent that I'd recognize anytime, anyplace, for as long as I live. "Ya don't got no idea who this is, do ya?" he says.

150

"Well of course I do," I reply. "How can I ever forget the pure twang of a damned Yankee like you? This has got to be, none other than, the one and only, Bobby Browning."

"Yankee! Yankee!" he shouts into the phone. "Hell, Red Man, I'll get in my pickup truck right this minute and come down there and kick your sorry Texas ass. New York—shit!"

I can almost feel the telephone line pull tight and jerk me close to the wall. "Bobby Browning, you Carolina redneck," I say with a laugh. I scratch my head and smile into the phone. "The sound of your southern drawl is music to my tired ears." My voice catches, and I can't speak. I take a deep breath and start again. "Bobby, I never thought I'd live to hear your hillbilly-butchering of the English language again in this lifetime."

"Well, shit," he answers. "I been a gettin' myself by just fine without no help from no Texas peckerwood. You ain't showin' me nothin' 'bout a North Carolina right way of doin' things."

I find myself pacing back and forth as if I'm waiting on the birth of one of my children. "Well, hell, Bobby, doesn't the 'North' part of North Carolina make you a damn, card-carrying Yankee?" I tease him. "Your great-grand-daddy must have been there shooting down at Pickett's boys as they charged across the field at Gettysburg."

"That ain't one damn bit funny, Red. Here I been lookin' for you all these years and you up and roll my relatives over in their graves like this. You best be ashamed, and you best say you're sorry."

I laugh at how serious he becomes. "Bobby, I do apologize from the bottom of my heart," I say. From the extra refrigerator we keep in the pantry, I take out a beer. "I was just checking to make certain I was talking to the good man I knew from twenty-five years ago." I hold the phone between my chin and neck as I pop the pull-tab on the Miller. "You're the man I trusted my life to. Hell, Bobby, you are my brother. You kept me out of trouble more often than I did you." I take a quick swig and the beer catches in my throat as I struggle to swallow. "I have tears in my eyes right this minute. I'm not one bit ashamed to let you know that damn truth, either."

There is silence at the other end of the line. I hear a cough and then a clearing of his throat. He starts, "Red Man, I just—" He pauses again and can't seem to go ahead.

"Bobby, I know; I know." I'm fighting a lump in my throat too. "It's been a long time, my good friend. It's been a damn long time." I pause myself, unable to go on either. After I catch my breath, I add, "God bless you for taking the time to find my sorry ass, Bobby. I never thought I would ever hear a word from a one of you Charlie Company boys again—except in the night, in the darkness, in the shadows." I find the light switch in the small, closed pantry and begin to turn it on and off. It reminds me of the strobe lights we'd use to mark our positions in the bush at night to call for air support. "Hell, Bobby, the Nam has just become a bad spot in the back of my head." I sneak another quick swig of beer. "It squirms around like some kind of cancer gone wild. It won't grow on me and take me away. It just wants to lie there and pick at me when my guard is down." After a final swallow, I crush the can with my left hand. "No, I never thought I'd hear a real live voice from any of you, Bobby." I stop flicking the light switch and leave it at "on." The glare is harsh and blinds me for a few moments.

"Shit, Red Man, just like in the Nam, you're gettin' way too deep for a country boy like me," he says. "I just told my wife that I had to find you. Told her I needed to talk to the Red Man. Said I couldn't die right if I never found you back here in the real world. I explained to her how you were my main man, brother. Told her I trusted you to cover my ass. And I did, Red, I did for a fact. I still do for that matter. I still do."

"Well," I say, "that's back at you, my brother." I pull a can of beans off a shelf and begin to peel the label from it. My hands shake. "How in the hell did you find me after all these years?"

"My wife got her one of them computer things couple a months ago," he answers. "Ever since then, all she does is play on the damn thing. Now don't get me wrong, I'm not bitchin' 'bout that, ya hear? It keeps her outta my hair, and gettin' on my ass about other shit. Believe me, it's just fine with me if she's on the damn thing all day." He laughs, and I can hear his love for her in his voice.

"You still got hair, Bobby?" I question him. "Seems to me it was gettin' a little thin last time I saw you, and that was a quarter of a century ago."

"You can kiss my country ass," he says. "That was my Marine Corps 'white wall' haircut. I still got the best head of hair in all of Raleigh."

"Well, Raleigh must be a damned shiny place to be when they turn on the lights at night," I fire back, laughing.

Bobby laughs too. Time melts away like ice in August and it seems as if twenty-five seconds have passed instead of twenty-five years. I feel as if I can reach out and grab his hand and pull him to me in a bear hug. I'd lift his tall, skinny ass up high and squeeze him tight. In return I know I'll take the stomach punch he'll jab into me when I let him down again. "Damn it, Bobby, it is just as smooth as Wild Turkey whiskey to hear you again. But hell, I got us sidetracked. You were explaining how you found me after all these years."

I can see him thinking across a thousand miles. "Well, my wife started lookin' up her old friends on the computer I got her for her birthday," he starts. "She began findin' some girls she hadn't seen since grade school. Now me, I don't know a thing about it, but Susan, she's a damn wiz. So, I say to her, 'Baby, you gotta find me the Red Man from the Nam.'"

"You mean all you had to do was type in 'Red from the Nam' and you got my phone number, just like that?" I ask.

"Hell, no, dumbass. I only wish it was that easy. I remembered your last name was Reese, or somethin' close to it. Now, I knew your first name wasn't 'Red' but I thought it was Leo or somethin' like that, so that's where she started. Then some of the other guys tried to help out."

I begin to flick the lights on and off again. "Other guys?" I ask. "Who else have you been in contact with?"

"Well, there is Lieutenant Galyean—now he's the one who started gettin' us all back together," he answers. "Then there's Sergeant Matt, and John O'Brien, and David Thompson, and Paul Julson. Well, there is a bunch of guys they have been able to track down, too. But nobody could find you. We decided that you worked for the FBI or the CIA or some secret shit like that. Everyone thought you just fell off the far edge of the world. You always were a sneaky little bastard, Red. They thought you were on some kind of 007 mission shit."

I stop working with the lights and leave them turned off this time. I stand still, and the darkness begins to calm me. "How did you finally track me down?" I ask.

"I remembered you was from Oklahoma, or Texas, or Arkansas, or some damn place like that," he answers. "I couldn't seem to be right sure. O'Brien says it was Texas and Thompson says so, too. Hell, them two have the best memories of all of us, so I decide to search through Texas for your ass. It took a hell of a long time. I called every Leo, and Leon and Leonard R-e-e-s-e or R-e-e-c-e I could find. Do you know how many damn Reeses there are who are not your relatives in Texas? Every weekend I'd find some time to rest and get a glass of good whiskey in my hand. Then I'd just sit with Susan and she'd go from town to town in Texas. Anyway, the damn long road led me to tonight and to a little boy on a phone who says, 'Let me get my Daddy.' Hell, Red, 'Let me get my Daddy' is a pretty nice way to find a man you don't even know is dead or alive, so far as I see it. Last time I saw your skinny ass you were walkin' up the back ramp of a chopper in the Nam. I thought "gone" was the only part of the Red Man I'd ever know about again."

"Bobby, I hate to challenge your manly man concept of yourself, but from one grunt to another, I love you, my brother," I say.

Bobby gives a cough. I can tell he's trying to hold himself together. "Back at ya, Red Man," he responds. "Back at ya."

I turn the lights back on and find another can on the shelf. I peel its label in small strips. "Bobby, tell me about your family," I ask.

He begins to give me a rundown on the lives of his children and grandchildren. I can tell he is proud of each one. He talks about the sports they are in, the plays and the concerts they performed, the races they won. He explains how his youngest grandson loves to fish with his Paw-Paw. He brags about dogs that became members of his family since his children left home. He tells me how they live in the house, sleep in his bed, and are every bit as spoiled as his own kids ever were. The more he bitches about them, the more I can tell how much he loves them, too.

He tells me about the trouble he is in at his job. Explaining that he can't get along with the chicken-shits he works with, he begins to lose his temper. "Hell, I can't seem to tolerate none of their sorry asses," he says. The pitch of his voice rises. "They ain't never faced no real danger in their cushioned lives. They don't know a damn thing about 'bad.' Shit, they ain't never slept in the mud or sipped shit clods in their water. Ain't never had to piss on a brother who is skin-dry with heat stroke to try to save his life. It angers me how they just laugh when I tell 'em 'bout fear and shittin' in your trousers 'cause the patrol can't stop out in the open so you can squat down and take a decent dump."

I hear a glass breaking in the background. "What the hell was that, Bobby?" I say. "Are you okay?"

"Yeah, I'm fine," he answers. "I just tossed a beer bottle at the trash can and missed. I'll clean it up later. No problem."

"Calm down some, Bobby," I say. "There isn't any need to get all riled up."

"I know, Red," he answers. "It just makes me so mad I feel like I gotta hit someone. But I hold it together. I hold it together till they start to talkin' 'bout the Nam boys dyin'. Then one smartass says that they died for nothin'. That's what he says to me, Red—for nothin'. Here's when I couldn't take it no more, so I started swingin'. Two or three of them wise asses go down fast. Then the manager hits the floor, too, when he tries to break it up. I told him while he is lying down on the ground, I say, 'You can take this fuckin' job and stick it up your ass.' Then I walk right out. That's just what I did to those pansy little draft-dodgin' sons o' bitches."

He stops to rest. I can hear him breathing hard over the telephone line. "Damn, Bobby, are you okay?" I ask. "I mean, right now while we are talking to each other? Bobby, I need you to slow down, my brother. I need you to take some deep breaths and get yourself together." I try to talk to him in a calm manner even though my anger rises, too. "This is Red, Bobby. It's just like the Nam. I need you to have your head on straight, now, Bobby. It's all right. It's all going to be all right. You are the only one who can pull it together for you. So, do it now, just like back then. We need to be right."

He starts again, but at a much slower pace. I can hear the sadness in his voice calling like the slow tones of a last dance. "Shit, Red, it's just so bad. They laughed at me, and they kept on actin' like it was all some kind of a joke. I just had to stand up and take them all down. Red, they can't talk 'bout our boys like that. Fuck 'em. That ain't the way it's supposed to go."

"Bobby, you're right. You are right, but I need you to calm down for tonight. I need you to take some more deep breaths and get yourself together. Do you hear me, Bobby? I need you to cool off, brother."

I hear the top of another beer pop and the sound of Bobby taking a deep swallow crosses the line. "What time is your wife coming home tonight?" I ask. "Do you have anyone around there you can talk to? Bobby, you shouldn't be alone right now. Listen, I'm not messing with you. I'm telling you the truth. I won't do anything to hurt you—ever. You know that."

Bobby's voice is now distant. Through the phone line I feel I can see him staring at the wall. The sound of his silent despair causes my heart to weep. "There ain't anybody here but you and me, Red Man," he says. "And I'm lost. I'm lost as hell. My head just keeps runnin' in circles and I feel like a merry-go-round's wooden horse with a chipped, painted face. And here I am, just goin' round and round, and up and down. And I got me no damn job, neither."

"Bobby, how can you be lost when you just found me after all these years?" I ask. "Answer me that, brother. Remember who called who?"

A sniffle comes across the distance. "Oh yeah, that's right," he says. "That's right. I finally found your silly ass today, after all these years of searching, didn't I? Damn, this is a fine day, a very fine day."

"Yes, you did find me, Bobby." I softly console him. "Yes, you did, and that's a fact, you Carolina hillbilly."

This seems to bring him out of his funk. "Hillbilly," he says. "Hillbilly, I'll show you hillbilly."

"Answer me something, Bobby," I ask. "When is your wife getting home tonight?"

"Hell, she's out with her girlfriends watching some damn movie—women shit," he responds. "They say it's their 'girls' night out.' She'll be home in about an hour or so. She doesn't trust me to boil the eggs right for the dogs' dinners. Hell, her and them damn dogs. They gonna drive me crazy."

"Well shit, Bobby, that's not going to be a very long trip, now, is it?" I ask. We both laugh at that. "Well Bobby, we'll just have to talk for a while longer and catch up on some more shit that matters." I change the subject away from those things that seem to make him mad. It isn't all that easy. A hell of a lot of things set him off when I bring them up. We take the time to exchange addresses and I get his phone number. He talks more about his family, and I talk more about mine. I talk about my wife and kids. I tell him how blessed I've been to love a woman who chooses to love a troubled man like me in return.

I ask if he is trying to see anybody who might help him with his anger issues. He says he is thinking about going to work on it. "I've been tryin' to get me an appointment to talk to somebody at the damn VA."

"That's a good idea, Bobby," I explain. "There isn't anything wrong with asking for some help. There is no shame in that at all. Hell, you have earned all the help you can get."

After a good bit more of our catching up, his wife comes home. We talk a little while longer, then it comes time to say goodbye. Before we get off the line he shares the phone numbers he has of the other guys from Charlie Company. We pledge to keep in touch and promise each other we will get together as soon as we can.

I end the conversation with, "Bobby, don't you ever forget how important your friendship is to me."

"Semper Fi, Red Man, Semper Fi, my old friend," he replies.

"Semper Fi," I respond. "You are my brother. And Bobby, you know my number now. You call me when you just need to talk to someone who has been where you are now. When you need to hear the voice of someone who knows the Nam we shared and who also knows you, then you call me. You take care of yourself, Bobby. Hell, I need your ass to be right when my down times come around. I'm struggling, too. I make it day to day, just like you. You are not alone. Do you hear me? You are not alone."

"Yeah, I do know that, Red," he fires back as if he's peered through the smeared windows of my mind. "I do for a fact." I can hear the dogs barking in the background and Susan telling them to hush up. "Red, I need to go. Now, you best know that I'll be gettin' back to ya. It took too long to find your ass to lose you again." He pauses for a moment with the same catch in his voice as I'd heard a while ago.

"Bobby," I say, "it's been really good talking to you. Thank you, my old friend, for taking the time to dig me up from the dead like this. I promise you I'll stay in touch."

"I'll be lookin' forward to it, Red Man. Yes, I will." I hear a 'click' and the line is dead. I hold the phone in my hand and stare at it for a few seconds before placing it on the pantry shelf. My legs feel heavy and I can't move. I reach over and turn the light off again. Alone in the dark, I feel caught between Texas and the Nam. Stranded between the supportive love of my family in our cozy home and the destruction in the rice paddies and jungle trails of my nightmares. I feel as if I am tearing apart from the center. My inside is turning out. For a moment the nightmare wins, and I am back in the Nam, alone within a dense thicket. I hear rustling grasses and voices whispering in Vietnamese. Noises surround me like Indians around circled wagons in a B-movie Western. The sounds close in and the voices become louder. "Are you there?" I reach for my rifle. "Are you in there?"

The fog lifts, and I make out vague outlines of packages and cans packed together like friends at a party. I turn on the light and open the pantry door. Cindy stands before me with worried eyes that ask questions I cannot answer. "It's all right," I mutter. "It really is." She comes to me when I reach out my open arms. I hold her close and she returns the urgency of my squeeze. More than holding her, I am holding on to her like a man falling from a wire reaches out to cling for one last grip. We stand together in the silence. She kisses my neck and the side of my cheek. "Do you want to talk about it?" she asks.

I turn it over in my mind. "No, not right now," I say. I take a step back and hold her out at arm's length. "But it is time. We will talk soon. I promise. I promise it will happen soon." I let her go and watch as her eyes look down at my feet. The floor is covered with the bits of paper I have torn from the cans that now sit, faceless and undefined, on the shelf. "But not right now," I add. "Not tonight." I laugh and reach for her hand, "I'll clean this mess up later. For now, let's go talk to the kids. I made a promise to my son. I need to read him a book."

# Chapter Thirty-One

### Suite Thing

**DATE: July 1995**

Bobby's call started a chain of events that brought me back into the fold of Charlie Company. With the number Bobby gave me, I was able to contact Lieutenant Galyean. We talked for almost an hour and he gave me more information on other members of our unit. Mike Malloy was commander of $2^{nd}$ platoon during some of our worst times and the period when the men I served with were closest. There were times before when the platoon was tight and times after as well. But, in the Nam, the four months Lieutenant Malloy was platoon commander enmeshed our lives and was the time when I felt the closest to the men around me.

The lieutenant asked that I call him "Mike," a damn difficult thing for me to do, even harder than to call my father-in-law "Angus" instead of Mr. Jameson. However, I will always call them both "Sir" in deference to their rank within my own priorities of respect. During our visit, Lieutenant Galyean explained how he decided it was necessary to reunite as many of Charlie Company as possible. Talking to him after hearing from Bobby made me feel a sense of renewed pride to be a part of something meaningful again, as if a hole in the side of my heart was plastered over by the memories with dry-wall mud. I felt the blood flowing smoother, with less pressure through my veins. With Lt. Galyean's support, I arranged to attend the $1^{st}$

Marine Division reunion in San Antonio with my wife in the summer of 1996.

A hot July day arrives to find Cindy and me on a flight from Dallas to San Antonio. Unable to hold a conversation, my thoughts slipping back and forth from the Nam to now, I hold my wife's hand and gaze out the window at faces in the clouds. Lieutenant Galyean and his wife, Nancy, pick us up at the airport. She and Cindy cry when we meet at the gate. Lieutenant Galyean wears a 1st Marine Division cap and a proud smile. He laughs and holds it together while my eyes turn red and wet. When we get to the hotel, the Galyeans leave us so they can be a part of a function on the River Walk. I wait by our bags in the lobby while Cindy walks over to the desk to check in.

When it reaches her turn in line, she asks the desk clerk if there is any way we might upgrade our room for a larger one. She explains that her nephew is a distributor for Miller's and arranged for us to have cases of beer and snacks brought to our room to share with our friends. She tells him that having a larger room serves us better as a place to gather. He explains to her that, because of the reunion crowd, there aren't any larger rooms available. I can feel Cindy's frustration through her nervous body movements. Her shoulders sag, and she shifts her weight back and forth while she struggles to find something to say that might get us more space.

An older gentleman in a custom-fitted suit studies the interaction between the desk clerk and my wife from an area behind the polished counter. He steps forward. "Is there a problem I might help you with, ma'am?" he asks. Cindy's eyes show a sparkle of life and her body straightens. "Thank you, sir. I don't want to be a problem," she explains. "My husband hasn't seen any of the men from his platoon in Vietnam for twenty-six years." She looks down and begins to scratch her neck. "Please forgive me for making this so personal, I know it is special to all of them, but it was like giving a cat a bath to even get him in here."

She nods over her shoulder toward me, pulls her hair back behind her ears and leans closer toward the desk. She talks in a softer voice. "When we drove up in front of your hotel, he started to talk about going back out to the airport," she whispers. "That just can't happen." She hesitates again then stands tall. "He needs to be here. Can't you find any way to get us some place big enough so his

Marines can get together and talk to each other? Perhaps there's a cancellation, or an early checkout?" The gentleman glances down to a computer and types in some information.

He looks over toward a large column at one side of the lobby where I stand with our mismatched luggage at my feet. A misfit looking around the lobby, I feel like a shell-shocked loser. I pace back and forth, a sentry on night watch. Excited, yet afraid that I might see a brother among all the strangers passing by, I avoid eye contact as if I were a guilty shoplifter with candy hidden in my pockets. Lost and stretched beyond my limits, I feel I am back in the Nam on full alert while I wait for incoming rounds. "Tomas, I'll assist this nice lady," the manager says to the desk clerk. The desk clerk nods his assent and works his way down the counter to help another guest.

The manager looks toward Cindy. "Ma'am, my name is Vicente," he says. "First, allow me to say it is a pleasure to have you with us. I couldn't help but hear your predicament, so I made some inquiries while you and Tomas were talking. It just so happens that we do have a room that we keep open for certain special occasions. As chance has it, this room's been unassigned. I believe it is just the one that will serve your needs. Ma'am, it would be my privilege to provide it to you for the same price as your original room."

Cindy is at a loss for words for a few moments. "Oh, thank you sir," she finally responds. "I wouldn't ask, but it means so much to them all." Vicente listens intently as she continues, "This is a difficult time for him, for many of them for that matter. These are his friends—he calls them his brothers—from Vietnam and he wants to do right by them." She leans closer to the counter and whispers even more softly, "Vicente, you can never know how happy this makes us."

"Ma'am, it is my wish that these accommodations will meet your needs," he responds. "Allow me to arrange for some assistance with your luggage." Raising his hand, he calls for a man standing at the end of the counter. With a look back at Cindy, he continues, "And Ma'am, please know that the pleasure is mine."

"You have done so much already," Cindy explains. "We have only a few bags and you have done so much for us. We can handle it on our own."

"No, I will have someone take care of them, Ma'am—I insist," he states. The man he called stands beside Cindy. "Juan, please help these good people with their luggage." Vicente hands him a key-card for our room, then adds, "and Juan, this is to be done as a courtesy of the management." Juan looks down at the room number on the card and then glances back toward the manager. Vicente nods at him and says to Cindy, "It is my distinct pleasure, Ma'am."

My wife returns to where I stand and takes my hand. She tells me she worked something out. Looking back at the desk and with tears in her eyes, she nods and says across the distance, "Thank you, sir." Vicente smiles, salutes, and says loud enough for all those around us to hear, "Semper Fi, Ma'am. I had the great honor to also have served in the United States Marine Corps." Old men around the lobby begin to give "Ooh Rahs" and applaud, without even knowing what service has been rendered. They are only responding to their shared motto: "Semper Fi."

We follow the young man with our luggage to the elevator. He pushes the button to the second floor from the top. "Damn Cindy, you moved us up some," I say. "We are way up high." The elevator stops and we exit into a long hallway of few doors. I am so nervous and lost with all that is going through my head that I just follow Cindy and Juan like a trained puppy on a leash. They stop at a room with a sign to the left of the door that reads, "Presidential Suite." Juan unlocks the door. The room is long and wide with several groupings of couches and chairs. A bar area with refrigerator and sink line a section of one wall. Juan passes through this area with our luggage and opens another door onto a bedroom that is larger than half our house back home.

He opens the drapes to reveal a view of San Antonio that takes my heart and gives it a gentle squeeze. I'm sure it skips a beat as I find myself within the eye of a storm of illumination and glitz. Caught high enough for the city's lights to fail to dull the stars, yet still able to look down upon a sea of false glare full of laughing neon magic, we gape at the scene before us. Juan directs us back into the main room. He draws drapes like theatre curtains on opening night to reveal an even more impressive view of the San Antonio skyline.

I gasp for air and fumble for the right words. "I'm sorry, there must be some sort of mistake, this is far beyond our means," I explain. "Please check and make certain you have the right room, Juan."

"Sir, these are my instructions," he responds. "You will need to talk to Señor Vicente if you have any questions regarding the room."

"Cindy, do you know what the hell is going on here?" I ask.

"I honestly don't know," she answers. "I just asked the manager for some help with a larger room. He said he would take care of it. Then he ended it all with that, 'Semper Fi,' you heard." I turn from her to question Juan, but in silence he has left the room without even waiting for a tip. A few minutes later there is a knock on the door and two young men with Miller insignias on their shirts enter the room. They pull dollies of beer, ice, and snacks like children's wagons loaded with grownup's toys. After they unload and leave, Cindy and I walk to the windows. We stare out at the skyline. I take her hand in mine. I squeeze it tightly as if trying to hold onto a dream. "Thank you for all you have done," I say. I don't know what else to add.

I feel as if all breath has left my lungs. In deep water unable to reach the surface, I begin to panic within this "unknown" territory. Questions fill my mind with images of the Nam riding on a seesaw opposite the beauty of this day. I ask myself, how can this be so? Is this right? Is it fair? Why should some of us old men from Charlie Company be within the gift of this fine hotel tonight, while others we fought beside as young men are gone? How can this opulence be correct? Why in the world is this unbalance acceptable? How can it be the Presidential Suite for us, while the forever cold and dark earth embraces those brothers who fell to stray rounds or to the random-tossed jagged edges of angry red-hot metal?

Cindy pulls me close to her. My head rests on her shoulder. She runs her fingers through my hair and whispers in a voice too soft to move a candle's flame, "It's all right." She says, "It's all right. You are here with me, and it is as it should be." She slides her fingers to my lips and I kiss their tender words of support. "The two of us are together," she continues. "All of this other confusion is something we will learn to walk through together. I will never leave you to face any of this alone. You need to know that I am in this for the long run. Don't you ever forget that."

# Chapter Thirty-Two

### She is Not Alone

**DATE: July 1995**

Words tangle and go unsaid. Cindy releases my hand and moves closer to my side. She wraps her arm around the back of my waist and hooks her thumb through one of my belt loops. With a firm tug, she draws me even nearer to her. We gaze through shared eyes at our reflections in the window.

I turn to face my wife and we kiss, her lips warm and moist. Our embrace becomes a presence of its own between earth, sky, and all dimensions between. She hesitates, then pulls back to look up into my eyes. I raise my hand between us, and she allows my fingers to touch her mouth and catch her unspoken thoughts like soap bubbles in a child's hands. "There are no words to express my feelings for you. 'I love you' is inadequate."

"Then let's not say anything at all," she says. Reaching over, she takes my hand. An impish glow skips, like a nymph in the reflection of her eyes, and touches my heart. "Here, come with me," she says, then leads me to our bedroom.

Meeting with other members from my platoon after all these years is like finding a long-lost key to a locked box. I don't even know what prize lies inside. After all these years I never imagined that any good could touch me from the Nam. For all this time, only negative thoughts and unforgiving dreams carry hidden briers and barbs in their wake. Until now, a blanket of memories has overwhelmed any good remembrance in the way ivy covers an abandoned wall. An uneasy calm walks beside the "goodbyes" and "Semper Fis" as Cindy and I exchange hugs and handshakes with my old brothers and her new sisters on the hotel steps before catching our cab to the airport.

We hold hands on our flight from San Antonio to Dallas but have no conversation. We sit quietly at the gate on our layover in Dallas. "Do you want to talk about it?" she asks.

"No, not yet," I murmur. "But soon." We sit in continued silence at the gate until time to board. From Dallas to Longview, I hold her hand even tighter. Staring out the window with a cross-eyed gaze, all I see transforms into a blur of indefinable shapes. Clouds cover the sky. The pilot takes us higher to avoid turbulence. I look down on a sea of dark, angry clouds to find that everything beneath vanishes as though it never existed.

I need a constant reassurance of my partner's presence beside me. Our fingers intertwine and change positions like aged, tired drifters in search of a single place of shelter for the night. I can't bring myself to turn and look at her. My ever-present fear whispers that I am now a part of this separate world of shifting clouds. Their monotonous gray panorama threatens me. I fear that, seeing the Nam within me out in the open the past few days, she now knows the part of me that contains the things I despise most in myself. The same fear reminds me that I do not understand how she can love the man who lived the stories she heard. As I continue to stare out the small window, I fight the urge to break the glass and float away.

At some point the flight attendant taps my arm and instructs me to fasten my seatbelt for landing. With a slight jerk away from this touch, I turn to see her move further down the aisle. At the same time, I steer toward Cindy's smile like a lost ship to a lighthouse. I feel her warmth at my side and there is color in my world once again. Her heart draws me to the refuge that waits within the touch of her hand.

The drive home from the airport is short and quiet. "Would you care to sit on the porch with me for a while?" I ask. She nods and responds, "I would like that very much." I pour us each a glass of wine, then we go out back and take our seats. Our dog, Burke, comes to lie at my feet. I scratch behind his ears. Satisfied that we are home again and all is right in his world, he runs off to chase a rustle in the bushes with a great show of barking and bravado. The sun drops beyond the trees in the side pasture. Reds and purples magnify silhouetted branches as distant streaks of heat-lightning illuminate the drama of a false storm. Crickets and frogs interrupt the night's silence, while curious gnomes rustle in dry leaves and play games of trickery beyond the boundaries of our backyard. The smell of fresh-cut hay mixes with fading summer heat. A soft breeze cools and welcomes us back to our own sanctuary in the woods.

"Well, did you enjoy yourself?" I ask. I put my hand over hers. "Did you have a good time?" Cindy doesn't respond right away. Instead, she plays with her glass of wine, turning it round and round on the armrest by her side. "Did I do the right thing by jumping into this reunion, or did I screw it all up? Did I lose the answer of your love to the questions of my past demons?"

She doesn't hesitate. "Please don't ask me that. Don't ever demean my love for you." She stands up, steps to my front, and faces me. "It was just so intense that the words aren't here for me yet. I can't define what happened this weekend." She reaches over and sets her wine on the table between our chairs. Kneeling in front of me, she rests her arms across my knees. "Don't ever talk about losing me again," she says. "Since our first walk together, I signed on for the long haul." I continue to watch the fading colors and melting shapes of dusk beyond her, without response to her plea.

Her voice is like a knife. "Look at me," she demands. She slaps my leg and the sound throws echoes like cracking branches in an ice storm. "Damn it, look at me, I said," she demands. I raise my eyes to her face and feel the heat of her anger. It melts the strings that bind my heart, and I feel their grip begin to loosen. "Don't you ever say that to me again—not one more damn time." She slaps my leg again, drops her head and shakes it from side to side. "I swear, if you do, I will slap you for the first time in my life."

She lifts her eyes to face mine. Tears fill her eyes and run down her cheeks in an overflow of emotion. "I will hit you, and hit you, and hit you." Frustration shakes her body. She strikes out and pounds her fists on my thighs to emphasize each oath. I grab her hands when she gasps for breath between sobs. Going down on my knees, I wrap my arms around her. She struggles, but I continue to hold her with the last-breath grip of the desperate man I am.

"It's okay, it's all right," I plead. Her tears continue, and I start my prayer again. "I'm sorry. Forgive me; I am a fool." She ceases to resist my hold and her body goes limp within my arms. Her shaking slows. Surprised with hope as she returns my embrace with one of her own, we remain within the clasp of each other's arms until she says, "I'm fine now. You can let me up." I loosen my arms and she stands. "I need to get some tissues. I'm a mess. I'll be back in a minute."

She goes into the house, leaving me with the crickets and the frogs and the cloud-covered night sky. I rise from my knees and sit in my chair again. I try losing myself within a deep swallow of wine. But like loose wires, the sting of her tears continues to shock me. I take my hand and wipe their wetness away. Touching my fingers to my lips, I find the salted taste of an eternal sea. Lost and embarrassed within my own insignificance, I wait.

The back door opens. Cindy crosses in front of me to take her seat at my side again. She takes my hand in hers. We sit and listen to the sounds of the night. "I'm afraid I fell so far off-center," I finally say. "It frightens me to lose control of my thoughts. It's as if they were in control and I was just along for the ride." She takes her hand from mine, reaches her arm around my shoulder, and pulls me tightly to her. I allow my head to bend and touch hers. Her touch eases my troubled mind and I continue, "Each hidden thought that revisited me this weekend scares the hell out of me, Cindy.

"Voices from the Nam echo in my head. The images are alive." I sit up and turn to her while she continues to look straight ahead into the dark. "Without my consent, they control my thoughts when I close my eyes," I say. "Without my brothers, I must face the Nam alone." Cindy turns to me, begins to speak, but decides against it and returns to a blank stare forward. "Caught by a false step onto quicksand, I find myself sinking, and I fight against it. But the more I struggle, the deeper I sink."

I refill our glasses. The cabernet is complex and leaves a dark, full taste in my mouth. "Cindy, it always comes back to the same thing," I say. "I just don't understand how you can love the man I am. It terrifies me that you now know the way we lived—the things we did to survive—the horrors that occurred in combat." The wind through the trees blows harder and branches sway as if in a dance. "I'm so afraid. I dread that, with this knowledge, you discover the reality that I don't deserve your love." The wind dies down and slowly comes to a stop. All is still.

Cindy turns to face me. I see the pain in her eyes and look down into my folded hands. In confusion I shrug my shoulders. "Cindy, I'm just lost here," I say. "There is not a memory of an ambush, or a firefight, or any damn bit of those thirteen months that frightens me more than the thought of losing you." I play with my fingers, weaving them together and twisting them around. I look up to face her. "I have trust in you and in your love," I say. "I just don't have any sense of worth within myself when it comes to my deserving that love."

She takes a tissue, wipes her nose, then dabs at her eyes. "You must accept this as a fact and never question it again," she says. "You and I will take on the Nam together." Again, she takes my hands into hers and squeezes them tight. She begins to smile through her tears like the sun shining through falling rain. "You will never be alone with the Nam so long as you allow me to remain a part of you." Releasing her grip, she moves both of her hands upward to take my face and holds it with the soft touch of an artist working clay. "I feel even closer to you now that I know more about the power she continues to hold over all of you." She takes a deep breath and adds in a soft voice, "I love you, and I always will." Cindy removes her soft touch and reaches for her wine. After a slow drink she sighs and pulls her legs beneath her on the chair. We join hands, soothed, touch on touch.

We remain in our quiet intimacy for ten or fifteen minutes. "Okay," I say. "Once again, do you think the trip was worth it?"

She stares at the red liquid in the crystal glass. "I didn't know what to think at first," she answers. "It was so good to see you open up and talk with such ease about Vietnam with your friends. You never shared any of those stories with me before. It made me wince to see the image of you and your friends walking so close to danger and death. But I've also never seen you smile and laugh at any mention of the Nam before. When you were with these men, you were different."

Her words cause me to think back upon the reunion: We each ran within our youth again. Many stories revealed foolish pranks and jokes we played on each other. We remembered unthinkable times with reverence and respect for those hurt or killed. Each wound brought pain and bled as a shared injury, for every death stole a piece from each of us. Many more men shared the meeting room with us than just those we could see and hear. Each new name joined us and became a living presence in the room. The boys were all there with us. Our shared memories warmed our hearts yet broke them at the same time.

"While you men shared your stories, the wives and I drifted off to the side," Cindy says. "As we moved away, y'all moved closer together. You slapped each other's shoulders and clasped the back of each other's necks. It seemed like you needed to touch one another to keep this shared 'return' from slipping away. It wasn't a dream. It was alive for you to hold with the strength of your combined will.

"The other wives and I watched you from the opposite side of your bridge in time, a span we knew we could never cross. Severed from you, separated from the part that is the 'all' that you give to us, we watched the 'something else' that exists apart from us. You each danced with the Nam, in turn, with joy and with pain.

"As we talked about your behavior, a strange thing happened. One of the women would make a comment and the rest of us would point out, 'My guy behaves the same way.' We recognized a common bond that lay in our shared experiences of being married to Marines of combat. We talked about your strange reactions and responses to loud sounds and slight movements. We discussed the way you avoid crowds and shy away from new acquaintances. It surprised us to find that almost all of you act the same way."

Cindy stops and looks away. Her eyes close and her head lowers for a few moments. She then turns to face me. "At some point I cried," she says. "Tears flowed, but I couldn't stop them. I apologized to the women; however, I couldn't explain what was happening to me."

**\*\*\*\*\*\*\*\*\***

"Cindy, we all reacted the same way you have on our first date with our boys and their Bitch, the Nam." Nancy puts her arms around me. "This is your first time," she says.

"We thought we were seeing men we never knew before," Cathy adds. "They all talk with one another in a way that they never talk to us or to anyone else."

"Seeing it happen makes me feel happy inside for their camaraderie," Alice points out. "But it also makes me feel a deep sadness. Being separated from them hurts. When we see them together, we face the truth that they are not all ours."

I look around and all the women, every one of them, has tears in her eyes. Alice blows her nose on a wad of tissues she twists in her hands. "It hurts to be blocked off from the man you love," she says. "You are forced to face a part of him you know you will never completely understand."

"It is a sorrow to know that the man you love withdraws to a secret place you'll never see," Janet says. "It makes you face a jealous part within yourself, a part you'll detest. I just want to get into an all-out cat fight with their damn Nam Bitch."

"I'd be happy to scratch her eyes out," Cathy joins in. "I might not win, but she'd sure know she'd been in a fight."

We pause in silence for a few minutes to pour fresh drinks and reach for some snacks. Each of us needs a break from the intense conversation. We have to catch our breath.

"This is your first time to see the Nam at work on each of them at the same time," Sandra says. "You think it would be the other way around. But she is the one who gangs up on them. You've seen glimpses of her on your own. But you've never seen her hair blowing wild in the wind like tonight. She holds an almost mystical power over them all. You can see it in their eyes." She notices my confused look and laughs. "One of the emotions that you haven't been able to identify yet is anger. And Cindy, look at me. It is all right to be angry with the Bitch. You have a right to ask, 'how dare she have such a strong hold on the man you love?'"

Alice looks over at the group of men talking in a large group beside a couch. "Look at 'em," she says. "Look at their faces. They are all on a high as their stories merge together and become one. Watch how one laughs while another looks away. Then, the very opposite occurs within the next sentence. They keep it all to themselves. It's hidden within so no one else can see." She pauses as we all stare across the room at the men in their masks. "But when they get together like this, memories fly like eagles from a cage. Our guys transform from captive curiosities back into proud warriors. Nightmares combine in one shared story after all this time. Together they draw strength from each other and are young grunts in the bush once more."

"Look at them," Cathy remarks. "They are bad-asses for certain, far beyond the men we know. For these few hours their lives depend upon each other again. It is as if they are within their fighting positions. Their backs, one more time, protected by the only men they will ever completely trust—each other."

Nancy touches me on the arm. "You must understand that you are not alone in your hatred of the Nam," she says. "She is lipstick on the collar of our men who can't admit how it got there. We all despise that Bitch." She looks around to see the consensus. "We all know that a part of each of those boys is over there, because boys are what they are at this moment—each of these 18- and 19- and 20-year-old boys will always love a bit of her, despite their hatred for all she did to them. They can't stand the thought of her. But, like a mistress, the thrill of her presence teases them. She walks hand-in-hand with them through their dreams. Their bodies shake back and forth as she talks to them in their sleep."

She stops to take the Kleenex that Cathy offers her to dry her eyes. "And when they wake on sweat-wet sheets, they tell us they don't remember a thing," she adds. "Then they turn their backs to us in search of a place to reenter their dreams. They want just one more ride on her magic carpet."

"But we know the truth," Cathy says. "Deep down inside we know. And they know that we know every one of her moves. She scratches their backs while they face us from the depth of their darkness. The Nam rests by their shoulder in our beds each night. She whispers in their ear that she's got the true rush they crave."

I wipe tears from my eyes and say, "I just never knew. I thought I was alone in this fight with his demons. I had no idea that anyone else had the same kind of hurt that drives knives through my heart. I felt alone and inadequate—until now. I've never met other women married to men who went through similar circumstances. Wow. I am not alone." I try to say more but the words catch in my throat.

"You have to know that, Cindy," Alice adds. "Like Nancy said, we need each other. You are not by yourself. Sometimes you think you've lost him. But how can you lose that part of him you never had?"

I look at the faces of the women around me and ask, "Are we forever only partially loved women? Will there always be a line we can never cross? Is there some forbidden door we can never knock on, let alone pass through?"

Each of them looks away. Some stare down at their feet. Others look out the window, mesmerized by the blinking lights of San Antonio. Susan stands up from her chair. "I'm sorry, Cindy," she says. "But that's about it in a nutshell. They give us every bit of the 'them' that's left to share. Our problem is, they left so much behind. There is only so much that is theirs to give away."

"The Nam will always have that part of them," Nancy adds. "And you are right, it is unkind and unfair." She took the time to look at each of the women's faces in our circle. Her eyes came around to meet mine again. "Cindy, all we can do is let you know that we're your friends. Call us when you need to hear the voice of someone who understands." She gives a small laugh, looks at the other women, then says to me, "Welcome to the Nam."

**********

Cindy sets down her glass of wine, stands up, and comes to me. She sits in my lap. Her long legs rest over the side of my chair and her arms wrap around my neck. Kisses like winter's first snow refresh me with their soft brush across my lips. She reaches her hand behind my head and pulls me to her with force. Her gift is selfless and complete. It is deep and sincere in its honesty.

She breaks away and rests her head on my chest. I can feel the movement of her cheek against my neck as she forms words. "I am forever yours. You are forever mine. We will fight this Bitch of yours together. However, you need to know that the part of you that you two think belongs to her—well, you are both wrong. It's mine, too. I stake my claim. To hell with all this 'sharing' shit those women were talking about. You're all mine."

She pushes away from my chest and raises her hand to my cheek. She shakes her head as she looks into the sadness of my eyes. "Together, you and I are going to kick this Nam Bitch out of our bed and out of our lives. No matter how long it takes. No matter what moves she makes. She's going to lose. As I am yours, you are mine. She can exist within the fading images burnt onto your photographs as a memory from your past. These things I can accept. But I demand to have all of your 'here and now.' She's not welcome in our home. I will not share a damn thing with her. I will win. I will never surrender." Cindy lays her head back onto my chest. Her arm around my neck, she pulls her body closer to mine and whispers, "Your 'forever more' is ours alone."

# Chapter Thirty-Three

## Karaoke Night at T-Bone's

**DATE: March 2008**

Chris looks over at me with the grin of a fox. "How do you sign up to sing tonight, Red?"

"You just put your name down on the list by the door. So, you like to sing, Marine?"

"Yes sir, do I ever."

He walks to a table by the entrance and I see his friend, Andrew, give me a nod and wink. "Red, he really has a good time. You're in for a treat."

My wife and I drove to Houston from East Texas and met the four young men earlier in the evening for the first time. Chris is from Minneapolis, Jake's home is a small town in North Dakota, Andrew lives in a suburb of Atlanta, and Francisco is from a town just to the south of Houston. Their unit recently returned from a year's tour in Iraq. The young Marine grunts stopped to take care of some business before heading to their own homes for a month's leave.

Andrew taps me on the shoulder and hands me his cell phone, "Red, my dad wants to talk to you."

Dale Greene was Charlie Company Commander when I served in Vietnam from 1969-70. We came to know each other in the summer of 2000 when a group of us made a return visit to the area where we fought. "Red, I just want to say thank you for—"

I interrupt, "Dale, it's my privilege to be with these boys." The Houston Rockets are beating New Orleans, and the noise in the bar is so loud that I can't hear any more of what he is saying. I end our conversation with, "I'll take care of them, don't you worry. Tonight is special, and I promise you we're going to have a great time."

While Andrew was serving in Iraq I sent him several care packages of cookies and snacks. In the Christmas package, I also included 60 "pocket angels" (quarter sized pewter ovals with angel images) and on the back of each I did my best to engrave "C 1/1" (Charlie Company, 1$^{st}$ Battalion, 1$^{st}$ Marine Regiment). Each of the boys tells me they came to the bar tonight to meet me and thank me for doing this for them.

My nephew, Trevor, owns T-Bone's Sports Bar, and it is Karaoke Night. He and his girlfriend, Kate, wait to talk with us before leaving to attend the Houston Fat-Stock Show and Rodeo. They'd been looking forward to the date for a long time. A cowboy's dream in her short dress and cowboy boots, Kate helps me put up two primitive poster-board signs announcing, "Welcome Home, 'C 1/1' Marines."

"Thanks, Trevor, for allowing us to meet here. I know you understand how important it is to make these boys feel welcome tonight." Trevor served in the Marine Corps during the Desert Storm era. He smiles as I give him a hug before they leave.

Fifteen minutes later, Trevor is back. "Kate wouldn't let me go. She felt this was much more important and insisted that I come back." I give her an appreciative kiss on the cheek and they help me arrange the tables and pull over some chairs for the boys' arrival.

The Marines arrive around 7:00 p.m. As they walk in the door, the entire bar rises as one and applauds. Embarrassed yet pleased, they come to our table with red, smiling faces. I present each of them with a cap that I designed for them with "C 1/1–Iraq" lettering and I proudly put on my own that reads "C 1/5–Vietnam."

The rest of the night is incredible, one of the most special ever. Trevor gives the boys whatever they want to eat and drink. It seems that every patron in the bar makes a point to drop by our table and shake their hands and add, "Thank you for your service," and "Welcome home, Marines."

After the Rockets win their game, the karaoke begins. One fellow with a wonderful voice belts out, "Proud to be an American," dedicated to the boys. Then the beautiful Kate paints a stirring picture by telling us to let freedom ring in "Independence Day." The young Marines stand tall as everyone applauds for the singers—and for them.

Finally, Chris gets his call to perform. He strides to the mike and commands everyone's attention with his confidence. The music starts in a rap beat. Then he surprises us all when he suddenly jumps into the air, rips off his tee shirt, and throws it to the crowd. The group attracts more than a few girls this night. To screams of "Go Marine, Go," he launches into his song and the young lady at my side turns to me and laughs. "My goodness, that boy sounds terrible; he can't sing a lick, can he?"

She is right. "I've never enjoyed a song more in my entire life," I say. Within the next few hours, Chris sings several more songs with the other boys howling along, a good distance from anything resembling a melody. Trevor and I join them in the spotlight to sing behind Andrew's lead to Neal Diamond's "Sweet Caroline," and I have no doubt that this, "good time never sounded so...bad." Warmth and an enthusiastic round of applause follow each performance by the Marines.

Trevor's townhouse lies directly across the street from T-Bone's. We insist that the boys stay the night, so they won't have to be on the road. The following morning, these fine young men, representing the very best of what the Corps stands for, go on to take care of the real reason for their stop in Houston. They go to spend time with the mother of Lance Cpl. Matthew S. Meldicott, then accompany her to visit the grave of her son and pay their respects to this member of their squad, killed in an ambush on August 25th in Al Anbar Province, Iraq. During their visit they give her one of the "C 1/1" caps and, in honor of her son and their friend, present her with their own service nametags.

I hope these young Marines have a positive memory to carry with them through their years. As for me, I know with certainty that I will never forget the honor of spending Karaoke Night at T-Bone's with these fine young men and singing, along with Chris's rap and Andrew's Neal Diamond song, "The Marine Corps Hymn" to a crowd of appreciative Houstonians.

On Saturday night, prior to the karaoke and celebrating, I took the time to give the following toast: "God bless you fine young men—we appreciate your service; God bless Matthew Medlicott—may he rest in peace; and God bless the United States Marine Corps—Semper Fi."

# Chapter Thirty-Four

## Broken Equipment

**DATE: June 1969**

One of the biggest differences between Marine boot camp and infantry training is the opportunity to receive liberty on weekends. With our first pass, my friend, Lee Wolf, and I catch a taxi and head to the nearest town, Oceanside. First, we ask the driver to stop at a discount store where we buy jeans, bright shirts, and white tennis shoes. Looking at each other, we recognize that no clothes can disguise our burr haircuts in a California world of flower children and surfers. We laugh, knowing we can't even fool ourselves with these lame, new disguises.

We pay for the clothes, then ask the driver to drop us at a cheap motel along the main drag through town. While we head toward our room after checking in, a young woman crosses the parking lot and stops us, introducing herself as Bambi. "What was it before you reached southern California?" I ask, scratching the back of my neck.

With a taste of acid in her voice, she answers, "Mildred." Wolf jumps in with, "Ya gotta be shittin' me." He notices the anger in her eyes, then adds, "All things considered, Bambi is a good choice, babe." She slugs him in the arm. He fakes pain in return. She explains that she ran away from somewhere in the Midwest. Her long hair, parted in the center with the perfection of a centerline on a highway, hangs below her shoulders. She wears tire-tread sandals, dirty jeans, and a leather halter with peace symbols hand-drawn in lipstick over each nipple.

"The girl I came here with took off with some biker asshole and I'm left on my own without any bread," she says. Looking from Wolf's face to mine, she smiles in a coy fashion, then adds, "I sure need a place to stay. Would you Marines be nice enough to put me up for a couple of nights till I can figure out what to do next?"

Wolf and I look at each other and exchange oh-shit smiles. In an exaggerated, unrecognizable British accent, he responds, "Of course you are welcome to stay in our humble abode, my lady. We would be most glad to assist a damsel in distress." Too anxious to believe that our luck is real, and too horny to admit that it might not be, we don't take the time to see that something is probably wrong with this set-up. Bambi walks along with us to our room where she falls backward onto one of the beds as soon as we enter.

Our room has one of these coin-operated vibrating machines where you can drop a quarter in a slot and the bed will shake like hell for several minutes. I whisper to myself, "Damn, it just keeps getting better and better." I dig into the pocket of my new jeans for two quarters that I then drop into the box attached to the headboard. I lie down beside our sweet Bambi. Tucking my hands behind my head, I close my eyes with growing anticipation. Wolf goes into the bathroom for a quick shower, so it is just Bambi and me, hips touching as we both stare at the yellow nicotine stains on the once-white ceiling.

I glance over at Bambi and wait for the shaking to begin. There appears to be a bit of boredom in her eyes from this angle. The room is quiet as nothing moves—nothing. The bed refuses to gyrate in any fashion. I reach over and drop two more quarters into the damn metal box and hear them slam into the other two that already lie there in a silent tease. I fall back down beside our guest with less confidence in the magic of technology than I had a moment ago. When nothing happens, I get pissed and reach for the phone to call the manager and inform him that he needs to correct the mechanical problems that plague the first stage of my fantasy. This bed needs to work. As I dial for the office, Bambi reaches over and tries to stop me. When I push her hand away she begins pulling at my shoulder. The manager answers and I explain that I want some help in our room to make the magic, shakingbed function right.

As soon as I hang up the phone Bambi jumps from the bed and starts to look around for her shoes. At the same time, Wolf steps out of the bathroom with only a towel wrapped around his waist. He looks to me for an explanation. "I don't know what the hell is wrong with her," I tell him.

"He called the manager!" Bambi yells in desperation. "Can you believe it? He damn went and called the fuckin' manager." She drops down on her knees and begins to crawl around the bottom of the bed. "Where are my damn shoes? Shit, what happened to my damn shoes?" She looks up at me and accuses, "What the hell did you do with my fuckin' shoes?" There is a knock on the door that causes her to jump in the air as if shot from a carnival cannon. She gives a double take, looks at the door, then back to us. A second knock causes her to run across the room to where Wolf stands, frozen in place. As she slips past him she snarls, "I'm going to hide in the bathroom. Whatever you do, don't tell him I'm here. Do you understand me? Don't you dare rat me out."

On the third knock I open the door to stare into the face of the old manager, Mr. Weaver, according to his nametag. He stands with hands on hips and says, "Okay, let me look at this broken-bed business that is so damn important." He glances over at Wolf, who still stands with only the cheap towel around his waist. Old man Weaver nods his head and adds, "Oh, I get it now. I'll see what I can do so you boys can get back to your business."

I look over at Wolf and begin to see the scene through the manager's eyes. "Oh no. No, it isn't like that at all," I plead while shaking my head.

The manager walks toward the headboard and coin box. As he passes between the two beds he stumbles but catches himself on the nightstand. He reaches down to the floor and picks up a pair of women's sandals and displays one in each hand. His eyes shift from me to Wolf and back again. "Now, I don't believe these belong to either one of you boys, do they?" he asks. "They don't look very 'government issue' to me." His eyes go beyond Wolf to the bathroom door, then back down to the sandals in his hands. He walks past us, bangs on the door and yells, "Come out of there, Bridget. Now! Your game is up. I said get your ass out here. Now!"

We can hear the rustling of the shower curtain and after a few moments the knob turns and the door crawls open.

Bambi/Bridget/Mildred stands there with her head down, then she sulks on over to the manager. "I'm sorry, Mr. Weaver," she says.

He holds out his arms, and she takes her shoes from his hands. "Now, damn it, Bridget, I told you I never wanted to catch you working my place again." Stepping toward her, he reaches out to grab her arm but catches only air. "I let you go last time only because you swore to me that you were moving on. I need to call the cops right this minute. I've had it with you, girl."

Bambi/Bridget/Mildred grabs his arm and begins to cry. "Mr. Weaver, please don't. Please." Her head does a dance between Weaver, Wolf, and me. "Danny made me do it this time. I didn't want to, but Danny saw the taxi drive up. We were parked over at the gas station and saw these two boot jarheads get out and go into the office." She reaches behind her head and takes a handful in both her fists. "He grabbed me by the hair and said, 'Get your ass out there and wait behind the front row of rooms for them.'" Still holding her hair, she begins to cry. "Danny's all I got, Mr. Weaver. He ain't much, but he's all I got." Tears wet her face; she wipes them on her bare arm. "He would have left me right there if I didn't get out and take care of business. He slapped me and then pushed me out of the car. What was I gonna do?"

Mr. Weaver looks down at her and shakes his head. "Get out of here," he says. "Now. Before I change my mind."

She looks up at him with fear still in her eyes. "He's gonna beat me if I don't come back with something, Mr. Weaver. Sure and for certain, he will."

The old manager looks at Wolf and me and says, "Okay, dumbasses, this is gonna cost ya twenty bucks each or I'll call the MPs on ya."

"For what?" Wolf asks. "We didn't do shit."

"I know the MPs around here, boys, and they don't know you from Shinola. Hand it over or we'll see whose story they buy this time," the old guy insists.

Wolf starts to resist, but before he can start to complain I say, "It was my fault, Mr. Weaver. I'll take care of it." I hand the money over to the old man, then look over at Bambi/Bridget/Mildred. Gone is the mask she wore when we first met in the parking lot. Now I only see a lost little girl, beaten down much too early by the ways of the street.

"This is the last, last time, Bridget," Mr. Weaver says. "I give you my word on that." Reaching up, she takes the money from his hand, squeezes past him, and opens the door just enough to slide through. There is a soft sound as her feet hit the pavement. She's a memory.

Mr. Weaver looks at us with tired eyes that make him appear even older than his years. "I don't know where you two boys are from, but you're getting off easy. You can be happy it only cost you forty bucks instead of everything else you might have that is worth a shit." He nods his head toward the door. "That little girl can move like a cat," he adds. "She'd have been out of here with both of your wallets. You'd have been left with nothin' in your hands but the hard-ons you were using to think with in the first place."

Neither Wolf nor I have a word of response. We stand with our heads hanging and take his lecture on the evils of life in a military town—for a little while. Wolf gets restless, moves from foot to foot, and starts a nervous rubbing of his arms. I know where my friend's short fuse is heading so I speak up first. "Sir, we recognize we screwed up. Thank you for helping us out. We appreciate your assistance, and you can be sure it won't happen again."

"Yeah, yeah, but just let me know one thing," Wolf adds. "Do we stay, or do we go?"

"You boys can keep the room," the old man says. "But I don't want any more trouble out of either of you. You got that straight?" He begins to leave, then turns around to us and adds, "Oh yeah, the fuckin' magic vibrator's broken. Tough shit."

# Chapter Thirty-Five

## Cue Balls

**DATE: June 1969**

After five or six places refuse to serve us alcohol, we find a hole-in-the-wall dive that doesn't appear to have as high standards as the others. We walk into the darkness and wait a few minutes before we can see well enough to find the bar along the wall. We each grab a stool and order a Schlitz. The bartender looks us over, shakes his head, but doesn't ask for our IDs. He brings two cold drafts, sets them in front of us, and says, "I've been to the Nam boys. I know what's waiting there for you." He stares between us at something beyond the far wall. A strange smile crosses his face and he rolls his shoulders, as if waking from a dream. Then he adds, "Drink up, but don't you dare cause me any problems, or you are out of here."

Wedged between our stools and a row of tables lining the far side of the room, a pool table waits. Wolf and I start to play eight ball at loser-buys-the-next-beer stakes. Both pretty damn rusty, we stay close to even in games and beers. By eight o'clock, the small bar begins to fill up with locals. One group makes a lot of noise and acts friendly. Two of the fellows ask if we want to play partners for beers and we agree. As chance chooses to call it, Wolf and I begin to shoot at a skill level far over our heads. Beer and bullshit cause us to relax and shoot smooth sticks. To our amazement, as well as everyone else's, we win game after game. Their quarters continue to drop into the machine and our free beers go down cold and smooth. Undefeated, by ten o'clock we are damn near unable to stand upright.

"Wolf Man, I've had it," I say. "I need to sit down before I fall down."

Wolf lacks a "stop" or "pause" button. He responds, "Damn, Red...we got 'em...we got 'em on the run." Blurred speech on his part and blurred hearing on mine follows as we both laugh.

"Wolf Man, I can't stand...straight or see...straight," I try to explain. "Why don't you ask one of those...lovely ladies sittin' over there to be your partner? Shit, you might just get lucky. Why the hell not?"

The idea challenges him apparently. "You're just a girlie boy, Red Man," he says. "You don't think I'll do it. Well, just hide and watch." Like a Saturday matinee gunslinger, he moves toward a table beyond the jukebox. Approaching by a zigzag route, he attempts to make it appear as if this is his chosen path. I decide to follow for the amusement that Wolf always provides within his direct approach toward life in general, and women in particular. After his meander through the tables, he stands at the front of their booth and begins to speak. "Ladies—" He catches a belch before it makes its way out, then begins again. "Ladies, my partner here—" He puts his arm around my shoulder and pulls me close to his side. Once again, he attempts to make himself clear. "My partner, the great and powerful Rojo, from Houston, Texas, has decided to re...relink...oh shit, give up his part of our partnership so he might rest his weary bone...sses." He laughs, "No, I mean bones." He looks at me and adds, "Red Man, you do have a weary bone, don't ya?"

"Wolf Man, it is a tired, tired one, indeed," I say. "I don't think there is any way in hell I could wake him up. Not even if I wanted to." The ladies smile at my drunken attempt at humor instead of calling for the bartender and asking to have us thrown out. Wolf takes this as a good sign to continue. "Would one of you lovely young women care to be my partner in a game of pool?" he asks.

The shorter of the two nods and rises to join him. "Red, why don't you sit here and keep her seat warm?" he asks. They walk away to the pool table and I drop into the bench across from a redheaded girl in a loose-fitting turtleneck sweater. "Ma'am," I say, "my name's Red, but you can just call me—Red." She doesn't see much humor in this line, either, and gives a cool turn of her head away from my line of sight. Having used up the best of my drunken bullshit, I turn attention to the table and watch the pool game unfold.

Wolf breaks the tight rack of balls. He then sinks the thirteen and proceeds to drop two more of the high numbers before missing a bank shot. The taller of the two men who challenges the table chalks his cue with exaggerated precision. It is now his turn. He calls out an easy "three ball in the side pocket." With a confidence that hovers over the table like fog above a damp bog, he lines up the shot. He pops the cue ball low and hard to stop it dead and set up his next shot. To his great disappointment, the pocket doesn't take the speed of his shot and the three ball jumps back out of the hole. With contempt he comments, "Fucking bar table."

"Oh, shit. Such a shame," Wolf responds, then begins to walk around the table. More to himself than to anyone else, he giggles, "Such a damn shame." A look of cool calculation crosses his face and he adds, "That one shoulda gone. I was pullin' for ya, bud. I was, for a fact." He looks at the challenger and laughs loud and hearty. "I do feel guilty about that damn bit of disappointment for ya since my partner…" He turns to the young lady standing across the table from him. "What is your name, ma'am?" he asks. Before she can answer, he adds, "I'll just call ya, 'Sweet Thing,' if ya don't mind."

Looking back at the challenger he continues, "Sweet Thing is fixin' to kick your smilin' ass, my friend." She takes the stick Wolf hands her, sashays around the corner of the table, and picks up the small box of blue chalk to fine-tune her stick. With an inordinate amount of care, she licks her lips and twists the cue into the small hole. With a look over at "Smartass," she begins to swirl the cue round and round within the cube. Smartass becomes anxious and Sweet Thing winks at Wolf. She then turns her back and takes a provocative step to the side of the table. In a soft little voice, she names a twelve ball, double-bank shot that I don't even see exists until she challenges Smartass with the call. The cue slides smooth and straight through her fingers as she leans over the table. A lightning-quick pop sends the sweetest double-bank shot I've ever seen fly over and back, then cross once again to drop dead into the pocket.

From this point on, Wolf Man and Sweet Thing kick ass and take names. Frustrated and losing face with his friends, Smartass decides to push the point and turns on Wolf between shots to give him a dark stare. Wolf steps forward into his space and into his face. Not a word passes between them. Smartass blinks first, backs up, and sits down.

I continue to drink and enjoy the game, but the redheaded girl refuses to take notice of me. She makes it clear that she holds no interest in anything I might have to offer. As far as confrontation with the men who challenge the table, the night passes without incident. I am not close to being a badass, but Wolf knows I have his back if necessary. Wolf's Sweet Thing also makes it more than clear that she wants all he has to give. Every chance she gets she backs up against him to sway her ass from side to side against the front of his bargain-store jeans. Wolf's game drops in quality with each additional beer, but Sweet Thing's precision becomes more exact as the night wears on. She carries him, and they win again and again against all challengers.

The last-call announcement finds us in the booth with the girls. The redhead seems to be angry while Sweet Thing continues to crawl all over Wolf with her eyes, her hands, and her body. I go to the restroom and Wolf follows me. "Red Man, can you find your way back to the hotel on your own?" he asks. "I've received an interesting invitation."

"Wolf Man, it's no problem," I say. "Well, it's a problem that you're getting some and I'm not, but I'll find my way. You take care of business."

"This is something hot that may take some time, Red," he says. "I might just meet you back at the base and not make it to the motel." He reaches into his back pocket and pulls out his billfold. "Do you have enough cash to pay for the room?"

"No es una problema, Wolf Man," I answer. "Knock yourself out." I bounce through the bar from table to chair and somehow make it out the door. I have no idea which way leads me back to the hotel, so I guess to the right and head downhill toward the ocean. I come to a stoplight and choose left, more for the leaning of my stagger than anything else. Storefronts become familiar and the neon signs around our hotel point me home. I make it to the room and collapse on the bed. It smells of stale cigarettes and sweat. The air conditioner is on high and the mold beneath a consistent drip on the carpet puddles on the floor. I don't bother to put any quarters in the bed vibrator machine. Fool me once...

A knocking on the door wakes me up. A much louder pounding and the shout of, "Red! Red Man, it's me, Wolf," gets me out of bed and running. I open the door to see the bloodied face of my friend. He pushes past me and falls on the bed. I hurry to the bathroom, wet a towel, and bring it back to wipe the blood from his face. He only has a few cuts, none deep or long. Without the dried blood, he doesn't look so bad after all. He tries to talk, but I tell him it can wait for morning.

I cover Wolf up and crawl into my bed to crash once again. I awake to the sound of running water. Wolf is already up and dressing. "There is some sort of pancake place across the street. Clean yourself up and I'll buy you breakfast." He hits me with a pillow several times and laughs in the deep sound of a song that promises the world is a fine place once again. He leaves the room and a loud slam of the door follows.

I make it to the bathroom to take care of business, dress, and head out into the morning sun in about ten minutes. I hear a loud yell from across the street. "Red Man, yo, over here!"

Wolf stands at the door of a pancake house with each arm draped over a pretty young girl in cut-off blue jean shorts. I jog over and Wolf Man introduces me to Judy #1 and Judy #2. The pair attempts to explain their real names, but Wolf will not cooperate. He chooses to distinguish Judy #1 as the taller of the two. We eat breakfast together while the Judys talk in the everyday banter of California girls that sounds like beach music and breaking waves. Wolf uses his silly bullshit that makes them giggle and squirm in their seats.

They spend most of the afternoon with us. We walk on the beach and lie out in the sun. The sand on my feet feels like the beach in Galveston. I am home again—for just a little while. The salty air and the ocean breeze make me feel at peace with the world. The girls have to go, and we need to catch the bus back to Camp Pendleton. They both give Wolf a big wet kiss, and I get the cheek treatment. But, what the hell? Our little foursome shared a very good day.

Riding on the bus back to Pendleton, I ask Wolf what in the hell happened to him the night before. "Sweet Thing took me home," he explains. Her apartment was somewhere up in the hills. She made us drinks, then we went to her bedroom and began to make out. She pushed me back on the bed and started to undress me. I heard her roommate come home. She said, 'Oh, shit,' and started to get up, but I pulled her back and told her not to worry.

"I rolled over on her but she pulled me over and insisted, 'No, let me do you.' She pushed me back down and began to pull my trousers off. Despite her protests, I reached up and pulled her bra down. I found her breasts to be small and lacking form, but by now this was a minor issue. I thought I understood her reasons for being embarrassed and reassured her. We continued our exploration. She was winning and had me down to boxers and socks. I was only able to slide my hand into her panties by the force of frustration."

He looks at me and shakes his head. "Red Man, there was more in there than I expected to find," he says.

Lost, I don't understand what he means. "Wolf Man, what in the hell are you talking about?" I ask.

"Red, she had the same equipment pulled up tight down there that you and I've got. She be a he, Red Man!"

"You gotta be shitting me, Wolf. That's one of the best-looking women I've ever seen."

"Well, yes. I thought so too."

"Okay then, what the hell happened?" I ask.

"I jumped up and began to pull my trousers on," he explains. "All the while she is grabbing me around the neck, crying and begging me to stay. I pushed her back and said, 'My mistake, my mistake—just let me go home now. It's not your fault. I don't have a problem with you. It is just not the way I happen to be. Please just let me go.'

"It was all still good until the roommate barged in and jumped on me from behind. She knocked me onto the floor. Sweet Thing was hollering, 'No, no, no!' to the roommate. 'No, he didn't hurt me. Let him go. Let him go.' The roommate started swinging at me again when I worked my way to my feet, and then she began clawing at me with her long nails. That's when I started to bleed. That's when I got freaked out—when I began to taste my own blood.

"I took a swing at the roommate and used my arms to push her away. She flew back and hit the far wall. She yelled in pain at the impact. This caused Sweet Thing to begin swinging at my back and start to scream, 'You leave my baby alone! Don't you hurt my baby!'

"'Shit, bitch, or whatever,' I said. 'I just want out of here. Y'all let me out of here and it is all over. Just let me be gone.'

"But hell, they were lovin' the hell out of saving each other from me. You never heard such screaming and cussing in your life. I wasn't doing nothin' but pushin' them out of the way. You would have thought I was killin' 'em. Honest to God, Red Man. I didn't swing at either one of them hard enough to hurt 'em. I was just pushing them. I only wanted out—that's all.

"I finally grabbed my clothes and got the bedroom door open again. I ran until I found a road that looked familiar. I headed down that hill as fast as I could run. When I found the main street, I somehow found our hotel."

He shakes his head, laughs, and says, "And that's how the cow ate the cabbage, Red Man."

"Shit, Wolf Man," I say. "If I'd just had better bullshit than you, I'd have been their mark for the night." For the first time in my life I'm happy to have been the least attractive man in the bar. Wolf only laughs at me. He doesn't seem bothered one bit by the experience. That's just the way my brother Wolf Man takes life—the man is always in stride.

# Chapter Thirty-Six

### Best Man Blues

**DATE: June 1972**

My fellow Marine, the Wolf Man, calls my mother and asks that she contact me to let me know that he is getting married and wants me to attend the wedding. I arrive at an expensive reception in an exclusive section of Houston wearing the purple suit with flared lapels and bell-bottomed trousers I picked up while on R&R in Bangkok. I look like shit—purple shit at that. But it is the only suit I own, so fuck 'em if they can't take a joke. Wolf looks great in his tux, and his bride, Janet, is a classic beauty. Several of the groomsmen are old friends of ours from high school, but most of the other guests give me a "what the hell are you doing here?" look.

Wolf welcomes me with open arms when I reach him in the reception line. He seems so happy to see me that I feel I am at the right place in spite of my appearance. I tell him to point me to the bar and ask that he drop by and talk with me if he gets the chance. I drink more than I should—a good deal more. Self-medication with whatever is handy seems to be my only doctor, and there is a lot of prescription liquor available this night.

From my soft spot in a corner chair a short distance from the wet bar, I decide to see if the room might stay a little more in place if I stand up. It doesn't work; I need help to keep my feet beneath me. I back up against the wall. Wolf makes eye contact with me from across the room and works his way over to the spot where I help support the ceiling.

"Red Man, what's going down, my brother?" He reaches out, tousles my hair and laughs with the deep, full passion I have come to enjoy so much over the years. I have no choice but to laugh back at him, unable to resist his happiness and love for life. "Red, you are down way too low, my brother," he says. He grabs me by the shoulders and gives me a good shake. "Hell, it's my wedding. It's a party, man. Don't bring me beneath the line with you."

"Sorry, Wolf Man. I just get lost sometimes. I'm fine. Don't think about it. It's nothing."

"Red, come with me. I've got something that will help you lighten up." He grabs me by the elbow and directs our way through the crowd to the men's room located near the front door. We enter, and he walks us toward a stall at the far end of the restroom. He pushes open its half-door. From the top pocket of his tux he removes a thick joint of marijuana. "This is good shit, Red Man. Your drinking is just depressing you more. By itself, booze will only bring you down. You need something else to help lift you back up. A couple of hits of this shit will take you to a softer, more copacetic high."

He lights the joint, takes a deep hit, then hands it on to me. I pinch it, bring it to my lips, and take as much into my lungs as possible. The burn that accompanies it creates the pressure to cough, but I fight the impulse. Squeezing my chest tight, I attempt to force all the good stuff into my head. I intend to hold my breath until a cloud of gray can leak out through my eyes and drift like freed balloons toward the florescent lights above. Perhaps it will stop the sounds and snapshots that play in my brain if I can only hold on beyond an involuntary exhale and shut them down. Maybe I am strong enough to have it end this way. Here, in a restroom stall, beside the only person I know who can relate to the taste of an acid that eats a little bit more of my life away each day.

Wolf slaps me on the back. "Breathe, dammit, Red Man. Come back home." I fall forward and hit the wall of the stall. Catching myself, I turn around with my back to the tile and gasp for breath. My slide down to the floor resembles sleet on a hearth-warmed window. Wolf reaches for my hand, pulls the joint from my fingers, and laughs once again at my lost self. "Damn, Red Man, are you planning on blowing your head apart from the inside out?"

191

Three old men with big bellies and suspenders that struggle to keep their grip on sagging trousers enter the restroom and walk toward the urinals near the front portion of the room. They hear laughing from within the stall and glance our way to see me, with my legs spread out like a Raggedy-Andy doll, propped against the back wall. I look toward them and give the giggle of a schoolgirl, then glance over at Wolf. He takes another deep toke as he sits on the porcelain pot like a king on a throne. The absurd comedy of our situation tickles the hell out of me, causing me to chuckle even louder.

The old men continue to stare with disgust in our direction. The restroom is alive with the sweet, moldy smell of the burning marijuana, and the old men cannot miss the signs that the dumb-shit they see propped against the back wall is smoking some of the 'funny stuff.'

One of the gentlemen shakes his head. He says something that I can't understand, and the others laugh along with him. "I'm sorry, my friends, but I seem to have slipped. Please forgive me for diminishing the pleasure of your lounge experience on this night of nights."

Wolf slaps the wall with the cup of his hand that causes the sound of a gunshot in the echo chamber of this tiled restroom. The three old men walk back in our direction. I reach over, slide my ass further out of the stall and close the door so they can't see that it is this night's groom in the shitter with me. The men stop at my feet. "You are a disgrace," one says. "Do you know that?" The other two power brokers shake their heads in agreement.

"Gentlemen, you just might be right," I say. "I have had too much to drink and my pants are getting wet on this fine restroom floor."

"You are a worthless piece of shit to behave in this manner at a friend's wedding," the old man adds. I think about his words and consider the discretion of letting it all pass. Even though I know this old fellow has judged correctly, I think, fuck these piss-ant old farts. In a moment of weakness my give-a-shitter shatters once again, and with an inspired creativity I arrive at "Fuck you piss-ant old farts. I'm pretty much figuring that, if you don't like what you see, you can haul your pampered, arrogant, country club asses out of here."

Rising to my knees, I straighten up with my weight still trapping Wolf within the stall so they can't catch sight of him. I hear my friend begin to laugh again, which causes me to laugh even harder to cover his noise. "If you don't feel like backing off—well, then I'm just all right with that, too," I add. "But what you need to do is something other than just stand there with your dicks in your hands. You need to either 'poop or get off the pot,' as my dear, departed Nana would say." I place my hand over my heart and add, "God rest her sainted soul."

Wolf slams down the lid on the toilet. I can identify the deep inhale of another toke on his part. Our combined laughter fills the restroom and bounces off the walls like ping-pong balls dropped on mousetraps. The men look at each other, shake their heads, then turn and walk out. I push open the door to the stall and it hits Wolf in the head. He yelps and angles his body out of the way.

"What is this Bogart shit, Wolf Man?" I ask. I grab the small nub that remains and the high takes me away again. It drives me to the limit one last time. I draw the smoke in till the red ash burns my thumb and forefinger. While I cough and choke, Wolf takes what little is left, drops it into the commode, and flushes it away. Our heads are at a good place, and we agree that the swishing sound of the swirling water is hilarious.

With trouble, clumsily I slide up the wall back to my feet but continue to lean on the cold tile for support. After a few moments, our laughter slows to a stop, replaced by silence and distant thoughts. With great effort I lower my head and begin to shake it back and forth like a dog fresh out of a country pond. "Wolf Man," I say. "I'm losing it, my brother." He reaches out and pulls me to his breast with both arms. Grunts in the Nam once again, our lives are in each other's hands. We are two lost souls—or two men without souls.

"I'm sorry, Red. You are the one alone now. I know your head is ripping apart. I know what that feels like."

"I'm in the wrong place, Wolf Man." I pull away. "I should be no part at all of this day. Get your ass back there where you need to be." He doesn't make a move to get up. I slide halfway back down the wall to face him. "Listen to me. You go back in there, get smart, and let this all go. And I'll go back in there and get a little more wasted on your new father-in-law's dime." I push back up the wall, reach over, and grab Wolf by the arm. "Come on, Wolf Man; comb your hair and straighten yourself up. You are going to make it through this party just fine, my brother, just fine."

Wolf pulls up his pants and adjusts his coat. "Red, not a one of them out there knows shit."

"Well, I'm afraid that none of us in here knows shit, either, Wolf Man. At least none of my answers seem to be on target at this point. Every shot misses for me, no matter how hard I aim for the bullseye." I help him up, and we walk to the front of the restroom. I look into a large mirror that reflects a man I don't recognize. "Wolf, it doesn't mean anything. It really doesn't." My head refuses to stop spinning, so I give it another hard shake. "It doesn't matter. Not one shit." Cobwebs keep trying to snag my thoughts like nets seining for baitfish, and they confuse me even more. "Those old men who wanted to throw me out with the trash a few minutes ago," I add, "hell, they don't mean shit. Who knows? Maybe they are right. Maybe there isn't any place for me after all."

One of Wolf's groomsmen enters the restroom and calls out to him. The Wolf Man and I look at each other, brought back home by his presence. "Wolf, where the hell have you been?" the newcomer hollers. "Shit, you are the groom, man. You got a wedding going on." He gives me a look that implies, *Oh, I see, Red's here. That explains it all.*

I ignore them both and continue to stare at my own image in the mirror. The eyes of the three old men who left us in disgust slip into the reflection of my tired red ones and I feel their repulsion at the fool within me. "Wolf Man," I say. "I'm heading out. I don't belong here. You let the Nam go and you make it work. What you don't need is that bitch of a place back here with you any longer. There is nothing good to come from those damn thoughts."

I don't want to look at Wolf and his friend any longer, and I can't stand to see the man in the mirror, either, so I lower my head and spend a few seconds searching for a distorted reflection of some escape in my scuffed shoes. "Wolf Man, you make your world right. You owe it to the boys we left behind."

Wolf tries to stop me as I turn and walk away, but the groomsman grabs his arm and holds him back. I am right. Wolf knows it as well as me. Hell, the three old men had it figured out all along, too.

# Chapter Thirty-Seven

## Wolf Trap

**DATE: April 1973**

I live in Austin and work as a bartender at a strip joint called The Hook 'Em. A small dive on Guadalupe Street, it sells cheap beer and wine coolers a short distance from the UT campus. Early in the evening, the club's interior hides in dim lighting and dark shadows to conceal its shabby booths and stained carpet. The front door slams and a deep voice hollers out, "Red Man!" Although unable to see the entry area, I know there is only one body in the world attached to the voice I hear.

He takes a shortcut across the dancers' stage and heads toward the edge of the bar while I go to the end and come out from behind. My friend engulfs me with a great bear hug that squeezes the air from my lungs like paste from a tube, then lifts me off my feet and spins me around. Setting me back down again he says, "Red Man, how have you been, my old brother?"

"Better and better every day, Wolf Man, and much better with you here now." A smile crosses my face, bent like the first stage of a new moon. "It's been a long time—too damn long, and that's for certain." I lean back and give the howl of a lobo. "What's going down, Wolf Man?"

"Janet and I are in town for a few weeks." He slaps me on my back and laughs as I stagger backward. "We've been staying at my parents' lake house, but we're going camping for a few days. You and the Trout come out tomorrow night and join us. I'll cook some steaks and potatoes. We'll make us a fire, sleep under the stars, and catch each other in old lies." He steps back and up on the stage where he does a quick little two-step like a dancer in a minstrel show. "Janet is in the car, so I can't stay. I left the window rolled down a little bit." He gives me a wink as if sharing a secret. "She starts to howl if I leave her out in the heat too long in the summertime." I laugh along with him at the corny joke and think how good it is to see him again. "Come as early in the afternoon as you can."

From his back pocket he pulls out a wrinkled piece of notebook paper. "Here's a map. It oughta be easy for an old grunt like you to follow." He reaches over, puts his right arm around my shoulder, and pulls me close. "Hell, you're not a 2$^{nd}$ Lieutenant, you can't miss it." As he lets me go, he rubs the back of his head and becomes serious. "Red, I want you to be there. We need to talk."

Just as fast as he blew in, he's gone again. I talk to Trout about Wolf's visit and the camping invitation when he comes in for his shift. The Trout played football with Wolf in high school, and the two will always be teammates. He wants to go, too, but there is no one to cover for him at work. The bar towel he throws at me lands flat in the middle of my chest. "Hell, Red, you go on without me," he says. "We'll make it work another time."

I pack and am ready to go when I head to work the next day. After my early shift ends, I jump in my old station wagon, use the screwdriver I keep under the front seat to start her up, and head out of town. About twenty minutes later I find myself on a lonely stretch of hill-country back road. The rock outcroppings and scrub grass intermingle with cacti and mesquite. I have no air conditioner in my old Ford, so I take off my shirt and enjoy the crawling summer air washing over my skin like heat from an open oven.

Beyond a sharp turn in the road, I see a Volkswagen bug and an old van resting beside each other in a pasture. An old tarp hangs from bamboo poles to provide protection from the sun. The vehicles are near some bent oaks beside a large stock pond. I pull off to the side of the road and honk the horn several times. Vague shapes scurry around the van and I hear the response of honking from their direction. Down the sagging barbed-wire-fence line, I find the gap open and leaning back off to the side. After I make my way through the wire, I stop and reattach the wire gap to its loops in the old cross post just in case there are any cattle or horses in the pasture. I drive my way through the ruts and rocks and pull up beside the paint-chipped and rusted van.

Wolf runs out toward my vehicle before I come to a complete stop. Within the darkness of the club the day before I hadn't noticed how much weight he'd lost. Jeans hang from his hips, a cinched belt many sizes larger than his waist holding them up. His eyes are hollow and his cheeks are concave and pale.

We share the same embrace as the night before. My friend holds me out to arm's length. He searches into my eyes as if he might find some common truth hidden within the shared memories that gaze back. Janet comes around from the other side of the van and runs up to give me an exaggerated hug, too. She is a beautiful girl—such a beautiful girl. Taller than I, her long blond hair falls to her shoulders in straight lines from a center parting. A sweetheart, she wears the smile of an angel on a very good day in heaven. "I'm really happy you came, Red," she says. Between Wolf and me she stands so that he is unable to see her face. Her voice laughs in the sunshine, but clouds of concern shade her eyes. She makes a point to squeeze them shut and then reopens them with an awkward movement meant to send some sort of message that I take to mean things are not as they seem.

Wolf unties his belt. His jeans fall like loose rags to the ground as he runs toward the pond. "Let's go swimming, Red Man," he yells back over his shoulder. I follow his lead, strip, and run into the cold water of the spring-fed pond. Janet stands on the bank and laughs as we splash and reach to the bottom of the pond for handfuls of mud that we toss at each other like kids at church camp.

While we play, Janet adds wood to the coals from their morning fire. In a short while, flames struggle, then leap skyward. Wolf and I stop to rest in the soft mud by the edge of the pond and talk about nothing and everything. Now and then he gets up and walks to the other side of the van where an ice chest sits in the lengthening shade of the tarp. He returns with two beers and a fat, rolled joint behind each ear. Janet comes down to the shore and sits in a lounge chair to listen to our shared bullshit.

I'm not sure where the conversation starts, but we three know it will soon turn to the Nam. But not combat. Not combat in front of Janet. Instead we talk of the dirt, mud, mosquitoes, gook sores, and the boredom. Only grunts can ever share the burden of boredom in the bush on an equal basis. We remember sitting in the fuckin' heat in the relentless downpour of a rain that promises complete saturation—sitting and waiting. We recall humping heavy packs of ammo on patrol, sweating, and waiting for a break in the monotony.

We laugh, then laugh some more about the shared experience of the "nothing" time. We remember all those nights they would tell us that intelligence found out "for certain" that we would be hit. We recognize it was all a stay-on-your-toes experience to keep us alert. Yet we also remember how, just enough of those times, all hell would break loose and serve to keep us honest and on guard.

Here we don't tell war stories of killing and dying, an unspoken taboo. We laugh about shared fear and hoot at the memory of every sort of common discomfort. Memories of the stench of the rice paddies cause us to pause and inhale the sweet country air around us. Knowledge of the smell of spices within the enemy's sweat carried on the wind before an attack pass in a glance between the Wolf and me; they are not for Janet's ears. We remember how we knew when we were going to be hit—by the stink of our enemy's bodies and their proximity to our lines. We discuss the sappers and how we could smell the dope they were smoking before they'd begin their efforts to crawl through the wires of our base camps.

Janet sits on the beach and laughs at us, with us, more at the sound of our amusement than at an understanding of the hidden punch lines. Wolf gets up and walks to the other side of the camp to take care of something. His naked ass is skin and bones as he makes his way through the weeds by the shore. He disappears from our sight. "Red, Wolf has problems," Janet says. She leans closer to me as she talks.

"Hell, Janet, so do I. I'm not any sort of walking good example for anybody else, and that's a fact. I'm just hanging on here, myself."

"No, Red, you are the only one who is good for him. Today is the first time in months the old laugh escaped his lips—the real laugh from deep down inside." Tears form in her eyes and slide down her cheeks. They drop, then disappear in the cotton of her turquoise blouse. "You are the only one who knows. Hell, I try. His family tries. His other friends try. We can't reach him. He just slips further away from us, Red. Every day he slides a little bit more beyond our grip." She wipes her hand across her eyes, then slides it under her nose to remove the moisture that smears her face. "It hurts so bad for me to see it. It wounds all of us who love him to watch him go like this, Red."

"Janet, I'm only here balancing on a dead branch and an updraft myself," I respond. "I'm not the man to save anyone. Ya gotta understand that I love Wolf. He's the only one I know around here who can just look at a tree line with me in the early change from dusk to darkness, and know what I think when I lose it and yell, 'Oh, shit. Oh, fuckin' shit,' to the dead night air. Wolf knows what 'Oh, shit' I'm talking about. He understands my thoughts that go unsaid. He doesn't need an interpretation of the shit that I have no intention of...splainin' to Lucy."

Janet chuckles with a catch in her throat at my flawed Ricky Ricardo imitation. Then her voice again takes on a cold, serious tone. "Red, Wolf is falling far beyond you." She looks out over the pond and directs her voice to the water bugs that walk on a cushion of air over the slick surface of ebony. "You drink too much and smoke dope to self-medicate; I know that."

She stops to look up at the last of the clouds that cross over our heads. She squints her eyes as if trying to find meaning in their dying shapes. Her thoughts snag on treetops. She returns and brings her eyes back to mine. "I know you are lost, too. But Wolf travels to places you choose not to visit. He now hangs out with different people. I don't know them—and they don't want to know me. Wolf's losing weight because he doesn't eat. He leaves me for days at a time. And he comes back to me a total mess."

There is a sudden strong wind out of the North. I grab a towel and put it around her shoulders. "Red, Wolf can't even hold a job. We're only able to make it because his parents let us live at the lake house. They pay all our bills." The towel falls from her shoulders without her awareness. "I'm certain he's into some very heavy drugs. It's reached the point where he needs their artificial highs more than he needs today. I can't call him home anymore—not back to the here-and-now. I can't reach him like you have today with your bridge to that damn 'place' of yours. You two and your fucking Nam."

She rises and walks in a determined small circle, stops to stare back over the pond, then looks down at me. "Red, please help me. I do love him with all that I have to give. But there isn't much of the man you know left behind for me to hold onto." She shakes her head. "Red, I'm not going down with his ship, either. I refuse to do that to myself." She drops her face into her hands and begins to cry. She sobs for several minutes. I look away and stare at the pond. At a loss for feeling, I hear, yet don't hear, the sound of her pain. When she stops, I look over to find that she glares back at me. There is a cold, serious appearance about her entire body. "Does that sound terrible of me?"

"No, you must save yourself. There is no shame in that, Janet. No, there is no shame at all. I know for certain that Wolf would never want to drag you under with him. He's a good man. One of the best I've ever known. If drugs stole that from him, then take yourself away, too. I'll try to talk to him. But if he's where you say he is, it'll take more than my words to bring him back home to you."

She looks toward the van for a sight of the Wolf. "He has been gone too long," she says. Two mosquitoes land on her left forearm. She doesn't react to their presence. "When he comes back, you watch him. You see with your own eyes where he takes himself."

# Chapter Thirty-Eight

### Fire and Water

## DATE: April 1973

Janet and I sit in silence. Wolf comes back around the corner of the van. He walks on feet less steady than those he left on a few moments before. With a splash, he staggers into the pond and plops down at my side. The friend I love is gone to me now. His eyes look beyond the tree line and stare from within toward something that exists on the other side. His shoulders hunch forward, his hands fall limp at his sides.

I reach over and shake him. "Wolf Man, are you with me?" He doesn't respond. His eyes droop from the direct glance across the pond down to the ripples in the water by his feet. I place my hand on his shoulder and give him a gentle squeeze. "Wolf, I need you, my friend. Don't leave me alone here. Don't fall away from me now— not now."

His shoulders roll even more forward, and his chin again falls to his chest. I turn around and look to the bank and the chair that lies in the light of the falling sun behind us. It rests empty and alone—Janet is no longer there. To my side, I see the friend and brother who held my feet to the ground at times when I felt that I would float away, un-tethered and lost in swirling winds. He now sits unaware of my presence—empty and alone at my side.

We don't eat dinner this night. Wolf and I don't do shit but wallow in the mud. In the pond we sprawl with hands and feet

201

wrinkled from a long day in the cold water, like faces of old witches in the storybooks of my childhood. When he leans to the side, I catch him and pull him up to my shoulder. Beyond darkness, Wolf shakes himself loose, then rises to stagger up the bank again. I have nothing to say to the back of his head as he bobs and weaves along the shore. Soon after, I work my way to my feet and stumble up the bank to the lounge chair and fall into its center like dead weight onto a stretcher. Beside the lounge, I find a joint Wolf Man left here earlier in the day.

When I feel clear-headed enough to think about all that happened, I push myself up, work my way to the embers that remain of the fire, and lay the end of a dry stick into their middle. I walk to the side of his van and grab two beers held together by a thin plastic strip. As I return to my seat, I pass the fire and pick up the half-burnt stick to light the joint with the small flame at its end. I fetch the blanket I brought along from the back seat of my station wagon, then return to the chair.

Covering myself, I droop the beers over one arm of the chair and spend the next few minutes inhaling the last bit of smoke from the joint. With each drag I attempt to hold the tokes longer and deeper in my lungs. I wish to disappear within the relief that plays its way through each inhale. My hope is to float upward along with the diffused waves of smoke and nothingness.

When the end of the roach burns the pinch of my finger and thumb and blisters the yellow stain of my skin, I pull it to my lips and suck-in one last taste of the heat. With a squeeze to the ash, I throw the remainder into my mouth and chew the bit of rot and mold that remains. The top of a beer that hangs by my side pops and I take a deep swig of warm suds and foam from its depths. The stars in a spattered sky blink back at me like flirting young girls with false lashes. Shapes take form and look down upon me. I smile at my wandering thoughts and feel at peace. The cool breeze calls my name and laughs as it shakes the leaves and rattles the brush with an understanding of my insignificance.

At some point within my escape I hear Janet's whisper to me. "Red, Wolf needs you. I've lost him."

I struggle and feel the cold of the night sneak through the blanket and chill my bones. I begin to shake, then shiver even more with a violence that pulls me into a tight ball on the thin lounge. I look across the pond and into the tree line opposite my chair. Shapes in the night move and challenge me as an enemy. They stop and start again and again. I close my eyes tight and I jerk away as my own hand squeezes my thigh. I struggle to remember that, at least a part of where I am, is where I am not. I am not in the Nam. I am not within the grasp of its uncaring fingertips. I am at a pond's edge. I am not to be lost, at least not on this night.

The burden on my eyes becomes sleep. It carries me through the night until the rays from the morning sun challenge me to face the new day. My head tells me, rise, but my body responds, *no way*. I look around. Only Wolf's van and my old station wagon remain. Janet's VW is gone. Her call for help stings like a slap of insult on my ears.

Sounds of the early day greet me as the songbirds and small animals begin their rustlings of life. I walk to the pond and wade into the chill of the smooth water. A quick, deep breath, and I dive under the surface. My eyes peer through the cloud of soot and sediment I stir by my movements. I push further out into the pond to the clear, undisturbed places where I swim as if in flight. I hold my breath with the intensity of the night before when I trapped fire and smoke in my lungs. This movement, however, is fresh and pure with hill-country air cold and clean within my chest.

I dive below the surface and work my way toward the darkness. Disoriented in the distilled early morning light, I lose up from down. With strong strokes, I swim onward but feel neither bottom nor top. A fire begins in my chest within the cold that surrounds my body, and tentacles of panic grasp at my heart. At last my hands touch a slick slime and I twist my body, pull my feet beneath me, and push up. As I shoot through the surface, I gasp for fresh air. I tread water and look around to find myself in the middle of the pond.

Exhilaration from my brief flirtation with up versus down fills me with a sense of rebirth—within the simple contrast between "final breath" and "first breath." I continue to tread until my strength and confidence return, then I swim back to shore.

"Wolf Man, where are you?" I call. He steps out of the van and looks toward me. I see the confusion in his eyes as he struggles to find a point of reference. He looks at me as if I am a stranger. By the lost way he checks out the area, I can see that he has no idea where he is. Fear shines in his eyes. Like a lost thought, he stands alone against a world he fails to understand. When his search ends, he comes back to where I stand.

"What's goin' on, brother?" he asks.

"Wolf, I need your help. We have to talk." I gaze at the sky for the right words to say, then look back into his eyes. "I need you to help me work through some things."

A look of concern crosses his face, "Red, what is wrong? I'm worried about you, my brother. I didn't think you looked so good last night." He steps beside me and places his arm over my shoulders. "You carry too much weight on your back. This is not good. You've got to let it go." He gives my body a squeeze. "This shit will kill you from within, Red Man. Trust me, it'll cut you like a slice of shrapnel."

I step away and pull two camp chairs from where they rest against an old oak, carry them to the side of the fire pit, and unfold them. "Come sit down, Wolf Man. We need to work on some things."

"Wait just a minute, I need to make this right." He goes back into the van and returns in a few moments twisting the ends of a fresh joint. We stand beside the remnants of last night's fire. Wolf tosses a few dry logs on the embers and stirs the ashes around. I add some kindling and flames soon break through the coals.

He sits down while I throw some thicker branches on top of the others. "Wolf Man—well, you are one of the few who knows that I just stumble from day to day," I say. I'm searching for a direction that evades me like a fly loose in the kitchen. "When I am around other people, I feel smothered. I can't breathe." I kneel to ground level and blow on the ashes several times to keep the fire from dying. Flames catch, and the fire takes form. I step back and take my seat beside Wolf. "The ceiling pushes down and the sides of the room work inward on me. A child's game of Red Rover where everyone has their hands intertwined to stop me." I stand and watch the sun hide behind a cloud, and I feel the chill its absence brings. "But when I cross over, there is no place for me to break through. Locked arms block my way and throw me back again and again and again. The wall laughs, and I fall to the ground in frustration."

I rub my hands together to warm them. "Wolf, you made it back all right. You have Janet. She has a heart willing to accept you as you are. You blend in like a sprinkle of hot sauce in a pot of Texas chili, my friend." My hands held out over the fire, I lean closer to the flames. "Along with everyone else, you still have the ability to breathe while I continue to gasp for air. I need to make the dive and chance the loss." I look away from his intense gaze. "Fuck, Wolf Man, I need to go 'all in.' There are gooks in the bushes, my brother. I need to get it on!"

A long silence stands between us. "Red, I know where you are coming from, my brother, but I can't find anything here, either."

I interrupt him. "What in the hell are you talking about? What about your wife? What about Janet? Wolf, that girl loves you. Fuck, I don't even know what a love like that is all about." I reach down and grab another small stick and toss it at his legs. He doesn't try to avoid it and just looks down to watch it bounce off to the side. "Wolf, listen to me, dammit." His eyes rise to meet mine. "I do know that you can't let all you have slide by like it has no value at all. That's the 'dumbass' in you talking now."

He stands and kicks dirt into the fire, then steps to the woodpile and grabs several large logs. Like rocks in a pasture wall, he arranges the wood in even rows on the fire, then sits back down. "Red, her love is more than I can deal with. She wants a part of me—no, she needs a part of me. But how the hell can I give her a slice of something I have no control over?

"She keeps crying that she wants only me. She just wants the 'me!' Now, how the hell can I give her a part of 'nothing at all?' Fuck, that is all there is in here—nothing at all." He pounds a fist on his chest then hollers over the top of the flames. "There is nobody home!" He opens his arms wide as if trying to catch the wind. "Don't they get it, Red? There is no one here."

I lower my head and shake it back and forth. "Wolf Man, you have so much. You gotta find it within yourself to make it work. It isn't ever going to get any better than you've got right now, my brother. Right now."

# Chapter Thirty-Nine

## Walk Away

**DATE: April 1973**

Smoke from the fire flies Wolf's way. He coughs in the cloud as it passes him by. "How can you tell me that it is up to me to make it work? You don't believe any of this shit you've been talking about, Red Man. Do you?"

I pick up a small stone and toss it into the fire, then look to the sparks for an answer. "Wolf, I don't know shit. I wish to God I did so I could offer you some peace. But I've got nothing here that will work. You deserve so much more, but it just isn't here for me to tell. I have no truths. There are only questions without answers."

He spits on the fire. We watch the moisture bubble then disappear from the side of the log. "Red, the best thing that ever happened to me slips away while begging to stay. The pain in her eyes kills me. It cuts like shards of glass. In her misguided trust, I recognize that I am not the man Janet thinks she sees."

Wolf lights a joint. We smoke it through without the intrusion of words, passing it back and forth to share the lie of escape. When we finish, I go to the cooler for two more beers. I pop the tops of both cans and return, hand one to my friend, then sit again.

"Red, how do you live with it?"

I think about this for a moment and take a sip of the beer. "I go to bed at night and get up in the morning. I sleep with a K-Bar knife beneath my pillow. Most of the night I stand by the window listening for movement in the shadows." My eyes shift to the fire's flames that mesmerize and seduce with their changing shapes and hues. I force myself to blink and look away. "Fuck, Wolf Man. Don't ask me how, ask me how long. How much longer can this go on?"

Wolf chugs the remainder of his beer. "How about one more high before you leave, Red Man?" Without waiting for an answer, he rises and goes back to the van to roll another number. I pull off my trousers and shirt and walk out into the pond far enough for the water to reach my knees. I continue farther and the cold slaps my senses as it reaches my chest. Wolf returns in a few minutes, splashes through the shallows, and stands by my side, a lighted joint in his hand. I dry my hands on the hair of my head and take the joint he offers like it is a long-lost friend. The smoke rises within me once again. A quick release of tension escapes from my shoulders, and they collapse with an exaggerated exhale. I take a second toke before I hand it back to Wolf.

The light compression within my chest brings a high that carries me away. I close my eyes as it takes me to a place where I float above the treetops in the movement of treading water with my hands from side to side. When I look down, I see leaves beneath me sway back and forth on thin branches. I open my eyes again, turn to Wolf, and smile the universal smile of the shit-faced. He returns the same grin and laughs at the shared knowledge that lives within the fucked-up.

"You are screwing it all up on purpose, aren't you, Wolf Man?"

"Yep. It is the only way I know how to do it. I have nowhere else to turn. Janet's love smothers me. All I can see is how very far I happen to be from the man she thinks I am." He looks at me for several moments as if trying to find something in my eyes. "It's the ambushes, Red. It's the momma-sans in the hamlets. It's the babies in the dirt. It's the gooks in the wire." Wolf hands the joint back to me and splashes water in the other direction with a swift slap of his hand. His words are staccato. "It's the boys we ate chow with. It's the call of 'fire in the hole.' It's the day before yesterday, Red Man. There ain't a one of 'em who knows this shit that crawls beneath our skin. It's all within another lifetime."

"Wolf Man, I'm getting ready to head out." I pass the joint back to him. "Look at me. Janet leaves if you don't clean up your act. She is fed up with your bullshit, my brother. It's no longer a 'what if?' It is a fact. You lose this woman if you don't choose to make her love more important than whatever it is we lost in that fucking Nam."

Birds fly overhead. One drops a twig from its beak but keeps on flying. There is a small splash and ripples begin to move toward us. "Wolf, if you don't grasp this moment, you are one lost son of a bitch. There is no other place left for you to land. Please, don't let this one go. If you lose her, you lose yourself. If you don't hold onto Janet—well, then you'll have nothing left."

The sun crawls behind a cloud and the water turns colder. I shiver and my teeth rattle. Wolf's head falls to his chest beyond the high of marijuana, and I understand there is something more than THC in his veins. I know I lost him. I talk to ears that don't hear. "I love you, my brother. I do for a fact. But you're killing me, man." I reach under his arms and pull him back to shore. Still somewhere else, Wolf's eyes refuse to open. His body denies my presence and the only thing I understand is our shared knowledge that we don't understand shit.

I pull him onto a lounge chair, find a blanket in the van, and cover my old friend. I dry off and put on my clothes. Wolf lies with his head back in some sort of la-la land. A broken smile crawls across his face as he enjoys a treat unknown to me. I check the top pocket of his shirt that hangs on the back of a chair and find another joint. I light it with the ash end of a stick from the fire and sit by his side. The smoke brings me a sense of mellow distraction and a welcome detachment. I lose track of time. In short segments that enable me to maintain a lingering buzz, I smoke it alone.

The sound of a car behind me catches my attention. I look back toward the road and watch Janet refasten the wire gap in the fence. Wolf remains out to the world. Her car stops beside the van. I decide to remain in the chair at Wolf's side to see if there is anything I might do to fix this train wreck. Janet walks around the corner of the van and stops to stare at us.

I look up at her. "Hey, Janet, I was hoping you'd be back."

The hurt in her eyes cuts deeper than pain. She gives the scene before her a raised eyebrow of lost words. "When I made the decision to turn around I thought I was wrong to leave. But I didn't know. I didn't know it was going to be like this."

She stares at Wolf's unmoving form on the lounge chair at my side for a long time without moving. I say nothing at all. There are no words to say. I feel out of place as I recognize I have no relevance to this scene that takes place before me. I am less than one of the clouds that float over our heads.

Janet shakes her head in disgust. "I knew when Wolf told me that he wanted to find you and ask you out here that I was in big trouble. It's that fucking Nam. It won't let him go. And then you show up and you make it all even more real to him again." She starts to cry. "I'm sorry, Red. It isn't you. It's that fuckin' Nam bitch you bring along when he sees you. He dances with her all the time. He invites her home to sleep in our bed when you are not around to confirm her presence. Hell, Red, you give him a reason to believe she's real." Janet lowers her head and begins to shake it from side to side. Slowly, she raises her eyes up to meet mine. "He loves that place more than he hates it."

She sticks her boot out and catches the chair behind my legs. She gives it a strong push and sends me to the ground. I lay in a frozen position. My back is wet with mud that soaks through my clothes. The cold crawls about my hair like a dance of trained fleas. She says, "You two and your damned Nam."

I'm afraid to move for fear she might kick me instead of the chair this time. "Janet, it's cold down here. Can I get up without getting slapped around?" She nods her head and laughs despite her anger. She smiles, drops to her knees and hits me several times with balled fists. Her laughter turns to sobs. The force of her fists becomes harder and harder. Her hits turn to slaps, and the slaps turn to the grabbing of curled fingers that scratch and claw. She loses strength, stops her attack, and straightens her back.

Wolf shows no movement throughout our display of emotion. Janet remains in this position for a good while. "God, how I love this lost boy, Red. He was so good to me from the very first. He held me close, and I was safe and secure in his arms." She rises to her feet and I stand up beside her. "Most of all, he made me feel needed. He had so much desire for me. Such a great need for my love. It took my breath away. This beautiful man with the smile of a child. He carried the insatiable hunger of an untamed animal. He had everything I wanted. So much more than I ever dreamed possible."

She turns to watch Wolf as he lies still in his chair. "And now—now look at him. I've lost him to the drugs that take him higher than I'm capable of flying. He's not interested in sex anymore. When he holds me close, it's not like he used to. It's not in the way that a man holds a woman. There is no longer a need in his touch. He loves me like a friend, but never, any longer, as a lover."

I right my chair and pull another one from the side for Janet to face me. I motion for her to sit down. She hesitates then lowers herself into the chair. "Janet, you need to save yourself. I know for a fact this is what Wolf would want you to do." She begins to play with the ends of her hair. I lean closer to her and stare at the top of her head until she looks up into my eyes. "He'd rather lose you than hurt you."

I catch myself and go back over the words I just said. "Janet, I don't know shit. You were right when you identified me as poison for him." I sit up straight and look back into the fire. "I don't have any of the answers you need. You are right. I am a bad influence on him." I look from the flames to her face once again. "Shit, I can't keep myself from falling. How in the hell can I even begin to catch the Wolf Man?" I stare at her with tired eyes. "I'm your problem, not your solution. There's nothing I can do about it."

I see Wolf move on the lounge chair beside us. He reaches his arm up to cover his eyes, then drops it back to his side. With both hands he rubs his face. A great yawn escapes and he opens his eyes to look over at Janet. "Hey babe; you okay?" His voice is barely audible. "Hell, I've been dreaming about you." He smiles. "It was a very good dream, babe." Then he laughs the good laugh from days gone by.

Janet grasps for a straw in her memory. "Hey babe; you okay?" she asks. "I've been missing you."

"I guess I was lost for a while," he says. "Hell, it's the Red Man's fault. He carried me too far back." He spits into the flames and smiles when he hears the scorching sound of a hot iron. "No, no it doesn't go like that. I'm just kiddin'. I'm a grown man. I am responsible for my actions." He spits again but misses the fire. With the back of his hand he wipes his lips. "Red's here because he's my friend and brother—not because he's my excuse. I got fucked up all on my own account."

He comes around enough to talk a bit more. Time passes, and a curtain closes between us. The closeness we share evaporates like moisture on the small plants around us. We promise to meet again soon, but we both know that our shared tie to the Nam is too close. We can't be together and not also be "there." Neither of us can handle getting too close to the flame without falling back into the fire.

I walk away.

# Chapter Forty

## Shadows

**DATE: June 1973**

My friend Trout calls me at work at The Hook 'Em. He just returned from a visit home to Houston where he got together with some of our old friends from high school. "Red, I've got some bad news for you," he says. The phone is silent for a while. "Are you by yourself?" I can hear him breathing on the other end of the line while he hesitates. "I mean, are any of the girls there yet? Are you on your own?"

"What the hell are you talking about?" I ask. The rag I use to wash the beer glasses slips from my hands into the soapy water. I lean back against the cooler to catch my balance. "Shit, you're scaring me. What the hell is going on, Trout?"

"Well, Red, when I was at home I found out that Wolf died several weeks ago." He pauses and waits for a response. I can't speak. Words refuse to form in the dryness of my mouth. "Red, are you there?"

I feel like a boxer blind-sided by a sucker punch. "No—I mean—yeah, yeah. Trout, what the hell are you talking about?" I hear the words leave my mouth, but they don't seem real.

"Wolf Man died on us, Red." He coughs and clears his throat. "He's dead. I know you two had the war in common. I know it hurts. I don't think anybody had it in them to tell you."

"The Wolf Man dead—there's no way. Not Wolf—"

212

Trout cuts in. "Mike said they kept it very quiet. They just had a small service. Only family."

"Hell, somebody should have called me. We had the Nam, dammit." The volume of my voice rises with my frustration. "I should have been told! Shit, that ain't right."

"Red, it was a bad deal. I guess they just wanted it all over with."

"What do you mean, 'they wanted it over with?' Hell, Wolf was a hero, man. I don't give a fuck what any of them think about the war. He stood up, dammit. He walked the walk. He put it all on the line. Shit! Dammit, all to hell. I'm not listening to this crap." I slam the phone down and remain against the cooler unable to move. A rock song plays on the jukebox and music blares out from an external speaker behind the bar. Amanda finishes her thousandth enactment of "Teen Angel" for a small audience of salesmen on an extended lunch break. She ends her dance with an imitation of a man digging a shovel full of dirt from a gravesite.

Amanda has great tits—large and natural. At least this is what she swears is the truth. They bounce together then slap away again as she moves to the beat of the music. Yes, they are great tits. Large and talented. She can rotate them in opposite directions with one going clockwise while the other swings counterclockwise. She is even able to time their rotation so that they don't crash into each other while they twirl in perfect synchronization. Yes, Amanda has well-trained tits. I make my mind concentrate on Amanda's talented tits and their attached, multicolored tassels. Blocking everything else out of my head, the spinning shapes on the stage mesmerize me and I become disorientated and dizzy. I pour myself a beer from the tap and chug it down. The woozy feeling remains after the beer, as Amanda and the music move on.

The phone rings again. It refuses to shut the fuck up, so I answer and yell, "What?" into the receiver.

Trout is on the other side of the line. "Red, talk to me."

"What the fuck was it?" I catch myself and realize it is my good friend I am talking to. "I'm sorry, Trout. How did he go? What the hell happened to Wolf?"

"Mike told me it was an overdose. They found him in the bathtub at his parents' lake house. According to the autopsy, it was heroin."

"How long was he dead when they found him? How long did he lie there—alone?" I feel sweat on my forehead even though I stand beneath the flow of an air-conditioning vent. "Do they know that? Do they at least know that much?"

"Red, let it go. None of that stuff matters. He's just dead." After another long pause I know that he expects me to speak. But my part of the conversation catches like gum in a child's hair. I feel confused and knotted together, while the more I struggle to focus, the more entangled my thoughts become. "Red, I'll be there in about twenty minutes. Don't go crazy on me, now." He hangs up to end the conversation.

Trout arrives and takes the remainder of my shift. The corner booth becomes my home for the rest of the night. I drink beer after beer, make it to the restroom in time to throw up, then return for more beer. The Wolf Man I knew talks to me between dancing girls and loud jukebox rock. I sit with the fine young Marine I knew. One full of mischief and life who was always more concerned about everyone else than about his own needs.

I talk to the shadow in my head: "Wolf, you are dead. And to a fuckin' overdose, you dumb shit. You threw it all away to a needle and a high. I can't imagine the pain of your family. Hell, I sure can't imagine Janet's pain. She loved you for the man you were. Now she's gotta mourn the loss of the man whose needs you would never allow her the chance to satisfy.

"Wolf Man, I resent my own selfish loss. There are so few friends I can relate the Nam to—so few from our background at least. Who the fuck from Memorial knows leeches and ambushes and booby traps? With your exit, a door slams in my face. There are not enough passages home that I can afford to lose even one at this point. Without doubt, not one of your importance to my sanity, that's for sure.

"I can't get it out of my head. I'm angry at your decision to fuck with heavy drugs. Nasty drugs take you too far out. You didn't expect this rush would be the one to take you away, did you? But you knew how close to the fire you were passing your hand. You knew there were blisters to be had and you fucked up, dammit. You understood you were chasing the flame. Did you really expect death to reach over and grab your ass? Surely not. You didn't want out, did you? Did you? I imagine you only wanted to recreate the nearness to the high that accompanies the nearness to the death.

"The Bitch you want back whispers in our ears and passes us by in a forever chase, Wolf Man. The instant when the rounds zip past and suck your breath along with them—those seconds between the spark of ignition and the few moments that remain to dive for cover—the blink between the call of incoming and the reality of explosion that brings new meaning to 'who's on first'—they all were yours, but you chased them too far.

"Wolf—well, all right. You are one gone badass. I guess that a last 'goodbye' is in order. I feel so damn empty at this moment. For the past few years your life meant the concept of 'death' for you, anyway. Within this confrontation of my own reality you are only now, at this moment, laid to rest. No, wait a moment longer. Not the real truth—not the truth of truths. So long as I walk and breathe and remember your silly smile and your fuck-it-all attitude, you will still be around. Oh shit, Wolf Man, if I have your memory within me, you are here. If I am, you are."

# Chapter Forty-One

## We Have Not Forgotten

**DATE: May 2008**

Memorial Day arrives a week early this year. It isn't felt in the rhythm of marching bands through a colorful parade, nor is it seen overhead in a shower of fireworks lighting up a summer night's sky. It isn't heard in the roar of racing engines and cheering crowds, nor does its taste linger in the smoke of barbecue pits and simmering baby-back ribs. This year, Memorial Day arrives on the evening of May 20 at a dignified high school graduation ceremony in the small town of Magee, Mississippi, where, along with a brief round of applause from the parents and friends of the class of 2008, it takes the form of a congratulatory handshake from Principal Bo Huffman.

Forty-one years before this night, when the graduating class of 1967 met to receive their diplomas in Magee's Fighting Trojan stadium, William Davis Martin was not in attendance. Davis had been young, energetic, and full of life, with all its possibilities, when he chose to drop out of school and join the Marine Corps. There was a war going on, and Davis was not one to miss out on a good fight. His brothers tell of a time when a much larger boy was picking on one of Davis' friends when Davis spoke up, "You can go ahead and kick his butt if you really want to, but you're going to have to wait to do it until after you've kicked mine first." The bully was bigger than Davis, but the town boys all knew that there was not an ounce of "give up" in him. The bully backed down.

216

Davis was a rifleman, a grunt, and proud of it. When I arrived in Vietnam, he became my first fire-team leader. He was to teach me those things that must be learned first-hand in combat; those lessons that go beyond classroom lectures and field exercises. He taught me the skills that would serve to help keep me alive for my thirteen-month tour in the An Hoa River Basin, one of the most hotly contested areas in Vietnam. On the night of August 21, 1969, Davis was killed in an ambush while walking point near a place we called "The Alamo." Davis was nineteen years old.

In the summer of 2000, I returned to Vietnam with a group from Charlie Company and found the exact spot where Davis had fallen. My squad leader, John O'Brien, and I stood together, held hands, and said a brief prayer. We told Davis he had not been forgotten. I made a vow on that small piece of high ground where Davis fell that I would do my best to find his resting place back in the world and talk to him one last time.

In May of 2001, after spending a great deal of time tracking the information down, my wife and I visited Magee for the first time. I didn't know his exact name; we all called him Davie. I assumed that was his given name, although many of the guys went by nicknames. But searching through records I couldn't find a Dave or David who had been killed in our province near the end of August in 1969. A William Davis Martin was as close as I could come to a match. I called the local high school and talked with the principal.

He said, "I'm sorry, but I have never heard of a Martin killed in Vietnam. The war wasn't very popular here. No one talked about it very much—then or now." Just before ending our conversation he said, "Wait a minute, why don't you talk to our counselor, Kay Ethridge? She has been around here for ages, and she knows everything about everyone." He transferred my call and he had been right, Kay Etheridge did know everyone and everything.

She said, "Well, yes, I knew Davis. We played together as kids. He was my cousin."

I couldn't breathe. It was as if a clock had stopped inside of me and its hands refused to move onward. I said, "I'd very much like to visit the site of his grave. Do you happen to know where the cemetery is located?"

She said, "No, I don't," and my elation took a coaster ride downward. Then she added, "But why don't you call his brothers and ask them?" It was a carnival ride for certain, and I was shot back up into a cloud. She found the phone number for me while I waited. I copied it down and said, "You can't imagine what this means to me."

"No, I think that maybe I do," she said. "Just a little bit. You see, I loved Davis, too."

I contacted Billy Martin and explained who I was and what I was looking for. I said, "Would you and your brother be willing to meet with me, so I can see if Davis is the man I have been searching for?"

There was a silence on the line for a few moments. I heard him sigh and then he said, "All right, let me tell you how to get here."

I could hear the sadness in his voice that wavered like a song sung out of tune. I said, "Are you sure? I know this is a great deal to ask of you."

He said, "Yes, we will make it work. You deserve at least that much."

On Memorial Day, my wife and I drove from our home in East Texas to Mississippi. When we pulled up at the address Billy had given, I felt awkward and out of place. Cindy put her hand in mine and I couldn't let it go. I held on and squeezed it as if it were a lifeline thrown into deep water. Her fingers turned white, but she never pulled away.

I knew I was at the right place when one of the two men who came out of the house to greet us was an exact replica of my friend Davie—or at least an older version of the nineteen-year-old I had fought beside. The brothers invited me into the house where I met Billy's wife, Patty. She was gracious to us, but I could tell she was uncomfortable and worried about these two men she obviously felt great love for. She kept sneaking glances between them and Cindy and me. I looked to the wall and saw a picture of Davie in his dress blues and explained to them that their "Davis" was our Davie. We sat down and talked for a while, then Billy walked to the rear of the house and brought back a shoebox. He carried the cardboard container as if it were a crystal vase that could be broken by a false move. He said, "This is all we have of Davis's time in Vietnam. It contains some pictures and the letters he sent home to my daddy. Daddy died several years ago, and I inherited the responsibility for Davis's things."

I said, "Do you mind if I look through it?"

Billy said, "No, go right ahead. I need for you to be sure, so we can be sure, too."

None of them said a thing while I thumbed through the fading pictures that carried me back thirty-two years. At first the dryness in my mouth and the cobwebs through my mind made it impossible for me to form words. But it soon all gave way and broke loose like a rain-swollen dam. The Nam had me in her grip once again. I began to explain who the men behind the faces were and identify where the pictures had been taken. When I had gone through all the photos, Billy said, "There aren't many letters. Davis was there for only two months before he was killed, and he wasn't much of a writer. The one on top is the last our daddy got before we received word of Davis's death."

I asked, "Would it be all right with you if I were to read it?"

He said, "Yes, of course you can. In fact, I'd like for you to."

I eased the letter out of the envelope and unfolded its one yellowed page of Davie's handwriting. In it he talked about having been made a fire-team leader. He mentioned that one of the men in his team was from Texas and said, "He is a good man, Daddy. We will be fine." I had to pause and look away for a few moments in recognition that Davie had been referring to me in this last letter home. At the end of the letter he wrote, "We are fixin' to go into a bad area tomorrow. But don't worry about me, Daddy, I will be fine. I'll take care of myself."

His brothers, Billy and Buck, drove us out to a small cemetery about fifteen miles from town where Davis's grave lays beneath a Mississippi oak tree. Its branches hang low to the ground and its shade covers his stone throughout the day. We stood together, held hands, and said a prayer. We told Davis we had not forgotten him. When the others got in the car, I remained behind for a few minutes to say private words to my old friend.

The Martins took us to lunch in town. We filled the silence with small talk that held little significance after the emotions of the day. We said our "thanks" and "goodbyes" at the restaurant. It seemed a drab ending to a day of multicolored, distant memories.

On our trip back to Texas, I continued on a carpet-ride high for the first few hours, held aloft by updrafts from the excitement of having found an end to my search for Davie. But after the rush slowed, I stared at the highway's spaced white lines and felt the reality that lived within the monotony of dash after dash after dash. Tears visited my eyes and colored them red.

I said to Cindy, "I'm ashamed of myself. I never took the time to consider the effect that our visit would have on the Martin family. It was a selfish indulgence. I went there only for my own purposes. I thought I could ease my sense of loss by saying a last goodbye to my brother of the Nam." As we rode west down the interstate into the afternoon sun, I realized that I had allowed the visit to be too much about my own memories and my personal need for resolution. Only upon saying our goodbyes did I become aware of his brothers' distraught faces and recognize how very real and in the present their pain remained. The hurt was alive and existed as an open sore in their walk through each day.

At that moment, I made another vow. It was one that went beyond my initial pledge of finding where Davie rested. I swore I would find a way to let the Martin family know that I knew what they knew—that Davis's loss was more than a brief trip to a cemetery and a walk through old photographs and frayed letters. I made a pledge to myself that I would not become a fleeting memory that waltzed into town, shed a few tears, and danced back out again. The Martin family deserved more than a token drive-by from me—Davis deserved so much more.

Cindy and I spent the remainder of our ride back to Tatum discussing possibilities that might become a worthy remembrance. We were both schoolteachers, so the concept of a scholarship in Davis's memory soon began to rise to the top of our list of considerations. When we reached home at the end of the day, I called Billy and thanked him again for agreeing to open their lives to us. I explained to him the direction our trip home had taken and asked for his permission to present a scholarship in Davis's name at Magee High School the next year.

I said, "I was able to track down your family by calling the high school and first talking with Principal Huffman. He told me that he had never heard of a Davis Martin. Those words stuck with me. The idea that no one at the school even knew my friend had walked the halls angered me. I wanted them to know; I wanted them all to know of his sacrifice and of the sacrifice of your family."

Billy said, "Thank you, Red. I think a scholarship would be a wonderful idea. I know that the rest of the family will agree, too."

With the school counselor's help, I was able to make arrangements for scholarships to be awarded to the graduating class of 2002. The raising of money became a personal thing for me. I didn't hold any fundraisers—no golf tournaments, bake sales, or fish-fries. I just chose to send out letters to everyone I knew in a sort of "Christmas Card" listing. I asked my children, my brother and sisters, and my nephews and nieces. I asked my in-laws and my old friends. I especially asked for assistance from Marines by writing to those from Charlie Company I had served with and to those whom I only knew through the brotherhood of a shared heritage.

I couldn't get away from my teaching responsibilities to make it to Magee for the assembly in May. Billy Martin stood up for us and was there to hand out the scholarships that were awarded to members of the class of 2002. I asked him to read a brief statement to the assembly explaining that the awards were meant to have Davis's memory live on through the futures of those students who were assisted. He explained that they were also meant to tell Davis Martin that he has not been forgotten. When I talked to Billy that night on the phone, he told me how much it had meant to the family that we had done this thing for Davis.

I asked, "Would you like for us to continue the scholarships for another year?"

He said, "The family would be honored. It would be a wonderful thing to do again for all of us."

And so, the William Davis Martin Scholarships became a continuing endeavor. The next year we raised a comparable sum, and I was able to be in Mississippi for the awards assembly to make the presentations. Both Billy and Buck are uncomfortable speaking in front of groups, so I addressed the assembly. I told them a little bit about the Davis I knew and asked that the people of Magee never forget their local hero.

The following year I again made the trip to Magee on a Thursday night after I finished driving my school-bus route. But this year our old corpsman, Roger "Doc" Teague, and his wife, Barbara, had driven down from Missouri to join us. Doc had been with us the night of the ambush and had done what he could to try and save Davis's life. After the awards ceremony we went out in front of the auditorium and had a picture taken with the seven scholarship recipients.

We stood in front of that small auditorium: Davis's brothers, nephews, granddaughters, aunt, Doc and Barbara Teague, and myself. Another lovely lady whom I did not recognize joined our group. Billy introduced me for the first time to his mother, Mother Marty. She had come to the awards presentation for the first time. She had watched the ceremony from the back of the auditorium. Doc and I gave her a hug of warmth and love. She said, "Boys, I apologize for crying so much. I just can't think about my Davis without falling apart. Please forgive me." She cried and could say nothing more.

I said, "Mother Marty, don't even begin to worry about us. Doc and I feel it is more than a privilege to be here with you. Remember we are only representatives of all of his brothers from Charlie Company who wish to honor him." She smiled behind her tears. I added, "The Teagues and I are going out to the cemetery to visit Davis's grave. I brought some plants that we want to leave there with him. We just want to talk with him for a little while. Would you like to go with us?"

Mrs. Martin broke down again but pulled herself together enough to say, "I was just out there yesterday. I pulled some weeds and left some flowers myself." She began crying again and Buck stepped over to grab her arm and walk her to their car.

Billy pulled me aside and said, "Red, Momma couldn't go to the cemetery on the day they buried Davis back in 1969. It was too much for her. It was all too painful for her to accept. For the past thirty-five years she has never been able to deal with visiting his grave." I put my hand on his shoulder and gave it a squeeze. "Red, yesterday Momma made her first trip out there. She told us she wanted to be sure it looked nice for his buddies from Charlie Company. It is important to her that y'all have a good visit with her boy."

We stopped by a convenience store on our way out of town and bought a six-pack of beer to take with us. We pulled off the main road at the far side of the cemetery. A short piece down a gravel lane, we turned in and parked. I had brought along a folding chair for Barbara to sit in and placed it close to Davis's grave. Doc and I stood and talked for a few minutes about the ceremony and meeting Mother Marty. I dug several small holes for the plants and wet them from a jug of bottled water. Doc, Barbara, and I opened our beers. I popped one for Davis and sat it on his marker. We proposed toasts to Davis, the Marine Corps, and to our absent brothers. With a promise that we meant no disrespect, we poured Davis's hot, foamy beer over his headstone and shared another swallow together. We held hands, said a prayer, and told Davis we had not forgotten him.

On the way back to the Martin home, we cruised through the downtown area looking for a florist shop. Doc and Barbara had me stop so they could buy a flower arrangement to give Mother Marty for Mother's Day, which fell on that Sunday. Both of their own mothers are now deceased, and they wanted to honor their memory through a gift to Davis's mom. When we went back to Billy's home after our visit at the cemetery, Mother Marty wasn't there. She had asked Billy and Buck to tell us that she just couldn't hold herself together to see us again at this time. But she did want us to know that she appreciated our being there for her boy.

The scholarship has continued to be an annual undertaking. Each year I follow the same formula: I compose letters asking for help, and mail them out to my family, friends, and members of Charlie Company. The response has been beyond all expectations. Over the past seven years, we have awarded approximately 55 scholarships, totaling over $50,000.00, to graduates of Magee High School. Davis has not been forgotten.

The senior awards assembly has become an opportunity for many of us to gather at the Martin home. Marines and corpsmen who haven't seen each other in years come together from all parts of the country to pay their respects. They stay on to enjoy the Martin hospitality and to feast on some of the best southern food imaginable. If you can name a country pie, cake, meat, or casserole, I'm sure that it sits somewhere on the long line of tables in the Martin family room. Most important is that we find ourselves surrounded by Davis's loved ones: his mother and aunts, his brothers and their children and grandchildren. This year I was blessed to hold in my arms Davis's namesake, Myles Davis Martin, born just a month ago. I held him close to my heart, kissed his forehead, and said a silent prayer for Davis. This time I told Davis that he has not been forgotten.

As our group of Marines and corpsmen walked onto the stage at the awards assembly to announce this year's recipients, the faculty senior sponsor, Felicia Robinson, stepped out before us. She took the microphone in her hand and addressed the crowd. She said, "I have a very special surprise for our Marines today. Something extraordinary has occurred over the past few days. At this time, I am very excited to let you, these Marines, and especially the Martin family, in on our secret. This year's senior class met earlier in the week and agreed that they wanted to do something for Davis."

The section of the auditorium reserved for the seniors came to life. They began to nudge each other and smile in our direction. They could see that we had no clue as to what was going on. We could tell by their movements that they loved this opportunity to turn the tables on us. Each previous year we held the surprise of the scholarship recipients in our hands. Today the "unknown" was theirs. Mrs. Robinson continued, "The class wanted to show how much they appreciated what Davis's memory has done for so many Magee graduates over the past years." The seniors were becoming louder and, with a continued smile on her face, Mrs. Robinson gave a hand signal for them to calm down. She went on, "Each of the more than eighty seniors signed a letter they had composed. They submitted it to the school board last night before its scheduled meeting. In the letter, they asked that Davis Martin be made an official member of their class. They also requested that he be a part of their graduation ceremony, and that he have his picture displayed along with theirs in the yearbook." Those of us on stage standing behind Mrs. Robinson shared a synchronized jaw dropping. The seniors laughed at our comic response.

She continued, "One member of our school board was also a member of Davis's class of 1967. He stated that he would consider it an honor if he were to be the one to officially present the proposal. He asked at the board meeting that all unfulfilled graduation requirements for William Davis Martin be waived. He then requested that Davis be an official member of the graduating class of 2008. The vote of approval was unanimous."

At the end of her announcement, the audience rose and gave a standing ovation. Mrs. Robinson stepped back, gave me a hug, and handed the microphone over. It was now my time to award the year's Martin scholarships. I looked down at the speech I had prepared and was unable to read the words I had jotted down. When I did look up to begin, there were tears running from my eyes. I said, "Damn, you've gone and made an old man cry. In this case, I hope you are as happy about that as I am." I then presented Davis's scholarships for the year.

I later talked with Felicia Robinson about how special their unselfish gesture had been. She said, "Red, as a teacher, I feel that it is important for students to get their math, science, English, and other subjects. But I also feel that the scholarships offered in Davis's memory have provided a special opportunity for the students of Magee to learn more than the facts that exist in their schoolbooks. I feel that the scholarships you men give after all these years in the name of your fallen brother are about friendship, dedication, and sacrifice. I believe this is, perhaps, the most significant message about life our students can take with them as they leave Magee High School." She pulled a Kleenex from her purse and wiped her eyes, which had grown wet as she spoke. "This has been my way—our way—of saying friendship lives beyond death. We have tried through this action to say to you Marines and to his family, 'Davis, Magee has not forgotten you, either.'"

**\*\*\*\*\*\*\*\*\***

I am back in Magee on this Tuesday night, May 20. I sit in a row of honor at the foot of the home stands at Trojan Stadium, along with Davis's mother, aunts, his brothers, and their wives, at the graduation ceremony. Out of the far end zone, the class of 2008 begins to march single-file onto the football field. They sit in a neat arrangement of folding chairs in front of their parents and friends. Along with the seated graduating seniors is an empty chair—one that has been left empty in the alphabetical arrangement for William Davis Martin. Many here tonight see only a vacant chair. His family and I see a nineteen-year-old Marine looking squared-away, sitting straight and proud in his dress blues. There is a smile on his face.

This year's valedictorian is a young lady named Dolly Welch. She is the niece of Patty and Billy. Her address is a wonderful speech that mentions the many possibilities that lie ahead for these graduates. She talks of hopes and dreams, of goals and aspirations. She ends her speech with a catch in her voice as she says, "We remember our classmate, William Davis Martin."

As their names are called out and the seniors file up to the area where the official guests and Principal Huffman wait to hand the graduates their diplomas, they are all smiles. They beam with pride at finally reaching this significant stage in their lives. When it comes time for Davis's name to be called, Mrs. Robinson pauses the ceremony to take the microphone. She gives a brief overview to the audience of Davis's story. She explains the meaning of the many scholarships that have been awarded in his memory over the years.

I look once again at an empty chair. Davis is gone now. He has joined the row that has risen and moved toward the presentation table. When his name is called, his brother Billy and I stand and walk forward. Billy accepts Davis's diploma, and we both shake the hand of Principal Huffman. We return to our seats and Billy pauses to present Davis's diploma to his mother. When he steps aside, I take her in my arms and give her a hug and a kiss. She is crying, but she has a big smile behind the tears—her son has just graduated from high school.

The diploma is not an honorary one by any means. In the graduation program; in the marching-in and seating of the seniors; in the awarding of diplomas; and in the official records of Magee High School and the state of Mississippi, William Davis Martin is a documented graduate of the class of 2008.

Yes, Memorial Day arrives a little bit early this year. Yet it also arrives thirty-nine years after Davis fell in the darkness of August 21, 1969. It comes forty-one years after he might have graduated with the class of 1967. But it has arrived nonetheless. Thank you, family, friends, and Marines for your generosity that made this day possible. Thank you, Magee, for the goodness in your hearts that also made this day possible.

Davis, you have not been forgotten. Semper Fi, my old friend; may God bless and keep you.

# Chapter Forty-Two

## What Degree Crazy?

**DATE: May 2007**

Crazy? Yes, but to what degree crazy? Am I baboon-run-naked-and-throw-feces-at-startled-zoo-patrons crazy? Am I spinning-gravel-on-a-small-town-speed-trap, deputy sheriff crazy? Am I bitch-slap-a-true-Harley-biker's-momma (not one of those piss-ant, yuppie-lawyer/accountant/CEO wannabes) crazy? Or am I rather lie-in-the-mud-and-weep crazy? Yes, this definition presumes enough for me to hold as truth. The idea that I am a crazy who sits shotgun with each night's long ride home suffices for me. At least not one of those yuppie-lawyer-three-cows-worth-of-leather crazies, I am not.

I do have a piss-in-the-alley leg-up on most crazies because I have documented proof of just how wacko I am. I hold a doctor's note with a government seal and a stamp at the top of each page that attests to my deviated state. Like squatter fleas on my cur dog, there is authenticity to my insanity—proclaimed in legalese and filed away.

The government that I raised my right hand and swore to "preserve, protect, and defend," the government that trained me to "kill...kill...kill!" as we thrust fixed-bayonets forward and across an invisible enemy, has deemed my craziness so. I can, with percentage-point accuracy, identify the degree of my sanity, or lack thereof. I have professional verification of being 30% sane. I grant you this is a concern for those of you who chance to sit near to me in a crowded bar late at night. However, I am also more than half-cup full, 70% crazy (which is a passing grade of "C", is it not?).

The VA directs me to meet a fellow in Tyler, Texas for a psychological evaluation to support my request for help. Unable to sleep and finding myself struggling like every other piece of river trash, I fight to keep my head above water. Every branch I reach for snaps in the false hope of a death-row reprieve. After a year's wait, some bureaucrat writes a brief letter to inform me the government, overloaded with claims, assigned me to a psychologist for a pre-requisite write-up.

I enter the dated office building and locate the appropriate name on the directory of insurance salesmen, real estate agents, and loan officers. I walk down the first-floor hallway and enter a door that bears my evaluator's stenciled nameplate. The waiting room is little more than an 8'x12', wood-paneled bunker with a frosted-glass, sliding-reception window on the facing wall beside an interior door. The small oscillating fan blows the scent of stale perfume and lemon-drop candy, leaving an underlying hint of urine and stale milk within its intermittent pattern across the room. I take three short steps across the waiting room to the blurred-glass barrier and tap for attention. A lack of response causes me to bang on the short shelf that reaches outward into the silent chamber. A further silence. I yell, "Yo, is anybody home?"

The shield slides back with the simultaneous opening of the door, and I receive a "What the shit?" look from a teenaged, candy-stripe-wannabe receptionist. A wrinkled penguin in the clothes of an overfed woman waddles through the door. By the arm, she drags a pint-sized mirror image behind her. With a double huff of mother-daughter arrogance, they do a two-step toward the hall door. The penguin says to the peppermint-stick power behind the desk, "I'll talk with you later, Lena Jean. I'll give ya a call after I carry my baby to the Walmarts 'fore it closes."

"Heck, Miss Corine, Walmarts never closes. That's a fact."

With the challenge of a stare, the penguin says, "I know, darlin', but this…'gentleman,' appears to be in such a hurry that we just need to get on along now. But I'll be checkin' back at ya, baby."

Darlin'/baby rolls her eyes, then answers, "I'm sorry, Miss Corine, it's just the way some of these…'people' act. You do know what I mean."

With that, Miss Corine and Little Miss Corine saunter out with a bit of awkward butt-twists and a final goodbye-slam of the hall door by Little Miss Corine. My eyes follow their exit, then I turn to hear darlin'/baby /Lena Jean say, "The doctor is busy right now. If you'd please take a seat, I'll inform you when he's ready to see y'all." There isn't anyone else in the room, so I assume that "y'all" must mean little ol' me.

The stained-glass shield slides shut. I turn and take a seat in one of the three elementary-school cafeteria chairs on the opposite wall and look up to find myself staring at a children's print of giraffes and elephants playing cards. On the floor to my left is a half-built Lego structure of a parrot/dog/truck. To the other side of my chair rests a rollercoaster contraption of multicolored wire and wooden beads. It appears frozen in time. I look to the ceiling's lone globe, with its light dimmed by the loss of one or more bulbs. It casts a yellow gloom over the room. My 'present' slips in this pseudo-moon's glow of long ago. I feel shamed and diminished in the same moment's breath at this display of contempt for my presence.

What the fuck! What in the hell am I doing in a child's toy-strewn waiting room? But wait is what I choose to do. I must play Big Brother's game; he holds all the aces. So here I sit. A lone goldfish in a slime-clouded tank stares in my direction from across the room, acknowledging my status as a fellow inmate. He turns and swims past bubbles that rise from a treasure chest and sunken galleon that rest on the colored-gravel bottom of its glass-plated prison. On shelves beneath the aquarium lie an assortment of torn magazines and cardboard Disney books with covers bent and yellowed by time.

The beat of piped-in music for juvenile ears pounds with tiny drums in my head. I close my eyes and see bare-bottomed village children huddled together in small groups for the cruel illusion of protection. Their small hands are held out like Sunday donation plates, begging for gifts of food or candy as we pass by on patrol.

The image shatters when the receptionist slides open her window of separation, motions for me to step forward, and says, "Y'all will need to fill these forms out before the doctor will see you." I pick up the papers and return to my seat. With a clipboard cut in the shape of a clown's face balanced on my knees, I begin to pencil in the required identifying data. However, I choose to leave many of the reason-for-visit spaces blank. After another long wait, the interior door opens once again and pseudo-powerful teen, Nurse Ratched, orders, "Please walk this way." Unable to fight the immature impulse, I stick my nose in the air and give an exaggerated sway to my ass as I follow behind her.

"Thank you very much, Ma'am," I say as I pass through the door into the interior room, partitioned off with a four-foot-long countertop.

Little Miss Ratched checks out my paperwork, then looks up at me with fire in her young eyes. She directs the clipboard at me like it's a pistol on a firing range and says, "Sir, the doctor will be unable to see you if these forms are not completed as required. And Sir, I know what 'N/A' means, but I don't know what game you are playing with 'NOYDB.'"

Pushed to its limit once again, my patience snaps with the crack of an AK-47 in my ears. With lips tight and white I explain, "Nurse Whoever-the-hell-you-are, it means 'None of Your Damn Business.'" I clasp my hands together in restraint behind my back and continue, "Now listen to me, little girl. I've been sitting for over an hour beyond the time to report here for my appointment."

I hear the volume of my own voice and pause to catch my anger. "My knees are on fire from being cramped in that undersized seat watching that prison-camp gold fish of yours die a slow death in that murky water. Hell, I damn near got seasick and barfed on the Legos." I feel my heart racing and know the pace of my voice matches it. "I answered every damn question on that list of yours that I felt necessary. But what you got there in your hands is all you are gonna get from me. Furthermore, I expect you to change your attitude and show some proper respect for a veteran of the armed forces of the United States." I take a step closer to her and add, "Not because it is me here today, and the balding old man that I am. But because it is a courtesy you owe to each of the good men I represent."

I step back, hold my hands to my head, and look down at the floor. I try to rein in my lost composure. Following several deep breaths, I look back up at her and say in a slow tempo, "I know that you know that I'm here because your boss is sub-contracting his license to the government to get paid some bulk-rate fee for agreeing to see old fools like me." I step up close to her again. "So here is the plan. This is the way it's gonna go. You say, 'Excuse me, Sir, for my rude, disrespectful behavior.' Then you waltz your prissy little self back to Doctor What-ever-his-name-is and tell him that Corporal Reese of the United States Marine Corps is ready to see him now."

I stop my tirade to look into the wide-eyed obstruction before me and realize that this young girl is clueless. I think, shame on me for the fear I caused. This is not the kind of man I wish to be. In my frustration, I bend forward and mime Edvard Munch's silent scream—aggggggggghhhhhh!

The back door to the room opens and a short, thin man with suspenders and a polka-dot bowtie steps in and says, "Oh, you must be my VA client. Lena Jean, I will take over from here."

She almost cries and says, "But, Doctor! Doctor, he didn't fill out all the forms. Remember, you told me never, never to let anyone past me without all of the forms filled in." She straightens her arm and points her finger toward my face. "He just wouldn't do it. He also used some very bad language. And you told me that I should never let a patient talk to me like that...and...and..."

"It will be alright, Lena Jean," the doctor interrupts. "Why don't you go on down the hall to the snack room. Maybe get a soda water and some Fritos and take a little break. Everything is going to be all right." Lena Jean squirms and twirls her hair with the fingers of her left hand. "Look at me, Lena. It is okay. It is all just fine. Now run along and relax a bit." She leaves.

The doctor turns to me and says, "Sir, I'm sorry for any inconvenience you might have experienced here. I did, in fact, hear the end of your conversation with my receptionist through the door. To my embarrassment, you are correct in almost every respect. I am a child psychologist trying to get by in a small city where the predominant answer to a youth's problems is, more often than not, 'let them alone and they will grow out of it.' I do take on a sub-contract with the VA to handle some of their incredible overflow of claims. And, just between you and me, you are also correct that Lena Jean is self-important and out of line." He shakes his head and pulls at his bowtie. "Hell, you should meet her mother." His eyes peek toward the ceiling. "But, her daddy and I have been friends since first grade. He is a good man and I value his friendship. Anyway, I put up with most of her foolishness and just wait for the summer to end and her fall semester to begin."

His smile fades, and he continues, "However, you are mistaken in one regard. I do care about your service to our country. I do take my responsibility to meet your needs as a serious charge. And if you will permit me to do so, I ask that you put this preliminary 'bullshit' behind us." He motions for me to follow him into his office. "I hope that you will allow me to go through the ridiculous rigmarole that you and I both know the government requires me to do." Reaching out, he offers his hand and says, "Sir, it is an honor to meet you."

I shake with guarded gratitude for at last being treated with a bit of respect and say, "Fine, thanks Doc, let's do whatever it is we gotta do."

# Chapter Forty-Three

## Too Many Questions

**DATE: May 2007**

Into a small office, I follow the doctor, then sit across from his desk with my back to the room's only window. Tired from my own child's-tantrum of a few moments before, I fall into the cushioned comfort of the worn chair. A series of three Winnie the Pooh prints angle down the wall behind his desk. Eeyore's sad face reminds me of the dispassionate ass I play in this day's comedy of errors, and I shake my head in disappointment at my loss of control.

The doctor takes his seat in a chair that rises higher than mine so that he looks down on me. "The interview works like this," he says. "I'm not going to play games with you; please trust me on this point. The government provides me with a required list of questions that I must ask of you. They instruct that I not deviate from their format in any way because this would jeopardize the standardization of the interview."

He pauses his rehearsed lines to open a folder from which he withdraws several pages. Tapping their edges on his desk, he aligns them in a neat stack, then begins. "You should also be aware that I am not to offer you any sort of diagnosis. Nor am I to provide you with any type of feedback or suggestions following this session."

He glances up and watches as I reposition myself in the chair. There is a lump in one side of the seat and I keep sliding toward the edge. Crossing my legs, I shimmy my ass back toward the middle of the cushion and look back at him with a blank face. He coughs, then returns to his directions. "The expressed purpose of this session is for me to walk you through this non-wavering process. When we are through, I will send them on to the appropriate office at the Veterans Administration."

The doctor stops reading and looks at me. Taking off his glasses, he sits back and twirls the frames by one of the earpieces. Caught in the rhythm of their spin, I can't seem to pull my eyes away from their orbiting motion. His words merge into a meaningless drone and my head begins to coordinate with the spiral movement. With an abrupt pinch of his thumb and forefinger, the Ferris wheel halts, and I nervously laugh out loud at the end to my brief ride. I change my focus to the doctor and find him smiling back at me. He puts his glasses back on and continues, "It is there where your final evaluation will be determined. Regardless of how offensive this statement is to the both of us, I am also directed to make certain that you know that this meeting is not a treatment session of any sort. Please confirm that you understand the process by signing these three documents."

From the stack on his desk he separates the top three pages and pushes them across toward me. I lean forward and scribble my name on them so the games can begin. The twitch of my nervous fingers causes the signature to appear shaky, as if there is an underlying quake in the earth below me. The counselor looks at me with what looks like a searching-for-absolution glint of shame in his eyes. "Do you understand the process as explained to you?" he asks. I nod in return, then respond with a "yes" to his prompt of "your answers must be verbal, so I am able to record them."

We work our way through a long list of questions that lead up to the obvious "biggies": In your time in Vietnam, were you ever in a situation where you felt as if your life was threatened? During your time in Vietnam, did you ever see one of your friends wounded or injured in any way? During your time in Vietnam, were you ever in a situation where you—

It goes on like this for longer than a long time.

"Were you ever involved in direct combat situations?" he asks.

"Yes," I say.

"Did you ever see a friend wounded?"

"Yes."

"Did you ever see a friend killed?"

"...Yes."

"Did you ever kill anyone?"

I slide back in my chair, grab its arms, and squeeze till my fingers turn numb. My heart begins to race. I lower my eyes and take a deep breath to slow myself down. My tongue catches in the dry cavern of my mouth. I am unable to speak. It takes a moment for enough saliva to wet my lips, so I can form the answer. "Yes."

The walls begin to move in like closing fists. I look back over my shoulder and out the window. Cars pass by a short distance beyond the sidewalk, their shapes distort in the pleats of thin drapes.

"Did you ever ki—"

"All right, Doc, that's all you fuckin' get." I raise my hand to stop him. "You go ahead and fill in the rest of the blanks however you want. But I don't owe you or anyone else one goddamned bit more than I've already given you." I rise from my seat to stand straight in front of his desk. "Doc, listen to me—please." My head feels as if it's caught in a vice. Blood pounds at my temples. "You are a nice guy. I can tell that you care. I really can. My first inclination to write you off was unfair, small-minded, and I am ashamed of the way I lost it." Swaying back and forth, I shift from foot to foot.

I know I need to slow myself down. I close my eyes, then open them and look into the wide eyes of Christopher Robin as they stare down on me from behind the doctor's head. I pause once more and try to organize my thoughts. My gaze switches to the print of Tigger talking with Roo, and I grow cold in the small room. I struggle with the words. "I...I can tell that you care. I really can." A dry cough catches my tongue in the desert of my dry mouth.

The doctor interrupts my silence. "Listen, Mr. Reese, I can see how difficult this is for you."

"Doc!" I surprise both of us by the harsh sound of my voice. I stand straight again and put both hands to my front to pause the situation. "Doc, only my brothers from the Nam get any more...any more of this bullshit. Hell, Doc, that's all I can give you. Don't you understand?" I drop back into my seat. My elbows rest on my knees. I lean forward, clasp my hands as if in prayer, and stare at the worn carpet at my feet.

"This is why I don't sleep, why I'm caught in a downward spiral of can't sleep—tired; then, can't sleep—more fatigue, and more memories; then can't sleep—more fatigue, and more—then, can't sleep—more fuckin' faces and sounds and memories, followed by more fear of—just the fuckin' ghosts of sleep—just the fuckin' ghosts."

Looking up at him, I see the worry and a little fear on his face. "What the fuck more do you all want from me, Doc?" My palms are wet with sweat. I pause to wipe them on my trousers. "I'm so damned tired of being tired, so afraid of the bullshit concept that sleep offers some sort of escape." My eyes begin to water, and I reach for the box of Kleenex on the small table at my side. I take several tissues, wipe my eyes, then blow my nose. Looking at him again, I shrug my shoulders. "Shit, my closed eyes offer only a fuckin' threat, Doc. Dreams are no sanctuary." Head shaking, I look back down at the floor. "I'm so sick of feeling like shit about myself."

The doctor plays with the papers on his desk, then closes the manila folder of my war. "We are finished with this questionnaire." He looks at me with true concern in his eyes, "Are you okay? Are you going to be all right?" My head drops to my chest. I don't speak or look up. He stands and walks around his desk to sit in a chair beside mine. "Are you going to make it through this shit?"

Surprised by his change in attitude, I jerk my face up to see a different man. "Yeah, I'm great—I'm just great." I notice again that his concern is real and add, "I'm sorry, Doc. I'm not doing too good here, right now." Placing my hands on the arms of the chair, I prepare to rise. "So, if that's all you need, it's time I get my sorry ass outta here."

"Well, the government is finished here," he responds. "It is just you and me now. Are you sure you are all right?"

I can't help it, but my voice rises in frustration, "Fuck, no! I'm losing it, can't you see that, Doc? Don't you hear me? I'm going fuckin' loony here. I'm hanging on by less than a thread." A car's horn blasts from outside the window to my rear and I duck down and raise my hands to cover my head. I take a deep breath, then continue, "I listen to your questions and try to come up with some sort of words, some sort of description for the feelings. But I've got only foggy answers, Doc. They slosh back and forth inside my head like a slop jar." I turn around and look again through the glass at the traffic passing by. "And all the while I sit here with my rear to this damn shoot-me-in-the-back window." I speak toward the drapes.

236

"I hear noises I can't identify. I'm trapped. I think about throwing myself to the floor. But—but, I still have the control not to. See, Doc, the thread that dangles from the edge of the cliff. Such thin glaze separates my two worlds: the world of the car-mirror-flash behind your head and the one that is the AK-47 muzzle-flash behind mine."

"You need help for this, you know that, don't you?" he asks. He leans forward and taps my knee with the back of his hand to get my attention. "You do know that, don't you?"

"Listen, I don't want anybody's sympathy. I don't want anyone trying to understand me or help me 'work it out,' or 'put it behind me.' I know for certain that shit just ain't gonna be." I turn away from him and look into the every-child's eyes of Christopher Robin once again. "Hell, I don't want to talk about it in any group setting that requires war stories and cryin'-in-your-beer pity. And, Doc, no offense, but I don't want to talk to you about it, either. You seem to be a good man, but you weren't there. That's pretty much it, as far as I'm concerned."

The doctor shakes his head in understanding. "I know. I know what you are saying. Wait here for just a minute. I want to get something for you—I'll be right back."

Left on my own, I think about our conversation. I really have tried to do the best I can. I've had a good life. I've been blessed, dunno why, with a wonderful wife, great children, a meaningful profession. It's all been so much more than I'd ever imagined while lying in those damned rice paddies. Without thought, I pop my right fist into the palm of my left hand and the sound startles me.

Hell, there were so many nights in the Nam that I never thought it possible that I would live to see sunrise. I sit here now, with the gift of forty more years. Shit, and what am I doing? I'm bitchin' and moanin' that I've gotta have some sleep. Hell, I went those damned thirteen months without sleepin' more than the two hours between my turns at watch. Even when I went on R&R in Bangkok, or the few times 2$^{nd}$ platoon was in the rear and we got out of standing lines, my clock was so set on one-hour-up and two-hours-down that I was stuck on it.

The first two months I was home I'd sleep on the floor with a K-Bar knife in my hand, locked in the back room of my mother's apartment. Every third hour I'd peer out through the Venetian blinds at random lights in the night, stare in silence, and watch for enemy movement. Hell, I was much more afraid of those nights when I lay there alone, without anyone at my back. At least in the Nam I slept two good hours when one of my fire team was on watch. I slept the sound sleep of exhaustion that came in a New York minute in the bush, with the knowledge that my ass was covered.

Damn, I'm uncomfortable with my back to this fuckin' window and only that silly-assed little Daddy's girl on the other side of the door standin' watch. Hell, I feel a shit-load more vulnerable here, at this moment in time, than I ever did in the Nam.

The doctor returns to the room. "Excuse me for taking so long. There is something I want you to have before you leave."

"Shit, Doc, just get me in the system in case it all comes falling down on me. I need to find something besides the self-medicating booze I've been using to dull my senses—something to buffer the endless—" I catch myself in this humiliating begging and feel a flush of heat rise to my face. How far I have fallen. I pull my shoulders back and say, "Fuck this shit, Doc, write up whatever you think is right. You be the one to play their sorry game. I'm gonna make it with or without you, and I refuse to kiss ass any more than I already have to get some…" I lower my voice and add, "help."

There is a long silence.

"Doc, just fill out the damn forms. I'm out of here." I rise and head for the door.

"I'm so sorry," he responds to my back. "And as I said before, I'm bound to not offer any assistance, theory, or advice at this time. I am only to fill out these required forms and mail them in." He throws up his hands as he rises from his seat. "But off the record, I wish to say these few things to you before you leave.

"First of all, you are, without question, the personality type that should never have been permitted to go to war." He reaches out and puts his hand on my shoulder. "Your personality type is too sensitive and too vulnerable to have gone through all that you did. Please don't allow this to offend your sense of being a Marine. I know that you did everything the Corps asked of you, and more. You were the 'grunt' they required you to be. Always know that you earned the right to be proud of that. Nevertheless—it should never have been men like you.

"Since I am unable to offer you any form of assistance from this office, let me give you this phone number of a good friend of mine. He was very much in Vietnam, too. He saw his share of combat, and he tries to help—well, men like you. Hell—grown men who are still the lost boys of the Nam."

Leaning back, he reaches into his wallet and pulls out a business card with his friend's contact information. "Call this man. He walked the walk. It won't be like talking to me because, as much as I might want you to, I know that a man like you won't open up about this to a man like me. I know that I am not the man you will confide in. But I also know that you need help. And this man, perhaps, can walk you through this."

I take the card, pull out my wallet, and slide it into the dead-file midsection of its tri-fold. "Thanks. Kind of you. I appreciate that you have gone far beyond what's allowed of you to even suggest this contact to me."

He hesitates, half-smiles, and says, "You aren't going to contact him, are you?"

I look down at the card and smile along with him. "No."

**\*\*\*\*\*\*\*\*\***

My old blue pickup truck waits for me in the afternoon heat. Its unwashed-and-rusted appearance reminds me to stop by the County Line Tavern for a cold beer or two, or two more than that, on my way back home.

# Chapter Forty-Four

**DATE: The Present**

My wife and I, several members of Charlie Company, along with a few others from different units who fought in our area, made a journey back to Vietnam in the summer of 2000. My Platoon Commander, Lieutenant Mike Galyean, and his wife, Nancy, were very special members of this group. One of their personal goals for the trip was to make the effort to find a lady who had been a Vietnamese, civilian-employee of Mike's in Da Nang following his time with 2$^{nd}$ Platoon in the bush with us. He and the lady became friends and he thought very highly of her.

Our guide told Mike that one of the most helpful means of attempting to do this was to contact the local Catholic Church and see if her name was familiar to anyone. In the process, they were introduced to Padre Antoine, a Catholic Priest in the area for many years. He promised them that he would do his best to locate her and that he would get back to them via e-mail before our time to leave the country. However, so much had occurred following the surrender of South Vietnam to the North, that they shouldn't get their hopes up too high.

So many people were moved around following the North's victory, especially those who had worked directly for the Americans in various capacities, including those many who spent a great deal of time in the various re-indoctrination camps established by the Communists.

After a short time, Mike and Nancy received a message from Padre Antoine. The brief e-mail explains the results of the priest's search and, in many ways, the ultimate purpose of this book as well.

… Original Message …
From: Antoine Nguyen Truong Thang
To: mike galyean
Sent: Saturday, July 01, 2000 11:35 AM
Subject: hello.

Dear Nancy and Mike,
Thank you for the Email and the news. I am sorry because I cannot help you in searching your girlfriend Lan. But I hope one day you will receive a good new about her. With the time. We, aged men, we need to live with memories. Our generation had passed a trouble and sad time. Many young men from both region of VietNam and America were died for a nonsense war. Many of my friends and relatives were fallen in the battle. The war had passed but the sorrows remained. These wounds continue to torture us every day. It's our tragedy. For politicians and generals, the war is finished, but to many families in VietNam or in USA, the sufferings are endless. But we, as Christians, we must always be optimists with the God's help. Thank you for your good appreciations to our country and our people. And I hope in a very near future day, USA and VietNam are closest friends.
May God bless you. Bye, Padre Anton.


AND SO IT GOES ON.

# About the Author

Leonard Reese is a retired school-bus driver who makes his home in the country outside of the small, East Texas town of Tatum. During his time as a bus driver, he taught English and History at Tatum ISD for thirty-five years to supplement his bus-driving income. He is married to his college sweetheart, Cynthia Jameson Reese, and they have two children, Elizabeth and Downs, who rule their world. Leonard was a rifleman in Quang Nam Province, Vietnam with the 2$^{nd}$ platoon of Charlie Company, 1$^{st}$ Battalion, 5$^{th}$ Regiment, 1$^{st}$ Marine Division from 1969-70.

# Dedication

This book is dedicated to my wife of 43 years, Cindy; she is my bridge and my life preserver. She is my love and my life.

# Acknowledgements

My thanks to Cindy Reese, Dr. Joy McLemore, Stephen Woodfin, Caleb Pirtle, Chris Wheeler, Elizabeth Reese, Leonard D. Reese IV, Susan Berger, Mike and Nancy Galyean, Roxanne Villarreal and the group at Roxie's Readings, and family and friends along the way, for their immeasurable efforts and encouragement; to the men of 2nd platoon, Charlie Company, 1st Battalion, 5th Regiment, 1st Marine Division; and also to those who didn't make it back, and to the many who never quite made it all of the way home. You are not forgotten.

CPSIA information can be obtained
at www.ICGtesting.com
Printed in the USA
FFOW02n1505160518